PROCEEDINGS

OF THE

HARVARD CELTIC COLLOQUIUM

Volume 42, 2023

Edited by

Dylan R. Cooper
Rachel A. Martin
Graham D. S. O'Toole
Samuel Ezra Puopolo

Published by
The Department of Celtic Languages and Literatures
Faculty of Arts and Sciences, Harvard University

Distributed by
Harvard University Press
Cambridge and London
by the President and Fellows of Harvard University,
Department of Celtic Languages and Literatures
©2025
All Rights Reserved

ISBN: 978-0-674-29838-5

The cover design is based on the medallion of an
Early Christian belt shrine from Moylough, Co. Sligo.
Drawing by Margo Granfors

Designed and typeset by the Fenway Group
Boston, Massachusetts

Contents

Preface iv

Place and Emotion in Medieval Irish and Welsh Narrative 1
    Helen Fulton J.V. Kelleher Lecturer, 2023

How to train your *näcken*: Death, dismemberment, and the
dissemination of some maritime fabulates 23
    Gregory Darwin Keynote Speaker, 2023

"his honour would remain forever . . . ," A reassessment of the
relationship between royalty and physical impairment in
medieval Irish society 58
    Dylan Bailey

Animal Studies Meets Medieval Studies Meets Celtic Studies:
An Invitation 81
    Matthieu Boyd

Women's libraries in medieval Brittany, thirteenth through the
fifteenth centuries 106
    Yves Coativy

The Gaelicisation of Two Medieval Irish Romances:
Beathadh Sir Gui o Bharbhuic and *Bethadh Bibuis o Hamtuir* 120
    Benedetta D'Antuono

Creating a Welsh-Language Historical Map of Swansea 152
    Geraint Evans

The Irish Progressive: Investigating Early Hiberno-English Texts 169
    Dolores Fors

The Early Medieval Topography and Toponymy of Armagh City:
Trían Saxan and Connections with Anglo-Saxon England 180
    Mícheál B. Ó Mainnín

Old Irish in the PaVeDa: Issues, Perspectives, and Two
Case Studies 212
    Elisa Roma and Chiara Zanchi

Abstracts of Presenters at the Forty-second Harvard
Celtic Colloquium 239

PREFACE

The annual Harvard Celtic Colloquium originated in a graduate student conference convened in 1980 by students in the Harvard University Department of Celtic Languages and Literatures. Since then the conference has developed into an internationally recognized event drawing together scholars and students from around the world to present papers on all facets of Celtic Studies. The Colloquium is the oldest graduate-run conference in the field of Celtic Studies, and, true to its origins, it remains entirely run and organized by the graduate students of the Harvard Celtic Department. The principal organizers of the Colloquium then become the editorial board for the publication of its Colloquium proceedings.

Papers given at the Colloquium may be submitted for publication following peer review in the journal, *The Proceedings of the Harvard Celtic Colloquium (PHCC)*. The journal is distributed by Harvard University Press, which also handles subscriptions and single volume orders. Information on the Colloquium and *PHCC* may be found through the Harvard University Department of Celtic Languages and Literatures website. The editorial board and managing editor for *PHCC* may be contacted directly at phcc@fas.harvard.edu. With this issue, *PHCC* changes to an A5 page size.

Acknowledgements

The editors are indebted to Professor Catherine McKenna for her advice and encouragement, and to the Celtic department staff, Ms. Mary Violette, and Mr. Steven Duede, for their help with the Colloquium and administrative matters. We also wish to thank the managing editor of PHCC, and the staff of Fenway Group for their help with the publication of this volume.

Dylan R. Cooper
Rachel A. Martin
Graham D. S. O'Toole
Samuel Ezra Puopolo

Organizers of the Harvard Celtic Colloquium 2023 and Editors of PHCC volume 42 (2023), 2025.

Place and Emotion in Medieval Irish and Welsh Narrative

Helen Fulton

It was a great honour for me to have been invited to give the annual John V. Kelleher lecture. John Kelleher was an outstanding scholar of Irish history and literature, with an incredible range from medieval to modern, as much at home with Irish genealogies as he was with the work of W. B. Yeats and James Joyce. I first came across his work when I was a graduate student in Celtic Studies, and his article on "Humor in the Ulster Saga" made a particular impression on me, mainly because his own writing was so witty. Having ploughed through the seemingly endless series of single combats in the *Táin Bó Cúailnge*, I found it liberating to read Professor Kelleher's verdict that "Most of the duels are treated seriously enough; but as the series is extended a suspicion of burlesque enters."[1] That phrase, "a suspicion of burlesque", is perfect because in fact we are never quite sure what is parody and what is an exaggerated brutality that signifies the violence of all-out war in a pre-industrial society. The saga plays on our emotions, making us unsure how to react, and in this paper I hope to explore some of the implications of this style of writing.

Anyone who has a special place where they feel they belong, or a happy place where they feel most like themselves, whether it is a country or a city or a beach or a mountain, will understand the link between place and emotion. The dramatization of such a link is particularly characteristic of modern literature, that is, the literature of the last three centuries, when the rise of the liberal-humanist individual, who appears to have agency and freedom of choice, has encouraged our belief in the value of personal connections with specific people and places, and in the legitimacy of our emotions as expressions of our own individual and unique identities. The recent turn to eco-criticism in literary studies, exploring representations of the natural world in relation to environmental concerns, further legitimizes our sense of a personal and increasingly urgent connection with nature and landscape.

---

[1] John V. Kelleher, "Humor in the Ulster Saga", in *Veins of Humor*, ed. by Harry Levin (Cambridge, MA: Harvard University Press, 1972) pp. 35–56, on p. 49.

PLACE AND EMOTION

This habit of validating our emotions by reference to particular places has precedents in medieval literature, though the viewpoint is less individualized. One of the loveliest poems in the corpus of Old Irish poetry is this one, whose modern title is "The Scribe in the Woods":

Dom-farcai fidbaide fál,
fom-chain loíd luin, lúad nád cél;
húas mo lebrán, ind línech,
fom-chain trírech inna n-én.

Fomm-chain coí menn, medair mass,
hi mbrot glass de dindgnaib doss.
Debrath! nom-Choimmdiu-coíma,
caín-scríbaimm fo roída ross.

A hedge of trees overlooks me;
a blackbird's lay sings to me (an announcement which I shall not conceal);
above my lined book the birds' chanting sings to me.

A clear-voiced cuckoo sings to me (goodly utterance)
in a grey cloak from bush fortresses.
The Lord is indeed good to me;
well do I write beneath a forest of woodland.)[2]

Like a modern poet, the Irish cleric refers to himself in the first person and gives us a personalized account of his relationship with the natural world, connecting his work as a scribe with the work of nature. The human activity of scribal copying, an activity associated with the technology of writing and the culture of production, is made to seem as natural and God-given as the timeless and ineluctable movements of the woodland. By locating himself, imaginatively if not literally, in the woodland, the scribe indulges his nostalgia for his homeland and the kind of mental peace and harmony that the later Romantic poets came to associate with the natural world.

What comes through the narrative voice is an expression of individual feeling that is embedded in collective values. The link between a people, the landscape, and a Christian worldview carries with it a range of prescribed emotions. The apparently personal relationship with nature

---

[2] Text and translation from Gerard Murphy, *Early Irish Lyrics* (Oxford: Clarendon Press, 1956), no. 2, pp. 4–5.

expressed in the poetry is actually rather conventional—it has a universal application, reminding readers and listeners of the inevitability of the human condition and the commonality of emotions such as the longing for God's grace and the awe inspired by God's creations. The Irish scribe in the woods found peace in the woodland because the natural world represented God's creative power.

When we turn to medieval Irish and Welsh narrative, we find ourselves confronted with rather different literary traditions and modes of writing, but ones which continue to articulate the values of a collective society. Early vernacular lyric poetry drew its inspirations from Latin poetry, both religious and secular, attaching itself to a European tradition of reflective thought and emotional expression. Vernacular prose in Irish and Welsh, on the other hand, is *sui generis*, of its own kind, emerging from specific social and political contexts and serving a purpose understood by audiences in those countries. The narrative voice is not a first-person speaker describing the places in which personal emotion flows forth, but a more distanced, impartial, third-person voice for whom emotion is a matter of observation rather than empathy.

My objective in this paper is to look at two prose narratives from Ireland and Wales in order to examine the ways in which place is linked to emotion, the ways in which storytellers position their readers to understand that particular places carry with them a kind of emotional charge which is often left implicit rather than directly stated. My two case studies are the Irish saga *Táin Bó Cúailnge*, "The Cattle Raid of Cooley", and the Welsh Arthurian narrative, "*Culhwch ac Olwen*", "Culhwch and Olwen". These two texts form an interesting pair as, despite many stylistic and contextual differences, they are comparable in three particular ways. Firstly, they both construct a distant and mythological past, an origin history for specific peoples. The exact dates of composition are unknown—the Irish tales which make up the saga of the *Táin* almost certainly emerged earlier than the Welsh tale, with traces of ninth-century language, but both survive in versions extant from the late eleventh or early twelfth centuries.[3]

---

[3] The earliest surviving versions of the *Táin* are in Lebor na hUidre (The Book of the Dun Cow), dated to c. 1100, and the Book of Leinster, written in the mid-twelfth century. A complete version of "Culhwch ac Olwen" survives in Llyfr

PLACE AND EMOTION

Secondly, they are both concerned with the importance of place, of geography, topography, place names, and features of the landscape, including hints of the otherworld that lies parallel to the human world. As Muireann Ní Bhrolcháin has said, "In Irish tradition, stories are not only about events; they are also about the sites where events take place . . . [The landscape] was seen as a living thing with a name for every feature."[4] Both tales demonstrate similar mechanisms for linking place and emotion, mainly through the displacement of individual emotion on to the socially constructed landscape so that personal emotions, which are potentially threatening to the social order, are contained within collective values and practices.

Thirdly, the two texts adopt a similar mode of storytelling, a mode of naturalism that is particular to medieval Ireland and Wales and which contrasts with the more realistic mode of narrative adopted by French and English literature of the same period. This naturalistic mode of storytelling generates a particular kind of affect within the texts, that is, the relationship between individual and society in terms of how emotion is managed, or what we might call the politics of emotion.[5] In both the Irish and Welsh narratives, words for specific emotions, such as anger, happiness, grief and so on, are rarely used by the narrator. Instead, the narrator acts as a camera, showing us how characters are feeling through their actions and in their speech. This means that the reader or audience has to do a lot of the work in determining how to respond to the texts, and how to recognise and rank the emotions that seem to hover below the plot lines without being fully examined.

Coch Hergest (Red Book of Hergest), written between c. 1380 and 1410, with an incomplete text in Llyfr Gwyn Rhydderch (White Book of Rhydderch), dated to c. 1325. The earliest recension of the text itself has been dated to about 1100.

[4] Muireann Ní Bhrolcháin, *Introduction to Early Irish Literature* (Dublin: Four Courts Press, 2009), p. 7.

[5] Lawrence Grossberg defines affect as "an articulated plane whose organization defines its own relations of power and sites of struggle . . . the recognition of an articulated plane of affect points to the existence of another politics, a politics of feeling." See Grossberg, "History, Politics and Postmodernism: Stuart Hall and Cultural Studies", in *Stuart Hall: Critical Dialogues in Cultural Studies*, ed. David Morley and Kuan-Hsing Chen (London and New York: Routledge, 1996) pp. 151–73, on pp. 167–8.

HELEN FULTON

Naturalism as a narrative mode

I will start by explaining what I mean by a naturalistic mode of storytelling compared to the more familiar mode of realism.[6] In a realist text, the events are narrated by what is often called an 'omniscient narrator', that is, someone who knows from the beginning what is going to happen, who understands the characters and what motivates them, and who deliberately organizes the story so that it unfolds in a particular way. We, the audience, are carefully led in certain directions, shown what is important, or not shown if there is to be a surprise ending; we are allowed to know certain information while other information is delayed or withheld, and yet we are scarcely aware of being led in this way. The more we lose ourselves in the story, the less we notice what the narrator is doing with us, we only care about finding out what happens. This is the lure of the realist novel, the realist film, the realist medieval text such as Chaucer's *Canterbury Tales* or the romances of Chrétien de Troyes. In the mode of realism, emotions are explicit, recognisable, relatable, and attributed to individual actors.[7]

In contrast to this, the naturalistic narrator never claims to be omniscient. The narrator aims to describe what can be seen and what events occur, without much conscious arrangement or mediation, as if they have stumbled across these fragments of story and are listing them as found objects. This is what one version recounts, this is what another version recounts, says the naturalist narrator, as if they themselves are nothing more than objective conduits of information. The narrator seems to have no

---

[6] The distinction I am making between naturalism and realism is largely my own, though I have drawn on narrative theory to some extent. Most literary (and film) critics regard naturalism as a sub-type of realism, whereas I identify significant stylistic differences between the two and consider them to be two separate modes of narrative. I have outlined some of the features of naturalism in a previous article, "Magic Naturalism in the *Táin Bó Cúailnge*", in *Narrative in Celtic Tradition: Essays in Honor of Edgar M. Slotkin*, ed. Joseph F. Eska, *CSANA Yearbook* 8–9 (Hamilton, NY: Colgate University Press, 2011) pp. 84–99.

[7] Associated with the visual arts as well as with literary texts and film, the concept of realism has a large critical literature associated with it. Useful texts include Pam Morris, *Realism* (London and New York: Routledge, 2003) and Catherine Belsey, *Critical Practice*, second edition (London and New York: Routledge, 2002).

PLACE AND EMOTION

viewpoint, no particular line to push, and little or no authority over the text. There is no distinction between what is important and what is trivial, we are not told which characters are trustworthy and which are not, which emotions are authentic or why. We simply have to make our own judgements, or perhaps not make any judgements at all but just accept the events as the empirical record of a historical moment. The naturalistic style betrays its origins as a scientific method, based on principles such as determinism, empiricism, and causation.[8]

In the mode of naturalism, emotions are among the found objects observed and recorded for us by a disinterested narrator, sometimes named but more often left to be inferred from a character's behaviour or direct speech. In both the *Táin* and "Culhwch ac Olwen", the narrative contains very few words that signify emotion. Instead, emotion is almost entirely performative, embodied in speech and action. In speech, emotions such as anger, pride, betrayal, pleasure or amusement are expressed at similar levels of intensity. It is in their actions that characters reveal the scale of their emotions, so that these actions are often dramatically or humorously exaggerated in order to convey the depth of feeling.

For example, in the opening section of *The Táin*, the so-called 'Pillow Talk' found in Recension II, where Ailill and Medb compare their possessions, Medb's messenger, Mac Roth, is sent to the house of Dáire Mac Fiachna to ask for the loan of his great bull, Donn Cúailnge, to even up the score between Medb and Ailill. Mac Roth makes his offer to Dáire:

> "Tair-siu féin lat tarb ⁊ fogéba comméit th'feraind féin de mín Maige Aí ⁊ carpat trí secht cumal ⁊ cardes sliasta Medba air sin anechtair."

---

[8] Naturalism is a term associated particularly with philosophy and the privileging of scientific knowledge and the natural world. The critical literature on literary naturalism is not large, focusing mainly on American and French naturalistic fiction of the nineteenth and early twentieth centuries, which had a particular political project. For a useful summary, see Raymond Williams, "Naturalism", in *Keywords: A Vocabulary of Culture and Society* (London: Fontana, 1976) pp. 181–4.

Ba aitt la Dáre aní sin, ₇ ram-bertaig co raímdetar úammand a cholcthech fái.[9]

"If you bring the bull yourself, you'll get a piece of the smooth plain of Aí as big as all your lands, and a chariot worth thrice seven bondmaids, as well as the friendship of Medb's thighs."

Dáire was well pleased by this. He leaped up and down on his couch and the seams of the flock mattress burst beneath him.[10]

The offer to Dáire is completely pragmatic, and there is no particular ranking of the gifts that are offered. The land and the chariot are offered in exactly the same spirit as "the friendship of Medb's thighs", even though these things are qualitatively different. The narrator does not position us to react to this list of gifts, including the implication of Medb's promiscuity, which seems to be taken for granted—of course she would offer this because that is who she is. In the same way, Dáire's response is simply recorded—he was "well pleased"—and it is only the factual detail of the burst mattress that indicates to the audience how excited he actually was. Dáire performs his feelings through the action of jumping up and down on his couch.

Emotion and Affect in the *Táin*

The naturalistic mode of narrative has a direct connection with the representation of emotion in both *The Táin* and "*Culhwch ac Olwen*". Emotion is projected from the cognitive to the material, displaced on to physical objects such as Dáire's couch or on to the physical surfaces of the landscape. With regard to the theory of emotions, I am locating my understanding of emotion within the larger concept of affect. As a human experience, affect has been theorized in various ways, including Brian

---

[9] Cecile O'Rahilly (ed. and trans.), *Táin Bó Cuailnge from the Book of Leinster* [Recension II], Irish Texts Society, 49 (Dublin: Dublin Institute for Advanced Studies, 1967), ll. 95–99, p. 3. All further quotes from Recension II are from this edition.
[10] Ciarán Carson (trans.), *The Táin: Translated from the Old Irish Epic, Táin Bó Cúailnge* (London: Penguin, 2007) p. 6. All subsequent translations from the *Táin* are from Carson's version.

PLACE AND EMOTION

Massumi's definition of affect as "intensity", or the scale on which emotional work can be measured, and Fredric Jameson's distinction between affect and emotion, arguing that while emotions can be named—love, hate, fear, pleasure and so on—affect "somehow eludes language and its naming of things (and feelings)".[11] In its broadest sense, affect refers to the whole human experience of interacting with the world—it encompasses consciousness, cognition, and identity and emerges from the space between the human and the material world. In his interaction with the natural world, the scribe in the woods generates an affect that "somehow eludes language".

In an attempt to narrow these definitions, I take affect to include the mechanisms and cultural practices by which feelings and emotions are articulated and positioned within specific social and political contexts. How do we feel things, how are we allowed or empowered to express feelings, how are feelings structured and transmitted, how are they gendered? One way of thinking about affect, then, is to think of it as the politics of emotion in a particular social context, the ways in which emotions are ranked and controlled.

In the *Táin* and "Culhwch ac Olwen", the social structures implied in both texts work to deny the validity of an individual's emotions, which are shown to be a challenge to the social order if not properly controlled. Society operates as a collective led by powerful individuals whose power has to be consented to by the rest of the collective. Feelings or moods are valid only when shared or endorsed by the collective, often through shared rituals and actions, such as boasting matches or the inauguration of kings, that reinforce the values of the dominant group. When Fergus is mocked by Conchobar in the final battle, Fergus attempts to kill him but is restrained by Cormac mac Loinges, who says:

---

[11] Fredric Jameson, *The Antinomies of Realism* (London: Verso, 2013) p. 29. Brian Massumi's discussion of affect in the context of how we experience the world can be found in his article, "The Autonomy of Affect", *Cultural Critique*, 31 (1995) 83–109. See also Margaret Wetherell, *Affect and Emotion: A New Social Science Understanding* (Los Angeles and London: Sage, 2012). Studies of affect and emotion in medieval texts have been published by Glenn D. Burger and Holly A. Crocker (eds), *Medieval Affect, Feeling, and Emotion* (Cambridge: Cambridge University Press, 2019).

HELEN FULTON

"Ben a trí telcha tarsiu. Toí do láim. Slig immud do cach leith ₇ nísnairle. Imráid ainech nUlad nádcon fárcbad. Nícon fáicébathar muna fácabtha triut-sa indiu."[12]

Strike out at those three hills yonder. Turn your hand. Strike anywhere. Be as reckless as you like. But remember that the honour of Ulster has never been compromised, and never will be, unless by you today." (Carson, p. 203)

Like most other emotions in the tale, Fergus's anger is not explicitly referred to—only the physical action of raising his sword against Conchobar indicates his mood. But his desire for revenge against a king is not endorsed by the collective rules of warrior society, and Cormac has to redirect Fergus's rage by reminding him that he is about to commit a dishonorable action.

The affect of the narrative is therefore based partly on the way that emotion is channelled, how it is allowed to be expressed and performed only within the social limits of the collective. Affect also arises from our relationship to the text, as reader or audience—we have to do the work of interpreting and assessing emotion, which inevitably creates a critical distance between us and the text. A realist movie which shows characters experiencing grief and loss may well make us cry. A naturalist story like the *Táin*, which lists hundreds of violent deaths, is very unlikely to move us in the same way, producing a very different kind of affect.

As in all societies, emotion has a political function, and the politics of emotion in both the *Táin* and "Culhwch" is collective rather than individual. Emotion works to inflame the warriors to perform acts of extreme violence while refusing to allow them to indulge in individual emotions that might destabilize the masculine social order of the tribe—a model of masculinity that we would now call toxic but which is socially normative within the bounds of the text. Fergus's relationship with Medb is barely hinted at and only in the context of sex rather than love, nearly always a dangerous emotion. Fergus's distress at his divided loyalties between Connacht and Ulster is not allowed to be acknowledged but turns outwards into ineffectual rage and loss of focus. Over-ambition and wilfulness, whether from Medb

---

[12] Cecile O'Rahilly (ed. and trans.), *Táin Bó Cúailnge: Recension I* (Dublin: Dublin Institute for Advanced Studies, 1976) ll. 4061–3, p. 122. All further quotes from Recension I are from this edition.

PLACE AND EMOTION

or from some of the warriors, threaten the collective and are shown to be disastrous. Cú Chulainn, on the other hand, shows a level of humility appropriate to the greatest of warriors. Despite being depicted as a unique individual, he belongs to the tribe. He fights for Ulster, not for himself.

The lament of Cú Chulainn for the death of his foster-brother Fer Diad is one of the longest poetic interludes in the whole cycle and one of the most emotionally intense and moving. The poetry in the *Táin* is typically used to express personal emotion, which is another way of managing emotion, by sectioning it off into a different genre of writing so that it is boundaried and controlled by the metre. It is a sign of Cú Chulainn's privileged status in the saga that he is allowed (by the scribe of Recension II) such a lengthy outpouring of emotion. It is represented as exceptional but, in the circumstances, appropriate, a fitting tribute from one warrior to another and an acknowledgement of their close relationship as foster-brothers. Cú Chulainn frames it as the tragedy of one man caught up in the greater politics of the conflict:

> *"Maith a Fir Diad," bar Cú Chulaind, "is mór in brath 7 in trécun dabertatar fir Hérend fort do thabairt do chomlund 7 do chomruc rum-sa dáig ní réid comlund ná comrac rum-sa bar Táin Bó Cúalnge."*
> *Is amlaid ra baí 'gá rád 7 rabert ne briathra:*
>
> *A Fir Diad, ardotchlóe brath,*
> *Dursan do dál dédenach,*
> *Tussu d'éc, missi d'anad,*
> *Sírdursan ar sírscarad.*
> (Recension II, ll. 3435–3444, p. 95)

"Ah, Fer Diad," said Cú Chulainn, "greatly did the men of Ireland deceive you and abandon you when they sent you to oppose and fight me, for to oppose and fight me on the Táin Bó Cúailnge is no easy task."
And having said that, he spoke these words:

Ah, Fer Diad, you were betrayed.
Our last meeting led to this,
my everlasting sorrow
that I live while you are dead.
(Carson, p. 154)

HELEN FULTON

Cú Chulainn's sorrow is socially acceptable because it is appropriate to mourn a foster-brother, especially one as brave and persistent as Fer Diad. It demonstrates Cú Chulainn's heroism and nobility of spirit, and his lament for Fer Diad is expressed through the discourse of social practices—growing up together, learning how to be warriors, fighting together in battle, recognizing the harsh truth of warrior life that, as Cú Chulainn says, "courage has a brutal core" (Carson, p. 158). Cú Chulainn's lament is personal but his emotion is channelled through the approved discourses of the tribe and its values. Individual characters who try to act on their own accounts, as their own agents, in the manner of the modern liberal individual, are constantly reminded that they are part of a social collective where the scope for individual agency is monitored and controlled.

The authenticity of Cú Chulainn's grief provides a counterpoint to the more humorous moments of emotion performed during the narrative, such as the grim gallows humor and the hubristic boasting of warriors hoping to beat the great Cú Chulainn. Such emotions work to calibrate the intensity and ambiguity of the affect, assisting us to navigate an emotional landscape which is not always made clear to us.

Place and landscape

I have been suggesting that the affectivity of the *Táin* is a politics of emotion which discourages self-indulgence in order to protect the tribe and which challenges the reader or audience to assess and rank expressions of emotion. Affect can be measured through a number of literary devices common to both medieval Irish and Welsh narratives, including descriptions, catalogues, and poetic interludes, but here I want to focus on a particularly significant element of affect, which is the function of place and landscape as frames for mood and feeling, a way of displacing emotion on to the materiality of the land and thereby controlling its impact. What anchors emotion and embeds it in both the *Táin* and "Culhwch and Olwen" is its association with place, creating an emotional topography built upon an actual landscape of physical places, many of them real places in Ireland and Wales. The politics of emotion, the cultural practices which control emotion, include a spatial element which determines the physical spaces, already freighted with meaning, where feelings can legitimately be expressed, transmitted, and if necessary neutralized. In the absence of clear

PLACE AND EMOTION

guidance from the narrator, references to the landscape help to prompt responses from the reader and absorb the emotions of the characters.

I am drawing my theory of place from a corpus of critical writing that is sometimes called literary geography or spatial humanities. Following theorists such as Henri Lefebvre, Edward Soja, and Doreen Massey, I am interested in the social and temporal production of space and the political organization of space.[13] In terms of their social production, there is no qualitative difference between physical geographically-situated places and socially organized space. Connacht and Ulster on the one hand, and south Wales and Cornwall on the other, are not simply pre-existing geographical places but are signifying spaces in a constant process of being created and sustained by successive power groups to ensure the survival of the dominant class. Affect is one way of thinking about the social construction of space, since our reaction to space is often an emotional one. The affect of both texts depends partly on this landscape of emotion which provides direction to the audience and which allows individual emotions to form the topographical contours of the land, the highs and lows of feeling as the characters move around the landscape. To take obvious examples, Emain Macha in Ulster and Celliwig in Cornwall are not just already-existing topographical sites, they are socially constructed spaces which carry a history of attachments and allusions that are designed to provoke responses of mood and feeling in audience and protagonists alike.

Our two texts are not unusual, of course, in prioritizing place and landscape. Onomastics is a major part of medieval Welsh and Irish writing, from the place-name stories embedded in the *Mabinogion* to the formalized Dindsenchas of Irish tradition. The function of these apparently empirical accounts of place is not only geographic and political, claiming significant sites in order to map territorial boundaries, but also historical,

---

[13] Edward Soja, for example, argues for a "postmodern geography" that must, among other things, "attempt to reinscribe and resituate the meaning and significance of space in history". Soja, *Postmodern Geographies: The Reassertion of Space in Critical Social Theory* (London and New York: Verso, 1989) p. 73. For Soja, and for other spatial commentators, "empirical descriptions [of space] which imply scientific understanding . . . too often hide political meaning" (p. 75). In other words, empirical accounts of geography, or of representations of place in literary texts, are no longer enough: recognition of the politics and history of space must also be articulated.

commemorating events that create a communal identity. It is not hard to see why place was important in the early tribal societies of Ireland and Wales. Place meant land, and land meant wealth, status, identity, and indeed survival. Land was mythologized, marked with sacred groves and portals to the otherworld. Both the *Táin* and "Culhwch and Olwen" are based on journeys around the landscape, and within each territory, key features of landscape and topography become the receptacles and validators of complex emotions, and also the proxies for those emotions, signifiers whose meanings are both literal and symbolic. The act of place-naming is a key generator of affect—in naming a place, a social group or institution marks its past and present connection with that place and transmits feelings and attitudes about their relationship to it.

Both texts, especially the *Táin*, contain numerous references to places and landscape, many of them real. As Paul Gosling has said, "Some of the scribes who had a hand in creating the epic had a keen sense of the landscapes in which they set the story. Moreover, they regularly employed real places not just as textual embellishments but for specific literary and dramatic effect."[14] The route of Medb's army from Connacht to Cuailnge in Ulster is mapped out through a long list of the places through which they travelled.[15] This incantatory list of place names indicates the enormity of the campaign but it also implies the determination of Medb to get what she wants, whatever the cost, and the scale of her ambition. Place names are coined by the progress of the army, such as Slechta, the Cut, where Medb ordered her army to cut down an entire wood so that her army and its chariots could take a short cut to avoid Cú Chulainn (Carson p. 27). This is another reference to her arrogance and recklessness which make her unfit to lead an army, and it is an ominous one as well, with the Cut and other places along the route leading only to the deaths of hundreds and the defeat of the Connacht army.

---

[14] Paul Gosling, "The Route of *Táin Bó Cúailnge* Revisited", *Emania*, 22 (2014) 145–67, on p. 145.

[15] The list of place names occurs in Recension I, p. 128. In his translation of the *Táin*, Thomas Kinsella provided a sketch map of the route taken by the Connacht army as it marched around Ulster. See Kinsella, *The Táin* (Oxford: Oxford University press, 1970) map 1. See also Gosling, "The Route of *Táin Bó Cúailnge* Revisited", for some important revisions to this map.

PLACE AND EMOTION

Some place names actually anticipate events that occur there, such as the reference to Tamlachta Órláim, Órlám's Burial Mound:

> *Dothíagat ass dano tar Irairu Culend ara bárach. Dosléci Cú Chulaind ríam. Dofuric araid nÓrláim meic Ailello 7 Medba i Tamlachtai Órláim fri Dísiurt Lóchait antúaid bicán oc béim feda and. (Recension I, ll. 869–72, p. 27)*[16]

> The next morning they [the Connacht army] went to Irairu Cuillenn. Cú Chulainn went on ahead of them. At the place called Tamlachta Órláim, Órlám's Burial Mound, just north of the sanctuary Dísert Lochait, he came across Órlám's charioteer. Órlám—Golden-arm—was a son of Ailill and Medb. (Carson, p. 54)

The narrator anticipates the death of Órlám by referring to a place name based on an event that has not yet happened. Órlám is not yet dead—Cú Chulainn is about to kill him—but the place name has already been established as Órlám's Burial Mound. He is a dead man walking, and the place name serves to prompt the audience towards a response of anticipation, which could be either gleeful or awful. The landscape is full of such names, commemorating the dead warriors cut down by Cú Chulainn's superhuman strength and Medb's hubris, creating a kind of killing fields across Ireland which marks its whole history. Place names and their stories therefore generate affect through the audience's responses to both the humour and the horror of the narrative.

The landscape in "Culhwch and Olwen" is drawn with less detail than in the Irish tale, with references to journeys, such as Culhwch's journey to find Arthur's court, which often have no specified landmarks or destination points. But geographic and topographic references are used to direct audiences to points of importance, such as when Culhwch demands entry to Arthur's court, saying to the gatekeeper,

---

[16] On the importance of Irairu Cuillenn as a threshold, see Mary MacKenna, "The Irish Mythological Landscape and the *Táin*", in *Ulidia 2: Proceedings of the Second International Conference on the Ulster Cycle of Tales*, ed. Ruairí Ó hUiginn and Brian Ó Catháin (Maynooth: An Sagart, 2009) pp. 262–73, especially p. 267.

HELEN FULTON

> *"Ot agory y porth, da yw. Onys agory, mi a dygaf anglot y'th arglwyd a drygeir y titheu. A mi a dodaf teir diaspat ar drws y porth hwnn hyt na bo anghleuach ym Penn Pengwaed yg Kernyw ac yg gwaelawt Dinsol yn y Gogled, ac yn Eskeir Oeruel yn Iwerdon."*[17]

> "If you open the gate, well and good. If not, I will bring dishonour on your lord and give you a bad name. And I will raise three shouts at the entrance of this gate that will be no less audible on the top of Pen Pengwaedd in Cornwall as at the bottom of Dinsol in the North, and in Esgair Oerfel in Ireland."[18]

These three place names function to mark out the length of Britain from north to south, and its breadth across to Ireland, making a large triangle of territory in which Arthur's dishonor will be broadcast, which would be a disaster for the porter. The geographical scale of Culhwch's threat is an index of the scale of his anger, but it is also a measure of his noble status compared to the gatekeeper. He has the authority to make such a threat and in doing so to express a legitimate emotion at the liminal border between outside and inside Arthur's court. The subsequent description of Culhwch riding his horse straight through that boundary into Arthur's feasting hall without dismounting confirms his status as a hero who belongs in Arthur's court.

Landscape is also used to create a feeling of foreboding in the description of Arthur's men journeying to the land of Ysbaddaden the Giant:

> *Mynet a orugant hyd pan deuuant y uaestir mawr, hyny uyd kaer a welynt, mwyhaf ar keyryt y byt. Kerdet ohonu y dyt hwnnw. Pan debygynt vy eu bot yn gyuagos y'r gaer nyt oedynt nes no chynt. [Ar eildyd ar trydyd dyd y kerdassant ac o vreid y doethant hyt yno.* (ll. 412–15 and n. 19)

---

[17] Rachel Bromwich and D. Simon Evans (eds), *Culhwch ac Olwen: An Edition and Study of the Oldest Arthurian Tale* (Cardiff: University of Wales Press, 1992) ll. 103–7, p. 4. All subsequent quotations from the text are from this edition.

[18] Sioned Davies (trans.), *The Mabinogion* (Oxford: Oxford University Press, 2007), pp. 181–2. All translations from *"Culhwch and Olwen"* are from this edition.

PLACE AND EMOTION

> They travelled until they came to a great plain, and they could see a fort, the largest fort in the world. They walked that day until evening. When they thought they were close to the fort, they were no closer than in the morning. And the second and the third day they walked, and with difficulty they got there. (Davies, p. 190)

There is already something uncanny in the landscape around Ysbaddaden's fort, some strange force-field keeping them away from the fortress, and this description foreshadows the ominous presence of the giant and provokes feelings of anticipation in the reader. The impressive scariness of the giant when he finally appears, with his eyelids propped open on sticks, has already been written into the landscape.

The most striking use of landscape and placenames in "Culhwch and Olwen" is the episode of the hunting of the great boar, Twrch Trwyth. This hunt is in the form of a military campaign which is like a shorter version of the hunting of the bull in the *Táin*. Like the Irish kings, Arthur raises a huge army from Britain, France, Normandy and Brittany to hunt the boar, and like the *Táin*, many warriors are killed along the way. The boar's route starts from Ireland and moves to Wales where its travels can be mapped fairly accurately across south Wales and into Cornwall.[19]

The topographical pursuit of the boar through the landscape, like Medb's pursuit of the Brown Bull of Cooley, underscores the extent of the losses—at every place-point, warriors are killed—but it also reinforces the need for Arthur to restore his authority over his territory in south Wales and Cornwall, the territory that is mapped out by the boar's rampage through the country. When Arthur finally drives the boar into the sea off Cornwall, he regains possession of his territory. Through the landscape, the story generates a drama about an external enemy, violent death, and a king's possible loss of authority, pointing the audience towards appropriate responses of alarm and relief.

Place and emotion

I have already argued that landscape and place are used to articulate and control the emotions of individual characters, but landscape is also used

---

[19] A map was provided by Bromwich and Evans in their edition of the text, on p. viii.

to prompt responses from the audience, in the absence of clear directives from the naturalistic narrator. By displacing emotion on to specific places, the narrative removes emotion from the human sphere to the physical materiality of land, the tribe's most valuable asset, thereby neutralizing the destabilizing potential of emotion and turning it instead into a memorial, part of the tribe's history written into the tribal lands.

We can find an example of this in the *Táin* after the tragic fight between Cú Chulainn and his foster-brother Fer Diad. After his long lament, Cú Chulainn lies down exhausted until his friends come to bathe his wounds:

> *In tan trá bátar in tslóig oc techt ó Áth Fír Diad sades, boí Cú Chulainn ina otharligiu andside conatatánicc ria cách Senoll hÚathach co mbaí-side ⁊ dá mac Fice and. Dolotatar la Coin Chulaind for cúlaib ailli do ícc ⁊ búalad a chrécht do uscib Conailli.*
>
> *It hé a n-anmanna-side: Sás, Búan, Bithslán, Finnglas, Gleóir, Bedc, Tadcc, Talaméd, Rindd, Bir, Brenide, Cumang, Cellend, Gaenemain, Dichu, Muach, Miliucc, Den, Delt, Dubglaise.* (Recension I, ll. 3143–48, p. 95)

> The Irish army drew back southwards from Fer Diad's Ford. Cú Chulainn lay there injured until he was found by an advance party consisting of Senoll Uathach and the two sons of Ficce. They took him to the streams and rivers of Conaille to cleanse and heal his wounds.

> These are those names: Sás the Repose and Búan the Steady and Bithslán the Longlife; Finnglas the Clearwater and Gleóir the Brightwater; Tadc the Tough and Talaméd the Silty; Rinn and Birr, the Point and the Peak; Breinide the Bitter; Cellenn the Hidden and Cumang the Narrow; Gaenemain the Sandy; and Dichú and Muach and Miliuc; and Den and Delt; and Dubglaise the Blackwater. (Carson, p. 163).

These names signify rivers and streams flowing across Conaille Muirthemne, which is Cú Chulainn's own home and the place he has almost killed himself trying to defend from the invading Connachtmen. The names of the rivers have meanings, which Ciaran Carson has indicated in his translation, words like 'repose' and 'steady' and 'long life' and 'tough', but

PLACE AND EMOTION

also 'bitter' and 'silty' and 'hidden' and 'blackwater'. Cú Chulainn's exhaustion and anguish at the trauma of his friend's death, emotions not described by the narrator, are instead written into the names of the rivers where he bathes his wounds, with the landscape standing in for his emotions, the need to be comforted by his own country, Muirthemne, but also the awful recognition of the terrible deed he has done. These are not real rivers—unless Dubglaise can be the River Blackwater in Ulster—so they have been called into being by the narrator not only to indicate the extent of Cú Chulainn's wounds that need so many rivers to wash them, but as a metaphor of his trauma. The initial reference to Áth Fir Diad, 'Fer Diad's Ford', is another example of great emotion being commemorated by the landscape, with the dead hero giving his name to part of the landscape, ensuring that his name will never be forgotten.

We see a similar absorption of emotion into the land in the episode I referred to earlier, when Fergus is prevented from killing Conchobar. After Cormac dissuades him, Fergus responds by killing a hundred Ulstermen, until he is stopped by Conall Cernach:

> "Ba ramór in bríg sin," ar Conall Cernach, "for túaith ⁊ cenél ar thóin mná drúithi."
> "Ceist, cid dogén, a fírlaích?" or sé.
> "Slig na tulchu tairrsiu ⁊ na dusu impu," or Conall Cernach.
> Sligis Fergus na tulchai íarom coro ben a teóra máela Midi dá thrí béimennaib.
> (Recension I, ll. 4068–73, p. 122)

> "You're very fierce," said Conall, "against your own kith and kin, and all for the sake of a whore's backside."
> "What then should I do?" said Fergus.
> "Strike out at those hills yonder, and anything on top of them," said Conall.
> Fergus struck the hills and with three blows sheared off the tops of the Máela Midi, the Flat-topped Hills of Meath.
> (Carson, p. 204)

Once again, Fergus's anger must be redirected towards something more acceptable than the killing of his own people, and this time he slices the tops off hills. It is an onomastic story, indicating how the hills came by their name of Máela, 'bald' or 'flat-topped', and in taking on this name the hills themselves become an expression of Fergus's rage, which is now imprinted forever into the landscape.

Turning back to "Culhwch and Olwen", we find similar examples of emotion displaced on to a specific place. In the sequence known as the Oldest Animals, when Arthur's men seek advice from a series of long-lived animals about how to find Mabon son of Modron, each animal is associated with a specific place. Each place is used as a measure of the animal's great age, with the landscape changing over centuries of time. The Owl of Cwm Cawlwyd says:

> Pan deuthum i yma gyntaf, y cwm mawr a welwch glynn coet oed, ac y deuth kenedlaeth o dynyon idaw, ac y diuawyt, ac y tyuwys yr eil coet yndaw. A'r trydyd coet yw hwnn. A minneu, neut ydynt yn gynyon boneu vy esgyll.
> (ll. 875–78, p. 32)

> When I first came here the large valley that you see was a wooded glen, and a race of men came there, and it was destroyed. And the second wood grew in it, and this wood is the third. And as for me, the roots of my wings are mere stumps.
> (Davies, p. 204)

This juxtaposition of the changing landscape with the Owl's changing appearance, her wings reduced to mere stumps, suggests emotions associated with loss and regret, displaced from the human world to the natural world. The Owl's experience of ageing is projected on to the landscape which absorbs and neutralizes any emotions that might be associated with the passing of time in the human world. The descriptions of the animals seem almost affectless in their refusal to record emotions, but affect is produced through the imagery of loss which permeates each scene, the iterations of the wood standing in for the passing generations of humans. All we have in the text are the place names themselves, suggestive of older versions of the folk tale embedded in the land itself.

Finally, the wise old Salmon of Llyn Lliw takes the men to find Mabon:

> Ac ysef yd aeth ar dwy ysgwyd yr Ehawc, Kei a Gwrhyr Gwalstawt Ieithoed. Ac y kerdassant hyt pann deuthant am y uagwyr a'r karcharawr, yny uyd kwynuan a griduan a

PLACE AND EMOTION

glywynt am y uagwyr ac wy. Gwrhyr a dywawt, "Pa dyn a gwyn yn y maendy hwnn?" "Oia wr, yssit le idaw y gwynaw y neb yssyd yma. Mabon uab Modron yssyd yma yg carchar, ac ny charcharwyt neb kyn dostet yn llwrw carchar a mi . . ."

Ymchoelut ohonunt wy odyno, a dyuot hyt lle yd oed Arthur. Dywedut ohonunt y lle yd oed Mabon uab Modron yg karchar. Gwyssyaw a oruc Arthur milwyr yr Ynys honn, a mynet hyt yg Kaer Loyw y lle yd oed Mabon yg karchar. Mynet a oruc Kei a Bedwyr ar dwy yscwyd y pysc. Tra yttoed vilwyr Arthur yn ymlad a'r gaer, rwygaw o Gei y uagwyr a chymryt y carcharawr ar y geuyn, ac ymlad a'r gwyr ual kynt. Atref y doeth Arthur a Mabon gantaw yn ryd.
(ll. 908–28, p. 33)

The ones who went on the Salmon's shoulders were Cai and Gwrhyr Gwalstawd Ieithoedd. And they travelled until they came to other side of the wall from the prisoner, and they could hear lamenting and moaning on the other side of the wall from them. Gwrhyr said, "Who is lamenting in this house of stone? Alas, sir, he who is here has reason to lament. It is Mabon son of Modron who is imprisoned here, and no one has been so painfully incarcerated in a prison as I . . ."

They returned from there and came to where Arthur was. They reported where Mabon son of Modron was in prison. Arthur summoned the warriors of this Island and went to Caerloyw where Mabon was in prison. Cai and Bedwyr went on the shoulders of the fish. While Arthur's warriors were attacking the fort, Cai tore through the wall and took the prisoner on his back and fought the men as before. Arthur came home and Mabon with him, a free man.
(Davies, p. 205).

In this extract, which is typical of the naturalistic narrative style of the tale, there is one clear emotion represented and that is the sorrow of Mabon son of Modron who explicitly laments his incarceration. He expresses his emotion through his moaning and through his own words, but the emotion produces no corresponding response in Arthur's men, who simply report back to Arthur, who then raises an army to attack the stronghold and release the prisoner. The writing avoids any reference to emotion in its recounting of events, refusing to offer any guidance to the reader. The intensity of emotion emanates entirely from the figure of Mabon and it is located in his place of imprisonment, the stone fortress surrounded by water from which no-one can escape without the help of an army. The fortress itself has a political implication, suggestive of Norman appropriation of Welsh land, with stone fortresses pockmarking the landscape as material representations of foreign oppression and Welsh suffering. The landscape of emotion, the affect, is raised just at this point, in the moment of Mabon's discovery, before flattening out again in the diachronic recital of events. Only that last phrase, "and Mabon with him, a free man", hints at the resolution of Mabon's sorrow and his ability to move forward towards a different future. Once again, the emotion of an individual is implanted into the landscape, where it has a metaphorical resonance in the political context of Norman Wales.

Conclusion

I have been suggesting that in the naturalistic style of medieval Welsh and Irish narrative, where the narrative voice seldom comments on the emotional life of the characters, expressions of emotion are mainly performative. Emotion is conveyed through the direct speech and actions of individual characters who function primarily as social agents rather than as the individual actors typical of realist narrative. In the absence of an omniscient narrator to guide us, the reader or audience is left to deduce individually how to respond to events, which is one of the reasons why we have so many debates about whether particular events are meant to be humorous or not, and how we are meant to interpret characters like the Oldest Animals who seem to give nothing away. We can respond to the language of individual emotions, such as Cú Chulainn's expressions of grief and regret, and Mabon's articulations of his misery as a prisoner, but these performances are produced in the context of a politics of emotion which prioritizes the collective over the individual.

I have also been suggesting that place can function as a generator of affect, a means of managing emotion in a social context. Displacing emotion into the landscape allows the naturalist storyteller to allude to

PLACE AND EMOTION

emotion indirectly, without the need for authorial commentary. But this displacement also functions to control and even neutralize emotion, transforming individual feelings into something more socialized, something that can be absorbed into the cultural practice of the collective. Given the importance of land in early Welsh and Irish societies, places are by definition socially organized and therefore carry an emotional charge, making them powerful vehicles for managing emotions as a social semiotic. I have given some examples of that process, and there are many others in the wider corpus of Welsh and Irish narrative. The incident of the barren landscape in the Third Branch of the *Mabinogi*, the story of Manawydan, its metaphorical force and the conflicting emotions it arouses, is one example. Another is the description of a warlike Bendigeidfran in the Second Branch wading across the Irish Sea, when his appearance as a walking landscape is described by a grieving Branwen. A third is the Old Irish *Acallam na Sénorach*, where stories from the past are linked by the landscape, itself a living material record of Irish history. As Amy Mulligan says, each site of story "allow[s] the landscape itself to provide material memory, continuity, to imbue it with events of the past".[20]

Place and emotion interact with each other in ways that are characteristic of, and produced by, the mode of naturalistic narrative that we find in early Welsh and Irish narrative. The result is a very particular type of affect in these stories, a politics of emotion that denies personal feelings by redirecting them towards a landscape that is mythological, material, and political. We are the ones who have to do the work of retrieving and identifying these emotions while picking up clues as to how to interpret them. Reading early Irish and Welsh narrative is therefore not only a linguistic challenge but demands a political hermeneutics in which place and emotion are inextricably linked.

---

[20] Amy C. Mulligan, "Landscape and Literature in Medieval Ireland", in *A History of Irish Literature and the Environment*, ed. Malcolm Sen (Cambridge: Cambridge University Press, 2022) pp. 33–51, on p. 51.

How to train your *näcken*: Death, dismemberment, and the dissemination of some maritime fabulates

Gregory Darwin

If, like most people, you come to Uppsala by train, one of the first things you will notice as you leave the central station is a fountain with a six-metre-tall bronze statue group, entitled *Näckens polska*, which was completed by Uppsala-born sculptor and painter Bror Hjorth (1894-1968) in 1967.[1] The core of the sculpture is formed by three rather phallic sunflowers; atop the middle and tallest one dance a young man and woman. Beneath this idyllic scene lurk more sinister forces: on the southwest face, a giant nude woman with arms splayed exposes herself to the viewer. Her back is hidden, a detail which suggests the *skogsrå*, a forest-dwelling spirit who resembles a mortal woman except for her hollow back, and who uses her beauty to lure men to their ruin.[2] On the north-east side, we see Hjorth's interpretation of the *näck:* an equally gigantic naked man, with a grotesque grin and pronounced phallus (an ongoing bone of contention for people concerned with how the city presents itself to visitors), playing a golden fiddle and providing the music for the two dancers.[3]

---

[1] Hjorth was commissioned to create the sculpture in 1951, although he had evidently formed the idea for it as early as 1930. The artist's sketches and maquettes for this work are held in Bror Hjorths Hus, a museum located in his former home and atelier in Uppsala. See Mattias Enström, *Bror Hjorth: konst och liv: en bok om konsten i museet Bror Hjorths hus* (Uppsala: Bror Hjorths Hus, 2017), 138-46.

[2] See Tommy Kuusela, "Spirited Away by the Female Forest Spirit in Swedish Folk Belief," *Folklore* 131, no. 2 (May 2020): 159-79.

[3] The museum's website notes that *"[många] var upprörda över näckens uppenbara nakenhet och skrev insändare redan innan skulpturen invigts. Att huldran inte heller hade kläder ansågs inte lika stötande."* ([Many] were upset by the *näck*'s obvious nudity, and wrote letters to the editor even before the sculpture was unveiled. The fact that the *huldra* did not have clothes either was not seen as equally offensive.") "Näckens polska, 1967," Bror Hjorths Hus, accessed April

HOW TO TRAIN YOUR *NÄCKEN*

The sculpture shares its title with, and was possibly inspired by, the musical setting of a poem by the Västergötland poet, priest, and folklorist Arvid August Afzelius, first published in 1812.[4] In Afzelius' poem, the näck is *hafwets Kung* (the king of the sea), who has fallen in love with a star, and who often comes to the surface of the ocean to play his golden harp and lament the divinely ordained impossibility of their love. Depictions of the näck as sinister amphibious musician figure in a wide range of popular literature and media from Sweden: recent examples that enjoyed some commercial success outside of Sweden include the 2017 survival horror game Unforgiving: A Northern Hymn, and the 2023 adventure game Bramble: The Mountain King.[5]

If you were to ask a typical educated Swede to describe a näck (and my long-suffering colleagues can tell you that I indeed have), you would hear something similar to what I have described: a being who resembles a human male, often unclothed (a description that is likely reinforced by the similarity between the definite form näcken and the adjective *naken* 'naked'), and who appears near rivers and other bodies of water often with a violin or another stringed instrument. He is a sinister figure who may drown those humans who are unfortunate enough to encounter him, but he is also a skilled musician and may teach tunes to humans who observe the proper protocols. The same ideas are reflected in the vast archive of material collected from oral tradition in Sweden in the nineteenth and twentieth centuries. To give just one example, Erik Gustav Andersson of Tösse, Västergötland, related the following account in 1928:

15, 2024, https://brorhjorthshus.se/verkstexter-bror-hjorth/nackens-polska-1967/. See also Enström, *Bror Hjorth*, 141.

Although the definite form *näcken* is more commonly used in Swedish, I have opted to use the indefinite form *näck* throughout, so as to avoid usages such as 'the *näcken*' (a pleonasm on par with 'the *hoi polloi.*') The exception is my title, as I could not resist the siren song of a tenuous and truly terrible joke.

[4] First published as A. Z., "Necken. Romanz," *Iduna: en Skrift för den Nordiska Fornålderns Älskare* 3 (1812): 87-90. A musical setting was published, along with an English translation, in Gustaf Hägg (ed.) and Henry Grafton Chapman (trans.), *Songs of Sweden: Eighty-seven Swedish folk- and popular songs* (New York: G. S. Schirmer, 1909), 5-7.

[5] Produced by Angry Demon Studio AB, Skövde, and Dimfrost Studo, Norrköping, respectively.

GREGORY DARWIN

Det var en gubbe väst i Fröskogs socke, han är nu död för månge år senna, han hade lärt att spele av näcken. Gubben och näcken kom överens om, att näcken skulle ha en blodsdroppe ur den högre lellfingern för det att han skulle läre gubben att spele. Den lellfingern blev stel alltsenna dess, så att det inte var nån led i den.

Han fick läre sej Näckens polske. När han spela den, om di aldrig hade dansat, så dansa bå små och store, onge och gamle då. Ja, den gubben lär ha haft liv i låtera.[6]

There was an old man west in Fröskog, who has been dead now for many years, who learned to play from the näck. The old man and the näck came to an agreement that the näck would get a drop of blood from the man's right little finger, and that he would teach the old man to play. His little finger became rigid afterwards, so there was no life in it.

He learned to play the näck's polka. Whenever he played this, everyone would dance, big and small, old and young, even if they had never danced. Yes, that old man learned to put life into his tunes.[7]

    Andersson begins his account by situating the action within a definite place and time: the parish of Fröskog, some fifteen kilometers west of Tösse, perhaps a few decades ago. While he does not name the man who made this bargain, one suspects that he could. This tells us that the näck exists within the realm of belief: in the mental world of nineteenth-century rural Swedes, the näck lurked by rivers and lakes outside of settled space, and could explain unexpected deaths and the unpredictable distribution of talent. The näck's gifts always come with a cost: a bit of blood, a cut of meat, or the sacrifice of a whole animal (preferably a black one).[8] If that price is not paid, then the näck's gift is dangerous or lacking in some way:

---

[6] Göteborg, Institutet för folklore vid Göteborgs Högskola (IFGH)1484:1, quoted in Bengt af Klintberg, *Svenska Folksägner* (Stockholm: Norstedt, 1986), 102
[7] Unless otherwise specified, all translations are my own.
[8] Bengt af Klintberg, *The types of the Swedish folk legend* (Helsinki: Academia Scientiarum Fennica, 2010), 125-7.

HOW TO TRAIN YOUR *NÄCKEN*

a man may be able to tune but not play his fiddle, or he may be unable to stop playing once he has begun.

In other accounts from southern Sweden, the term näck is used to signify an intelligent and often malicious water-dwelling horse. Both hippoid and humanoid näck have a similar profile, as dangerous and solitary water-dwellers with a penchant for drowning unwary travellers. Perhaps unsurprisingly, the näck-as-horse rarely acts as musician or music-teacher: violins are difficult to play with hoofs, after all. Like many other supernatural beings, it reacts negatively to hearing its own name, as in the following account, recorded in 1933 from Johan Sjödin, of Visselfjärda, Kalmar:

> *Näcken han kan uppträda som en häst, en stor fin häst. Det var några barn, som var ok lekte här strax intill vid en liten sjö, och då gick där en stor vit häst, som de inte hade sett där förut, och nyfikna och kliiga, som sådana pojkarna alltid är, skulle de ta och rida på de här hasten. De klev upp den ene efter den andre, men så var där en liten, och han kunde inte tala rent. "Jag näcken inte," sa han. "Jag räcker inte," menade han. Då satte hästen av i sken, och barnen trillade av hit och dit, och sen fortsatte han ner i vattnet, så att det brusade om honom. Se, det var bara för att den lille sa "näcken" – det tål han inte att höra.*[9]

The näck could appear as a horse, a great big horse. There were some small children, who were playing right next to a little lake, and then there came a big white horse which they had never seen before, and, curious like young boys always are, tried to get up on this horse. They climbed up, one after the other, but there was a little boy who could not speak properly. "Jag näcken inte," he said. "Jag räcker inte" [I can't reach], he meant. Then the horse set off, and the children tumbled off here and there, and the horse dove back into the water, which bubbled around it. See, it was

---

[9] Lund, Lund universitet folklivsarkivet (LUF) 4702: 11, quoted in af Klintberg, *Svenska folksägner*, 104-5.

only because the little one said "näcken", that word which it could not hear.

In Sjödin's account, the näck can take the shape of a horse, but it is not essentially a horse, and there is no question of it being a different sort of beast than the violin-playing *gubbe* or *karl*. Some tradition-bearers distinguish the *bäckahäst* 'brook-horse' and *bäckaman* 'brook-man'; whether these are distinct beings, *sui generis*, or different accidents of the same essence is not always clear. Elsewhere in the Nordic world, cognate terms are used to signify both a more-or-less humanoid water-dweller and a water-horse.[10] The following account, recorded in the early nineteenth century from Arnljótur Ólafsson, a minister in Bægisá, Iceland, presents the same motif of a would-be victim saved by a chance utterance of the beast's name:

> Einu sinni var smalastúlka að leita að fé. Hún hafði gengið lengi og var orðin lúin mjög. Sér hún þá hest gráan[11] og verður fegin, hnýtir upp í hann sokkabandinu sínu, leggur svuntuna sína á hann, leiðir hann að þúfu og ætlar á bak. En rétt í því hún ætlar á bak segir hún: "Ég trúi ég nenni þá ekki á bak."

---

[10] Danish *nøkke*, Norwegian *nykk* or *nøkk,* Icelandic and Faroese *nykur*. The Norwegian painter Theodor Kittelsen's painting *Nøkken* (1887-92), a mainstay of Norwegian gift shops, depicts the eponymous being as a vaguely humanoid form submerged in a lake, while *Nøkken som hvit hest* (1907) depicts the being as a white horse.

Cognates that denote sinister supernatural forces with aquatic associations exist in other Germanic languages: German *Nix* or *Nixe*, Dutch *nikker*, Old English *nicor*, etc. In addition to being used in *Beowulf* to describe some kind of aquatic monster, the Old English term is used in the Old English version of the *Epistola Alexandri ad Aristotelem*, where it corresponds with *hippopotamus* in the Latin version. Robert Dennis Fulk, *The Beowulf Manuscript: Complete Texts and The Fight at Finnsburg* (Cambridge, Massachusetts: Harvard University Press, 2010), 48, 50. See also Ryan Denson, "Ancient sea monsters and a medieval hero: the *nicoras* of *Beowulf*," *Shima* 16, no. 2 (2022), 113-26.

[11] "Sumir segja *brúnan*. Þessi saga er mjög algeng og sögð um nykra í ýmsum vötnum." ("some say brown. This story is rather common, and told about nykurs in various lakes.")

HOW TO TRAIN YOUR *NÄCKEN*

Þá tekur hesturinn viðbragð mikið og stökk út í vatn eitt skammt þaðan og hvarf. Stúlkan sá nú hvers kyns var, að þetta var nykur, því það er náttúra hans að hann má eigi heyra nafn sitt, þá fer hann í vatn sitt, en hann heitir öðru nafni nennir, og því fór hann er hún sagði nennir. – Sama verður og ef hann heyrir sagt andskoti.[12]

One time there was a shepherd girl who was looking for some sheep. She had been walking for a long time and had become very tired. Then she saw a grey horse and, overjoyed, she ties up her garter on him, lays her apron on him, and leads him to a grassy area and plans [to climb] onto his back. But right as she was thinking about doing this, she says, "I don't believe I feel like [climbing] onto his back after all."

Then the horse gave a start and lept out into the water, and then vanished straightaway. The girl now saw what sort [of horse] it was, that it was a nykur, for it was his nature that he could not hear his name. He went back into the water then. He was called by another name, *nennir* ['to feel like, care to'], and he left when she said *nennir*. The same would have happened if he had heard the name of the Devil said.

For those who are specialists in Celtic, some potential parallels with Gaelic tradition will come to mind: Cú Chulainn's two horses, Líath Macha and Dub Sainglend, in early Irish literature, and numerous oral traditions in Ireland and Scotland of water-horses who drown unsuspecting humans: *each uisge* in Irish and Scottish Gaelic, *kelpie* in Scots.[13] Accounts such as

---

[12] Jón Árnasson, *Íslenzkar þjóðsögur og ævintýri* (Leipzig: J. C. Hinrich, 1862), i 137.

[13] As discussed below, the closest parallels between traditions involving Cú Chulainn's horses and modern oral traditions of the water-horse are to be found in the Old Irish *Brislech Mór Maige Muirthemne* (also known as *Aided Con Culainn*) and the Middle Irish *Fled Bricrenn*. See R. I. Best, Osborn Bergin (eds.), *The Book of Leinster, formerly Lebor na Nuachongbála* (Dublin: Dublin Institute for Advanced Studies, 1954-83), ii 448-50, and George Henderson, *Fled*

those quoted above, in which the horse's would-be victims are spared after they accidentally say its name, are absent in the Gaelic world; instead we find well-established narratives with distinctly unhappy endings. A representative example was recorded by one Peig Judge of Croagh, co. Sligo, in the Schools Collection in 1937:

> Near the Ladies' Bray which is about 13 miles from Dromore West on the Sligo side there is a lake called Loch an Chroí. There once lived a farmer near this lake who had a very large farm of mountain and bog. The lake was a large one and the people of the district believed it was enchanted. They believed that under its dark waters lived great kings and chiefs of long ago.
>
> This particular farmer became very poor. All his stock died and when he bought some more to replace them they too died. Spring then came and he felt very distressed and lonely not having a horse to plough his land. He did not know what to do. One evening he was out walking on his farm—very grieved and down-hearted—when looking towards the lake what did he see but a most beautiful jet-black mare grazing along the lake. He went near her. She stood up—looked at him. He caught hold of her and took her home with him to his stable. He fed her and patted her and grew very fond of her. She ploughed and worked for him with cart and car very quietly. Each year she had a foal which the farmer sold and got well-paid for. He was now growing very rich. The mare worked willingly and quietly for him for many years. During all this time the farmer was very kind to her. He never gave her even one blow.
>
> At last one day as the farmer rode the mare to the lake for a drink he struck her with the bridle. The mare leaped and neighed three times. Immediately all the foals she ever

---

Bricrend: The Feast of Bricriu (London: Irish Texts Society, 1899), 38-41. The modern oral traditions are discussed by Bo Almqvist, "Waterhorse legends (MLSIT 4086 & 4086B): The case for and against a connection between Irish and Nordic tradition," *Béaloideas* 59 (1991): 107-20.

reared came round her. Then the mare with the man on her back, and all the foals dashed into the lake. It seems the farmer was killed, for it is believed that on the next day his heart was seen floating on the surface of the lake, and from that day the lake is called *Loch an Chroí* [lake of the heart].[14]

As *fabulates*, these narratives occupy an uneasy middle ground. On the one hand, as a form of legend they reflect real belief, belief in other-than-human beings who inhabit our world and interact with humanity in various ways (although, as Linda Dégh and others have pointed out, the question of how widely and how sincerely a community holds a particular belief is far more complex than it might appear at first).[15] On the other hand, unlike the brief *dite* and the personal *memorate*, the fabulate represents a stable narrative cluster which can be identified and observed repeatedly in the archive.[16] When the same cluster can be observed in multiple tradition-areas, this phenomenon invites comparative approaches. The narrative patterns of many fabulates can be found across geographic and linguistic boundaries, and while it is, of course, possible that similar stories may arise independently of each other, when discussing areas such as Iceland,

---

[14] Dublin, National Folklore Collection, Schools Collection, MS 167: 50-1. Collected by Peig Judge, 15 years old, from her grandmother in 1937.

[15] The conception of the legend as historical or true, in contrast with the fictitious or poetic folktale, can be traced back to the Brothers Grimm's *Deutsche Sagen* (1816). For an important account of the reassessment of the legend as genre which took place in the middle of the 20th century, see Linda Dégh and Andrew Vázsonyi, "Legend and Belief," *Genre* 4, no. 3 (September 1971): 281-304. For more recent overviews, see Timothy R. Tangherlini, "'It happened not too far from here': A survey of legend theory and characterization," *Western Folklore* 49, no. 4 (October 1990): 371-90; and Kaarina Koski, "The legend genre and narrative registers," in *Genre – Text – Interpretation*, edited by Kaarina Koski, Frog, and Ula Savolainen (Helsinki: Studia Fennica Folkloristica, 2016), 113-36.

[16] My use of these terms follows that of Carl Wilhelm von Sydow, "Kategorien der Prosa-Volksdichtung," in *Volkskundliche Gaben: Festschrift J. Meier zum 70 Geburtstag dargebracht*, edited by Erich Sechmann and Harry Schewe (Berlin: W. De Gruyter, 1934), 253-68; reprinted in Carl Wilhelm von Sydow, *Selected papers on folklore* (Copenhagen: Roskilde and Bagger, 1948), 60-85, with English summary 86-8.

GREGORY DARWIN

Scotland, Ireland, and Scandinavia which have a long history of trade and migration, only the most die-hard adherent of polygenesis would deny the possibility that stories migrate with people and take root in their new settings.

Fabulates are legends and cannot be understood independently of the belief which informs them. This fact invites several questions when considering those fabulates with international distribution. When and how does supernatural belief, especially belief in particular supernatural beings, travel across cultural boundaries? Can we, and when can we talk about belief in the 'same' being as existing across such boundaries—is the *näck-as-bäckahäst* the 'same' being as the *each uisce*? For that matter, is the näck of Småland the 'same' as the näck of Skåne? In the introduction to his influential catalogue of the migratory legends found in Norwegian tradition, Reidar Christiansen acknowledged the generic fluidity of fabulates.[17] Legends can be told as, and indeed catalogued as, wonder-tales. The narrative pattern of a legend has the potential to exist independently of a particular belief, entering the realm of pure story at the moment of translation, or being forced into the Procrustean bed of the 'traditiondominants' of the borrowing culture's belief system.[18]

In my title, I flippantly suggest that I will offer ways to train the näck. From the examples given so far, I hope to have demonstrated that it is indeed an unruly beast which needs to be brought to heel, but carefully. Death and dismemberment are the fate of most humans who encounter the näck and other such beings; but they are also the risk which such beings face when we let our own monsters run loose in an attempt to construct narratives to make sense of the archival material. In the remaining time, I intend to discuss a few examples drawn from the broader corpus of Gaelic and Nordic maritime legend, that portray beings who refuse to inhabit the neat conceptual boxes that we have set aside for them.

---

[17] Reidar Th. Christiansen, *The Migratory Legends: a proposed list of types with a systematic catalogue of the Norwegian variants* (Helsinki: Academia Scientiarum Fennica, 1958), 4.

[18] On the term 'tradition dominant', see Lauri Honko, "Four Forms of Adaptation of Tradition," *Studia Fennica* 26 (1981): 19-33.

HOW TO TRAIN YOUR *NÄCKEN*

The first example I wish to consider is the widespread legend about the man who compels a woman from the sea to remain on land and marry him.[19] The legend received the designation ML 4080 'The Seal Woman' in Christiansen's catalogue, on the basis of the one Norwegian variant available to him, as well as the handful of Icelandic, Faroese, and Danish variants, all of which identify the woman in question as a member of a pack of shapeshifting seals.[20] Christiansen did not include any of the numerous Irish or Scottish variants of the legend, in which the woman is more typically a solitary mermaid or woman from the sea; this difference is seemingly minor, but not a trivial one, as I will discuss later.

The earliest reference to this legend appears in Egbert Óloffson's 1772 account of his travels through Iceland. Note that, although Egbert distances himself from the legend, he does present this (and other accounts of seals) as items of genuine popular belief:

> *En anden Fabel eller Meening, som er ligesaa urigtig, skaffer Sælhunden et Slags Anseelse; nemlig, at den skulde være et Slags menneligt Slægt, kaldet Sæfolk, der skulde boe paa Havets Grund, og have en menneskelig Skikkelse, under den udvortes og bekiendte Sælhunde "Stabning", og denne skulde de lægge fra sig iblandt, naar de ville i godt Væir spadsere paa Strandbredden. Man skal have kommet over deres Fruentimmere og taget dem till Ægte.*[21]
>
> Another fable or tradition, equally fantastic, devotes special attention to the breed of seals, regarding it as a kind of human race, called merfolk, living on the sea-floor and possessing human shape under the familiar external seal-hide; this hide they are said to discard occasionally when

---

[19] This legend formed the subject of my doctoral dissertation. Gregory Darwin, "Mar *gur dream Sí iad atá ag mairiúint fén bhfarraige*: ML 4080 The Seal Woman in its Irish and international context" (PhD diss., Harvard University, 2019).
[20] Christiansen, *The Migratory Legends*, 75.
[21] Eggert Olafsen and Biarne Povelsen, *Vice-Landmand Eggert Olafsens og Land-Physici Biarne Povelsens reise giennem Island* (Sorøe: Jonas Lindgrens Enke, 1772), 535.

in fine weather they want to walk on the beach. Their women are said to have been caught and taken as wives.[22]

This is a summary, and not a sympathetic one, rather than a transcription of an actual performance, and so many details are lacking, but it does allow us to infer that the legend existed in Iceland by the late eighteenth century in a form resembling that which appears in the major nineteenth-century collections. I should quickly note that we cannot infer that the legend has its origins in Iceland from the fact that it is first attested there; for reasons which I won't explore in the interest of time, I think an Irish or Scottish origin to be most likely.[23]

The overwhelming majority of variants of the legend were recorded in Ireland: in my doctoral research I identified nearly four hundred versions from published and archival sources.[24] The legend is well-represented in Scotland as well, with sixty-six versions known to me; none of the other countries where the legend is attested—Iceland, the Faroes, Norway, Sweden, Denmark, the Isle of Man—have more than a dozen recorded versions. In Ireland, most versions of the legend fit neatly into what I refer to as the Northern or Southern oicotypes (localized folk tale), along with some more regionally restricted sub-types. I give the following account, recorded from Máire Ní Bheirn of Málainn Bheag, co. Donegal, in 1935, as a representative sample of the Northern oicotype:

> *Bhí fear i Málainn Bhig, agus chuaidh sé síos lá amháin 'na chladaigh fhad le áit a dtugann siad a Sludán air. Agus chonnaic sé cailín deas ag n-a taoibh, agus bhí sí a cíoradh a ceann. Thug sé'n brat abhaile leis, agus lean a cailín é abhaile.*
>
> *D'fhan sí aige (annsin) ins a bhaile, agus pósadh an bheirt annsin. Agus bhí triúr a mhuirghín aici. Chuir sé'n brat i bhfolach oirthí, nó dá bhfaghad sí an brat, d'fhágfad sí é i*

---

[22] Translated in Martin Puhvel, "The seal in the folklore of Northern Europe," *Folklore* 74 (1963): 326-66, at 327.

[23] See Darwin, "*Mar gur dream Sí iad*," 78-80.

[24] References to all known versions of the legend appear in Darwin, "*Mar gur dream Sí iad*," 266-99.

HOW TO TRAIN YOUR *NÄCKEN*

ndiaidh í a leanamhaint abhaile, agus bhainfeadh sí'n fhairrge amach.

Bhí 'n brat i bhfad i bhfolach aige, go dtí go rabh sé a déanamh cruach órna, agus chuir sé isteach i lár na cruaiche órna an brat i bhfolach. Dar leis go b'é an áit a b'fheárr é. Chonnaic duine de na páistí é ag cur a bhrat i bhfolach, agus d'innis sé do'n mhaithir nuair a d'imthigh an t-athair go rabh 'n brat astoig sa chruach ghráin. Leag sí anuas go talamh í, go bhfuair sí an brat. D'imthigh sí léithe 'na fairrge. Agus ó'n lá sin go dtí 'n lá indiu ní fhacthas í.[25]

There was a man in Málainn Bheag, and he went down to the shore one day to a place they called the Sludán. And he saw a beautiful girl combing her hair. He took the *brat* 'cloak' with him, and the girl followed him home.

She stayed with him and they were married. They had three children. He hid the brat from her, for if she found it she would leave him, after having followed him home, and return to the sea.

He had the brat hidden for a while, until one day he was making a stack of barley and he hid it in the middle of the stack. One of the children saw him hiding the brat there, and when the father had gone away to work, he told his mother that the brat was inside the grain stack. She knocked it to the ground and found the brat. She left for the sea, and from that day was never seen again.

The supernatural woman may be described as half-human and half-fish or, as in this account, simply as a 'girl' or 'woman'; invariably she is young and beautiful. The characteristic feature of the Northern oicotype is that the man hides the woman's *brat* 'cloak' (the description of this object varies) in a stack of drying hay. As these are temporary structures, the man has to regularly replace the brat, and the woman learns where it has been hidden

---

[25] Dublin, National Folklore Collection, Main Collection, MS 142:477-8. Máire Ní Bheirn, 68, housewife, Málainn Bheag, Tír Chonaill. Collected by Seán Ó hEochaidh, 31/12/1935.

from her children, who observe their father moving the brat to a new hiding place and ask their mother about this behaviour. While this detail is not included here, some versions of the Northern oicotype specify that the mermaid returns to comb her children's hair, bring them fish, or to otherwise care for them.[26] The Scottish versions can be seen as a subtype of the Northern oicotype: the brat is often hidden in a barn rather than a haystack, but both are structures external to the main domestic space, and the children play a role in the recovery of the object.[27]

An account recorded from Mícheál Ó Murchadha, Páirc an Teampaill, co. Kerry, in 1929 demonstrates the Southern oicotype:

> *Bhí fear thíos i gCill Chuimín i bParóiste 'n Litriúigh i gContae Ciarraidhe ⁊ bhí sé lá insa tráigh a' bailiú feamnaighe ⁊ chonnaic sé bean 'na suidhe ar leac cloiche ar lag trágha ⁊ í a' cíoradh a cinn. Tháinig se i leith ar drom uirthi ⁊ ní fhaca sí é go dtáinig sé suas léi. Bhí cochaillín draoidheachta aici in aice léi ar an gcloich. Rug sé ar a' gcochaillín draoidheachta ina láimh chomh luath is tháinig sé suas. Chromadar ar chainnt le chéile ⁊ dubhairt sé léi teacht abhaile in-aoinfheacht leis féin. Dubhairt sé le n'athair go gcoinneochadh sé mar bhean an bhean so ó'n dtráigh. "Álright," arsan t-athair, "táimse sásta má tá'n tú féinigh sásta," ar seisean. Phósadar ⁊ bhíodar a' déunamh go máith idteannta chéile ⁊ bhí cúigear cloinne acu. Do bhí an cochaillín draoidheachta istigh imála anáirde ar an gcúl-lochta fan na haimsire go léir.*
>
> *Do bhí fear a'tighe a' dul a treabhadh ⁊ do bhí sé a' soláthar gléas an treabhtha ar a' gcúl-lochta. I measg an chuid eile cad a chaith sé anuas ach an cochaillín draoidheachta. Nuair d'imthigh sé amach do phrioc an bhean suas an cochaillín draoidheachta. Nigh sí agus ghlan sí gach éinne de'n gclainn ⁊ chíor sí a gceann. Nuair a bhí san déunta aici d'imthi' sí amach a' dorus ⁊ rug sí léi an cochall go dtí an áit sa tráigh na raibh an leac-cloiche. Ansan do shín sí*

---

[26] Darwin, "*Mar gur dream Sí iad*," 57.
[27] Ibid., 49, 53.

HOW TO TRAIN YOUR *NÄCKEN*

an cochaillín os a comhair agus d'imthigh sí amach an fhairrge.[28]

There was a man down in Cill Choimín, county Kerry, and he was by the shore one day gathering seaweed. He saw a woman sitting on a rock at low tide, combing her head. She had a *cochaillín draíochta* 'little magical cloak' on the rock by her. He grabbed her cochaillín as soon as he reached her. They started talking, and he told her to come with him. He told his father that he would keep this woman from the shore as a wife. "Alright," said his father, "I'm happy if you're happy." They married and were doing well together and had five children. The cochaillín was in a sack up in the upper loft this whole time.

The man was going to go plowing, and was looking for the plowing gear which was in the upper loft. There with everything else, what else should he throw down but the cochaillín? When he left, the woman picked it up. She washed and cleaned all of her children, and combed their hair. When that was done, she went out the door and she took the cochall with her and went to the place at the shore where the rock was. Then she put on her cochaillín and went into the sea.

The main points of divergence between the Northern and Southern oicotypes are the hiding-place of the magical garment, and the method of recovery. Rather than in a haystack or a barn, the man hides this object within the domestic space, usually in the storage loft, and it is his own neglect of the domestic sphere, by carelessly tossing aside objects in search for something, which results in the supernatural woman abandoning him.

In addition to this North/South divide, there is another detail in the Irish and Scottish material which is subject to significant variation: the identity of the supernatural bride as a mermaid or seal-woman.[29] This

---

[28] Dublin, National Folklore Collection, Main Collection, MS 34:238. Mícheál Ó Murchadha, 80, Páirc an Teampuill, Lios Póil, co. Ciarraí. Collected by Séamas Mac hIcidhe, 19/10/1929.

[29] Darwin, "*Mar gur dream Sí iad*," 35-7.

correlates not only with the description of the stolen object—a mermaid possesses a garment of some sorts, or a detachable tail, while the seal-woman possesses a skin or hide—but also with her behaviour prior to her capture. The mermaid appears alone, sitting on a rock and combing her hair; while the seal-woman appears as part of a group of similar beings, and dances and frolics with her companions after excorticating herself.[30] Unlike the hiding place and means-of-recovery motifs, the variation between seal or mermaid does not constitute a clear isogloss. The seal is dominant within Shetland and Orkney, as well as Iceland and the Faroe Islands. While the mermaid is dominant in Ireland and Gaelic Scotland, versions involving seals are to be found with no geographic pattern. Even in versions of the legend where the woman is identified as a mermaid, there are occasionally details which suggest a connection with seals, such as an inherited taboo against killing the animal, or visitation by seals identified as the mermaid's kin.[31]

While there is overlap, there are reasons to conceive of mermaids and seals as different 'types' of beings in folk tradition. When the legend is connected with a particular family, the woman's identity is fixed: legends about the Mac Conaola of Galway or the Mac Codruim of Uibhist invariably present the woman as a seal, while those connected to the Ó Séaghdha of Kerry present her as a *murúch* or mermaid.[32] These connections are also represented in, and reinforced by, other traditions connecting the family with that being.[33] Other fabulates and memorates ascribe different behaviours to seals and mermaids, and recommend different strategies for humans who encounter them.[34]

As noted above, legends are related to belief, and the content of ML 4080 reflects beliefs about whichever being plays the role of the supernatural captive. Seals are social animals, whereas mermaids often appear alone at sea or on the shore in maritime memorates. When confronted with this variation, it is natural to ask which option is the

---

[30] Ibid., 46-7.
[31] Ibid., 58-9.
[32] Ibid., 352-69.
[33] As recently as spring 2021, the author heard a native speaker from co. Galway refer to a member of the Mac Conaola family who was not present as "*cloigeann aníos*" (literally "a head from below," a periphrasis denoting the common seal).
[34] Several examples are discussed in Darwin, "*Mar gur dream Sí iad*," 81-133.

original. In my dissertation, I suggested that the earliest forms of the legend presented the woman as a seal, and that the mermaid later became the tradition dominant throughout the Gaelic-speaking world, with stray survivals of the seal-archetype.[35] I am no longer convinced that this is the case.

The Icelandic and Faroese versions of the legend agree with each other fairly closely.[36] They describe the supernatural woman as is a seal who regularly visits a particular spot with her kin in order to assume human shape and dance and play for a period of time. As in the Northern oicotype, the seal-woman often returns to the shore after her escape in order to care for her children. Unlike in the Northern oicotype, these children play no role in the recovery of the object; instead, the man locks the sealskin in a chest, and his wife recovers it when he forgets the key in the lock one day. The relative uniformity of this tradition across a fairly large geographic area suggests that it is a relatively recent import; perhaps brought to Iceland and the Faroes via Shetland and Orkney, where we find the Northern oicotype and the woman portrayed as a seal. If that is the case, then the forgotten-key motif is an innovation introduced when, or before, the legend was brought to Iceland and Faroe. The same motif, however, also appears in about a dozen versions recorded in Ireland, mostly from counties Kerry, Cork, and Waterford.[37] This could, of course, be a coincidental independent

---

[35] Ibid., 79.
[36] Five Icelandic versions of the legend are known to me: Jón Árnason, *Íslenzkar þjóðsögur og ævintýri*, edited by Árni Böðvarsson and Bjarni Vilhjálmsson (Reykjavík: Þjóðsaga, 1954-1961), i 629-30, iv 10, 10-11, 11-12; Sigfús Sigfússon, *Íslenskar þjóðsögur og sagnir*, edited by Óskar Halldórsson et al., second edition (Reykjavík: Þjóðsaga, 1982-1993), iv 187-8. Six Faroese versions are known to me: Jens Christian Svabo, *Indberetninger fra en Reise i Færøe 1781 og 1782* (København: Selskabet til udgivelse af Færøske kildeskrifter studier, 1959), 53; J. H. Schröter, "Færøiske Folkesagn", in *Antiquarisk Tidskift udgivet af det Kongelige Nordiske Oldskrift-selskab* (Kjøbenhaven: Brödrene Berling, 1850), 190-3; V. U. Hammershaimb, *Færøsk Anthologi* (København: S.L. Møller, 1886), 345-8; Joseph Russell Jeaffreson, *The Faröe Islands* (London: Sampson Low, Marston & Company, 1898), 84-7; and Oslo, Institutet for folkminnevitskap, MN 1971 band 10, recorded by Mortan Nolsöe from William Tindskarð, Skálavík, 20/5/1971.
[37] Darwin, "*Mar gur dream Sí iad*," 54.

development, but the possibility that it might not, and that the legend may have travelled more than once, is worth consideration.

The Danish and Norwegian versions show the influence of the Northern oicotype.[38] The skin is hidden somewhere outside of the house (beneath the floor in Denmark, and in a barn or outhouse in Norway), and the children help their mother find it either by bringing it to her, or telling her where they saw their father hide it. The Danish version describes her as a *havfrue*, a term which in contemporary Danish signifies a half-fish, half-human mermaid such as the protagonist of Hans Christian Andersen's famous novella, but describes the stolen object as a *sælhundeskind* 'sealskin'. In one of the Norwegian accounts, she is a seal-girl (*kobbepige*); in the other, she is a young woman who comes up onto the land from the sea with her two sisters, and her would-be husband steals her clothing while she is bathing.[39] The latter version is unusually long, as it is a hybrid of ML 4080 with the internationally distributed wonder-tale ATU 400 "Man on a Quest for his Lost Wife" and, unlike in nearly all versions of the legend, the man is able to regain his wife through deception in this account. This version, published by Jens Andreas Friis in 1871 and recorded from an anonymous storyteller from Lebesby, is also noteworthy in that the storyteller was a speaker of Northern Sámi. Intelligent and human-like seals, to the best of my knowledge, do not figure prominently in Sámi tradition; absent this background of belief the borrowed narrative was presumably grafted onto an already-known tale.

A fairly straightforward narrative emerges: the legend originates in Ireland (or perhaps Scotland), and spreads via the Highlands to Shetland and Orkney, whence it is brought to Iceland, the Faroes, and continental Scandinavia. The Swedish evidence, however, complicates things. To the

---

[38] One Danish version is known to me: Evald Tang Kristensen, *Danske Sagn*, 2. Afdeling: Ellefolk, *Nisser og adskillige Uhyrer, samt religiøse Sagn, Lys og Varsler* (Århus: Århus folkeblads bogtrykkeri, 1893), 16. Two Norwegian versions are known to me: O. Nicolaissen, *Sagn og Eventyr fra Nordland* (Kristiania: B. T. Rallingsboghandel, 1879), i 27-8; and J. A. Friis, *Lappiske Eventyr og Folkesagn* (Christiania: Alb. Cammermeyer, 1871), 27-32.

[39] In Nicolaisen, *Sagn og eventyr*, 27-8, the woman is identified as a kobbepige, and the magical garment as a *kobbehud*, glossed as *sælhundeskind* 'sealskin'. In the account published by Friis, the woman is simply "*pigen fra havet*" (the girl from the sea).

best of my knowledge, five versions of the legend have been recorded in Sweden, although two of these versions were recorded from the same informant, Fredrika Pålsson of Brånalt, in Halland.[40] In the versions from Blekinge, Halland, and Värmland, the supernatural woman is described variously as a *sjöjungfru* 'mermaid', *havstroll* 'sea-troll', or *sjörå* 'sea-rå'; a solitary being who appears either half-fish or fully human. The man steals her clothing or her *hamn* 'skin, shape', described as a detachable covering over her legs, and hides it in a chest.[41] She recovers her stolen property when her husband forgets to remove the key from the chest, and in the Halland variants she is reunited with her former husband, another ocean-dweller.

A distinctively Swedish oicotype emerges, one which shares the forgotten-key motif with the Faroese and Icelandic versions, but which also disagrees with them, and the Norwegian-Danish versions, in several respects. One possibility is that this legend was brought to Sweden from Iceland or the Faroes, with the unfamiliar seal-woman replaced by a local tradition-dominant, although the diversity of names for the supernatural woman in Swedish versions of the legend, as well as the rarity of the half-fish sjöjungfru in archival materials, do not support this interpretation.[42] Another is that the tale may have been brought to Sweden from the south of Ireland, where both mermaid and forgotten-key motifs co-exist.

A very different account was recorded by Tomas Sandberg of Uddevalla, Bohuslän, in 1919, from an anonymous sailboat captain. In

---

[40] The versions recorded from Pålsson are Göteborg, IFGH, 3021:4 (recorded by Erik Johansson, 1931) and Uppsala, Institutet för språk och folkminnen (ISOF), 23019: 115:13 (recorded by Erik Brånberg, 1943). The other three recorded versions are: Per Johnsson, *Sägner och folktro från Blekinge* (Karlshamn: E.G. Johansson, 1921), 14-15; Göteborg, IFGH 3915:26-31 (recorded from Carl Eriksson, 69, of Eskilsäter by Ragnar Nilsson, 1937), published in Ragnar Nilsson and Carl-Martin Bergstrand (eds.), *Folktro och folksed på Värmlandsnäs* (Göteborg: Gumperts förlag, 1952-62), iii, 52-55; and Göteborg, Västsvenska folkminnes föreningen (VFF) 41:68-70 (recorded by T. Sandberg, Uddevalla, 1919).

[41] Fredrika Pålsson uses the terms *fiskhamn* 'fish shape,' *sjöjungfruhamn* 'mermaid shape' and *sjöhamn* 'sea shape' at various points in the two accounts recorded from her.

[42] "The mermaid (*sjöjungfru*) of international sailor lore with naked breasts and a fish tail has been documented only occasionally in Sweden." af Klintberg, *Types of the Swedish folk legend*, 111.

GREGORY DARWIN

Sandberg's account, the protagonist sees a group of seal-women on the shore one night, and steals one of the skins, compelling the woman to follow him home, and eventually marry him. They have children, one of whom finds the sealskin hidden under a rock outside the house and brings it to his mother. When the husband is away on a fishing trip, she escapes and is reunited with her former husband, but before she vanishes forever she tells her captor:

> *Farväl. Jag önskar dig att lycka och välgång. Jag älskade dig alltid, då jag var på jorden, men min förste man har jag dock älskat mer än dig! Jag väl vara på våra barn och må du bra lycklig tills den död.*[43]

> Farewell! I wish you luck and well-being. I have always loved you while I was on land, but I have always loved my first husband more than you. I wish well for our children, and may you prosper until your death.

Many of the details of this version, especially the woman's final blessing, are characteristic of Shetlandic and Orcadian tradition; Sandberg was aware of this discrepancy, as he identified his informant as a sea captain and stated that the legend "*är kanske icke av bohuslänsk ursprung*" (is perhaps not originally from Bohuslän). While Samuel Hibbert did print a version of the legend in 1822, Sandberg's account differs sufficiently in other details that I do not think it must be a re-oralized version of the legend.[44] Regardless of whether or not we regard the Bohuslän legend as 'fakelore', it does challenge the implicit assumption that seems to inform much work, including my own, on Gaelic-Norse contacts: that traditions only migrate once.

I will refer to the next legend under discussion as 'The Three Laughs'. Study of this legend is hindered by the fact that it was not included in Christiansen's catalogue of migratory legends, and it lacks a designation in the schemata used for classifying the legends of Ireland, Scotland, and Sweden. Christiansen and Seán Ó Súilleabháin included examples of this

---

[43] Göteborg, VFF 41:70.
[44] Samuel Hibbert, *A description of the Shetland Islands comprising an account of their geology, scenery, antiquities, and superstitions* (Edinburgh: A. Constable & co., 1822), 569-70.

legend under the type ATU 670 "The Animal Languages", an entirely unrelated tale, in the mistaken belief that a shared motif of ironic laughter pointed to a common origin.[45]

In counties Cork and Kerry, the legend exists as a sort of hybrid with ML 4080.[46] The captive mermaid is said to have only laughed on three occasions during her time on land. The reasons for the first two bouts of laughter vary—her husband (or a relative) trips over a stone under which treasure has been buried, a visitor refuses food or drink (not knowing that there will not be another opportunity to eat that day), the husband slaughters a sheep which is still able to produce milk and wool, among others—but the third laugh is invariably when she recovers her stolen property. Although beyond the scope of the current discussion, there are parallels in the Welsh legends about fairy brides discussed by Juliette Wood and others, of which the Physicians of Myddfai is the most well-known example.[47]

Ultimately this motif of a captive supernatural being, laughing at the ironies of human experience, can be traced back to the Babylonian Talmud.[48] One of Solomon's captive demons, Asmodeus, cries upon seeing a wedding (because the bridegroom will die within a month), laughs at a man purchasing shoes which will last for seven years (because he will die shortly), and laughs at a would-be conjurer performing tricks in the marketplace (because the man is unaware that a great wealth of treasure is buried beneath him). The earliest evidence for this legend in insular tradition is Geoffrey of Monmouth's *Vita Merlini*, composed in the middle of the twelfth century.[49] In the *Vita*, Merlin, like the Irish Suibne, has gone

---

[45] Seán Ó Súilleabháin and Reidar Th. Christiansen, *The types of the Irish folktale* (Helsinki: Academia Scientiarum Fennica, 1963), 137. See also Michael Chesnutt, "The three laughs: a Celtic-Norse tale in oral tradition and medieval literature," in *Islanders and Water Dwellers*, edited by Patricia Lysaght, Séamas Ó Cathain, and Dáithí Ó hÓgáin (Dublin: Four Courts Press, 1999), 37-49.

[46] Darwin, "*Mar gur dream Sí iad*," 51-53.

[47] Juliette Wood, "The fairy bride legend in Wales," *Folklore* 103, no. 1 (1992): 56-72.

[48] Alexander Haggerty Krappe, "Le rire du prophète," in *Studies in English philology*, edited by Kemp Malone and Martin B. Ruud (Minneapolis: University of Minnesota Press, 1929), 340-61.

[49] Basil Clarke (ed.), *Life of Merlin: Vita Merlini* (Cardiff: University of Wales Press, 1973), 65-7, 76-81.

mad after the death of his companions in battle, and fled into the wilderness. He is captured by king Rodarchus (Rhydderch) and laughs on three occasions. The first laugh, when Rodarchus picks a leaf from his wife's clothing, unaware of her adultery; the second laugh when a beggar asks for money, unaware that he is standing above buried treasure; the third laugh when a man buys new shoes, unaware that he will die before he will have a chance to wear them. The author of the second Lailoken fragment presents the same episode, although the captive madman is Lailoken (perhaps a doublet of Merlin), and the king is Meldred.[50] The earliest evidence for the legend being known in Nordic tradition is the fourteenth-century 'fornaldarsaga' *Hálfs saga ok Hálfsrekka*. In the saga we are told:

> Þetta haust reru feðgar tveir á fiski ok drógu marmennil, ok hét annarr Handir, en annarr Hrindir. Þeir færðu hann Hjörleifi. Konungr fekk hann í hendr hirðkonu einni ok bað hana gera vel við hann. Engi maðr fekk orð af honum. Kertisveinar glímdu ok slökktu ljósin. Í því bili sló Hildr horni á skikkju Æsu. Konungr sló hana með hendi sinni, en Hildr sagði hundinn valda, er lá á gólfinu. Þá laust konungr hundinn. Þá hló marmennill. Konungr spurði, hví hann hló. Hann svarar: "Því, at þér varð heimskliga, því at þau munu þér líf gefa." Konungr spurði hann fleira. Hann svarar engu. Síðan lézt konungr mundu flytja hann til sjóvar ok bað hann segja sér þat, er hann þyrfti at vita.[51]

That autumn, a father and son, Handir and Hrindir, rowed out to fish, and caught a *marmennil*. They brought him to [king] Hjörleifr. The king delivered him into the hands of a woman of the court, and bade her take good care of him. No man could get a word from him. The candle-servants were wrestling and put out the light. At that moment, Hildr [Hjörleifr's wife] tore the dress of Aesa [his other wife] with a horn. The king struck her [Hildr] with his hand, and she said that the dog, who was lying on the floor, was to

---

[50] Text: H. L. D. Ward, "Lailoken (or Merlin Silvester)," *Romania* 22 (1893): 504-26, at 521-5; translation: Clarke, *Life of Merlin*, 231-4.

[51] A. Le Roy Andrews (ed.), *Hálfs saga ok Hálfsrekka* (Halle: Max Niemeyer, 1909), 82-3.

blame. Then the king struck the dog, and the marmennil laughed. The king asked him why he laughed, and he responded: "because that was foolish of you, since they will save your life." The king asked him to say more, but he did not answer. Then the king ordered him to be brought back to the sea, and bade him say that which he needed to know.

The marmenill, evidently some sort of merman, utters a prophecy in verse about future military engagements, which I omit here. Before the marmenill returns to the sea, someone in the king's entourage asks him "*hvat er manni bezt?*" ("what is best for man?") The marmennil responds by saying:

> *Kalt vatn augum*
> *en kvett tönnum,*
> *lérept líki,*
> *lát mik aptr í sjó!*
> *Dregr mik engií*
> *degi síðanmaðr*
> *upp í skipaf*
> *mararbotnum.*[52]

> Cold water for the eyes,
> and meat for the teeth,
> linen for the body,
> let me back into the sea!
> No man shall drag me,
> from this day onward,
> up onto a boat
> from the depths of the sea.

There is only one instance of cryptic laughter in this account, rather than two or three, but the motivation for the laughter is consistent with that found in the other accounts: Hjörleifr's limited knowledge causes him to act against his own interests, and Aesa's disloyalty parallels the adultery found in the *Vita* and Lailoken fragment. At the conclusion of this episode,

---

[52] Ibid., 86.

the marmenill offers a gnomic triad about human well-being followed by a poetic resolution to never be caught again. This advance suggests another legend type found throughout Norway and Sweden which Christiansen designated ML 4060 'The Mermaid's Message'.[53] In some versions of this legend, the aquatic being—not always a mermaid—mocks the human for failing to ask the correct question; the beneficial knowledge they could have gained from this encounter is forever closed off to them. This motif may represent a development of 'the Three Laughs' legend, although that legend is not, to the best of my knowledge, attested in continental Scandinavia.

Jón Árnasson published three Icelandic versions of this legend in the nineteenth century. The earliest of these was written by the sixteenth-century eccentric poet and suspected sorcerer Jón lærði Guðmundsson.[54] In this early account, the captive marmenill laughs three times: first when his captor embraces his wife but kicks his dog, next when he trips over a sod of earth and curses it, and finally when he is unable to choose a pair of shoes from those offered by a merchant. Upon being released, the marmenill explains the reasons for his laughter: the man kicked his loyal dog and embraced his adulterous wife, buried treasure lay beneath the sod of earth, and the man had no need for shoes because he would be dead soon. In the other two accounts, recorded in the nineteenth century, the shoe motif is absent and the man finds the buried treasure.[55]

As previously mentioned, 'the Three Laughs' legend exists in Munster in a form combined with ML 4080: the mermaid only laughs on three occasions during her period of captivity, with the last laugh being one of triumph upon regaining her freedom. In counties Donegal, Galway, and Mayo, the legend involves a man who captures and eventually releases a leprechaun.[56] The reasons for the laughter are varied, but some common threads can be discerned: the leprechaun laughs when his captor is ignorant of hidden gold, or unwittingly reveals his caches to thieves, as well as laughing when visitors refuse hospitality. As is the case with ML 4080, the

---

[53] Christiansen, *The migratory legends*, 71-2; cf. types F4, F6, F44 in af Klintberg, *Types of the Swedish folk legend*, 113, 116.
[54] Jón Árnason, *Íslenzkar þjóðsögur*, i 126-7.
[55] Ibid., i 127-8, iii 202-3.
[56] Dublin, National Folklore Collection, Main Collection, MS 509: 374-8, 539: 218-20, 1063: 430-5 (Donegal), 451: 1-8, 1133: 374-7, 1311: 157-9 (Galway), 381: 70-3 (Mayo).

legend can be told about one of two supernatural beings, and the choice of being informs the form of the legend. While the mermaid and seal-woman seem like obvious substitutions for each other, the relationship between the mermaid and leprechaun is harder to explain without appealing to earlier literary sources.

Our earliest literary reference to this legend in Ireland is a relatively understudied tale which I have discussed at this conference before: *Imthechta Tuaithe Luchra ocus Aided Fergusa*, which was most likely composed c. 1300, somewhere in Ulster.[57] This text has some overlap with, and is often referred to as, a later 'version' of, the Old Irish *Echtra Fergusa meic Leiti*, which depicts Fergus' encounters with the *luchorpain*, portrayed as aquatic dwarves, and the water-monster living in Dundrum Bay.[58] While the 'leprechauns' of the latter text are not explicitly identified as water-dwellers, they have the ability to travel over and through water that we would expect from such beings. In light of this, the substitution of a mermaid for a leprechaun (or a leprechaun for a mermaid?) is perhaps more understandable.[59]

In this text, Iubhdán, the leprechaun king, is held hostage in Emain Macha.

> *Lā ann do chúaidh Iubdán co tech in banntrochta ⁊ síat ag dénum fhoilcthi ⁊ fhothraicthi ⁊ hic slemanchíradh a ġcenn.*

---

[57] See Gregory Darwin, "The deaths of Fergus mac Leite," *Proceedings of the Harvard Celtic Colloquium* 40 (2023): 184-201. To date, the only edition and translation is that of Standish Hayes O'Grady, *Silva Gadelica: a collection of tales in Irish* (London and Edinburgh: Williams and Norgate, 1892), i 238-53 (text), ii 265-85 (translation). A new edition and translation is being prepared by the author.

[58] For the Old Irish account, see D. A. Binchy, "The saga of Fergus mac Léti," *Ériu* 16 (1952): 33-48, along with Neil McLeod, "Fergus mac Léti and the law," *Ériu* 61 (2011): 1-28.

[59] The relevance of the Early Modern Irish text for the dissemination of this legend throughout the Gaelic and Norse culture sphere has been discussed by Davíð Erlingsson, "*Ormur, Marmennill, Nykur*: Three creatures of the watery world," in *Islanders and Water Dwellers*, edited by Patricia Lysaght, Séamas Ó Cathain, and Dáithí Ó hÓgáin (Dublin: Four Courts Press, 1999), 61-81, at 70; and Michael Chesnutt, "On hidden treasure, useless shoes, and the gullibility of husbands," *Copenhagen Folklore Notes* 1 (2000): 1-8.

GREGORY DARWIN

Tibis Iubdán a gen ghāire uime sin. "Cad fa ṅdernuis in gáiri sin, a Iubdáin?" ar Fergus. "Is fada ón chrēcht in t-innrach," ar Iubdán. "Créd tuicter trit sin?" ar Fergus. "A ġcinn do-níd na mná d'f[h]olcadh ocus do fhrichnam ar son a tón," ar Iubdán. "Ar is tís a-tá in crēcht ₇ túas a-tá in folcadh ₇ in fothrugadh .i. na cinn dā nighe ₇ dá sgíamghlanadh." Úair ann do chūaidh Iubdán co tech amhuis d'amhsuib in rígh ocus bróga núadha aigi aga ṅgabál uimi ₇ ro bī ag techt ar thanacht bunnaighedh a bróg ₇ ag cesacht orra. Do-rinne Iubdán gáiri uimi sin. "Cad fa ndernais in gáire sin, a Iubdáin?" ar Fergus. "Adbar gáire dam," ar Iubdán "in fer úd ac cesacht ar thanacht a bróg ₇ ní chesinn ar a shāeghal ar gidh tana na bróga úd ní chaithfi-som íad," ₇ rob f[h]ír d'Iubdán sin, úair do chomruig in fer sin ₇ fer eili do mhuintir Fergusa re chéili ₇ ro marbsat a céile (32vb) ré n-oidhchi. Lā eli do bí fer don teglach ag búain brodh d'édach a mná ₇ do-rinni Iubdán gāiri. "Cad fá ndernuis in gáiri sin, a Iubdáin?" ar Fergus. "Maith adhbar mo gáiri," ar Iubdán. "In fer úd benas na brodha d'édach a mná, a marbadh budh cóir dó, úair fuithe do bí in t-étach úd in trāt[h]-sa ₇ fer eili ag dul uiri."

Lá eli do batar in teglach ag imrádh gach neich co ṅdéndaís é ₇ ní dubratar "ma áil le Día" ₇ do-rinni Iubdán gáiri umpu ₇ do-rinde in láedh . . . [60]

One day, Iubhdán went to the women's dwelling as they were bathing and washing and combing their hair. Iubhdán laughed at that. "Why did you laugh, Iubhdán?" said Fergus. "The poultice is far from the wound," said Iubhdán. "What do you mean by that?" said Fergus. "The women are washing and cleaning their head, instead of their lower region. The wound is below, and the cure and cleaning are

---

[60] Edited from London, British Library, MS Egerton 1782, f. 32v; cf. O'Grady, *Silva Gadelica,* i 246, ii 278-9. The first and third laughs are omitted in O'Grady's translation; O'Grady, like many of his contemporaries, was evidently reluctant to publish sexually explicit material in English.

HOW TO TRAIN YOUR *NÄCKEN*

above, washing and beautifying their hair." Another time, Iubhdán went to the house of one of the king's warriors. That warrior was wearing new shoes, and he was complaining about how thin the soles were. Iubhdán laughed at that. "Why did you laugh, Iubhdán?" said Fergus. "I laughed," said Iubhdán, "because yon man was complaining about how thin his shoes were, and not his lifespan, for however thin his shoes, he will not live to wear them out." Iubhdán spoke truly, for that same warrior fought with another of Fergus' household, and they killed each other before nightfall. Another day, a servant was plucking a speck of straw from his wife's cloak, and Iubhdán laughed. "Why did you laugh, Iubhdán?" said Fergus. "I have a good reason to laugh," said Iubhdán. "Yon man who is plucking the straw from his wife's cloak ought to kill her instead, for that same cloak was underneath her when another man was on top of her."

Another day, the household were discussing everything they were planning to do, and they did not say "if it please God." Iubhdán laughed at them, and recited a lay . . .

    This episode corresponds quite neatly with the Irish and Icelandic oral versions of the legend, although there are some discrepancies. No mention is made of buried treasure here; instead, the author has inserted a crude misogynistic joke in keeping with the humour of the rest of the text. There are four rather than three laughs, and the final laugh is explained with a rather incongruous statement of conventional piety—incidentally, the only mention of Christianity within that text. This is a helpful reminder of the potential pitfalls of using premodern literature as evidence for the travel of motifs and narratives: our authors often made use of oral tradition for their own artistic purposes, but they rarely sought to preserve it for its own sake as later collectors did. In the same light, we may note that Iubhdán's utterance—the poultice is far from the wound—parallels a proverb recorded in Monaghan in the early twentieth century, while the other *seanfhocal* 'proverb' presented in the text, "*cacc i dtiobraid*" (shit in the well), is unusual and otherwise unattested, most likely a joke.[61]

In Scotland, the same variation between sea-man and sea-woman can be found in the admittedly sparse record. In versions recorded by John Gregorson Campbell from Barra and Tiree, a human captures a merman who laughs on occasions which mostly accord with the material we have seen so far: a servant who is fated to die complains about his shoes, a man brushes barley from the clothes of an adulterous wife, and a houseowner silences the barking dogs that were warning him of robbers.[62] Another version from Skye, preserved by Robert MacLagan, begins like many versions of ML 4080 with a fisherman finding a mermaid by the shore, capturing her, and bringing her to his house.[63] The man's wife is jealous of the attention he is paying to the captive mermaid and so takes a lover for herself. The mermaid laughs only once when the wife manages to trick her husband into ignoring evidence of her infidelity. As with many of the Icelandic and southern Irish accounts there is a happy ending of sorts, as the mermaid leaves behind a magical stone that remains in the family for several generations.

As in ML 4080, the nature of the supernatural captive can vary: merman (or marmennill), mermaid, or leprechaun. The question of which best reflects the archetype is unavoidable. Those versions of the legend that involve the leprechaun are, unsurprisingly, unique to Ireland and, given the leprechaun's association with shoe-making in later tradition, it is not surprising that it would become associated with a legend involving shoes (although it should be noted that the leprechaun does not actually laugh at someone buying or complaining about shoes in any of the twentieth-century examples from Ireland known to me). The presence of the leprechaun may represent a geographically limited innovation, a more generic being

---

[61] "*Is fada ó'n chreich an ceithrin.* The plaster is far from the wound. (Said if one suggested a far-away remedy for anything.)" H. Morris, "Some Ulster Proverbs," *Journal of the County Louth Archaeological Society* 4, no. 3 (December 1918): 258-72, at 261.

[62] J. Gregorson Campbell, "The Green Island," *The Scottish Historical Review* 5, no. 18 (1908): 194–5.

[63] University of Edinburgh, School of Scottish Studies, MacLagan MS 2682-9. According to MacLagan, this story was "[from] Skye M.S.S. 1888"; unfortunately, no further contextual information is provided.

replaced by a figure from the local tradition ecology. The opposite development may also be possible: when a legend involving a leprechaun was retold in tradition areas where belief in the leprechaun was absent, the part was recast with another water-dweller. Either way, it can be said with some confidence that the leprechaun-redaction of 'the Three Laughs' was in circulation in Ireland during the thirteenth or fourteenth century, when the redactor of *Imtheachta Tuaithe Luchra* made use of the legend. As I suggested earlier, we should not assume that legends cross linguistic and cultural borders once and once only: the Southern mermaid-oicotype could perhaps be a later importation from Icelandic tradition.

As noted above and earlier, the fact that 'the Three Laughs' does not have a designation in any of the major catalogues and classification schemata for legends in northwestern Europe is a hindrance to research. Obviously, it would be desirable to include a new designation, along the line of the late Bo Almqvist's MLSIT (Migratory Legend Suggested Irish Types), but where would it fit in these schemata? Most catalogues of migratory legends are grouped according to the broad category of supernatural being or force which is encountered in the legend: thus, in Christiansen's catalogue we have legends about the devil, witches, the dead, water spirits, trolls and giants, terrestrial fairies, and domestic spirits. From the perspective of a would-be cataloguer, is 'the Three Laughs' a story about a terrestrial being, an aquatic one, or even about a demon? Arguments can be made for all of these possibilities, and the question is not a trivial one as this framing would influence how future scholars approach the corpus of this legend.

Before concluding, I want to return to the figure of the water-horse and offer some brief comments. As is well-known, Ireland, Scotland, Iceland, the Faroe Islands, and continental Scandinavia all have abundant legendary traditions about aquatic horses. Like other supernatural beings, they are figurative double-edged swords: they may bring luck and prosperity to the humans who encounter and interact appropriately with them, but more often than not they will drown, or attempt to drown, those unlucky enough to find them. While such legends are known in Norwegian tradition, they are not included in Christiansen's catalogue. In her discussion of the Swedish material, Brita Egerdt distinguishes two main groups: *vattenhästen som ridhäst* 'the water-horse as riding-horse' and *vattenhästen som arbetshäst* 'the water-horse as work-horse'; the former can be further divided on the basis of whether the would-be riders are adults or children.[64] Further subtypes are distinguished in af Klintberg's catalogue.[65]

The examples previously quoted earlier are typical of the 'Water-horse as Riding-Horse' complex: an adult or several children finds a strange horse by a body of water and attempts to mount it. The horse sometimes drowns its rider (or riders), but is often prevented from doing so when someone inadvertently mentions the näck's name, or invokes the name of God. The legends involving children often have a didactic, and sometimes quite comical, tone:

> Min mor berättade, att de var några barn, som en gang sprang och plockade oxöron vid en liten bäck borta vid Bäckabro. Bäst som de plockade, kom där upp en liten gul häst, och han var så kelen så vilken av barnen som helst fick klappa honom. Så lade han sig ner och gossarna satte sig upp på rygge på honom, och ju fler de satte sig upp, desto längre blev han. Då var där en som ropade, "Dä va då en Guss långer häst!" Men då välte han av dem allihop och försvann i bäcken. Och barnen blev så rädda, så de sprang hem och talte om'et med desamma. Och att det är sant, det är så säkert, for mor har visat mig på det stället manga gånger.[66]

My mother said that there were some children who went out one time to go picking pasqueflowers by a little brook near Bäckabro. While they were picking flowers, a little

---

[64] Brita Egerdt, "De svenska vattenhästsägerna och deras ursprung," *Folkkultur* 4 (1944): 119-64. See also Bo Almqvist, "Upp flöt lever och lunga: en preliminär omtuggning av problemen rörande de nordiska vattenhästsägernas ursprung," in *Inte bara visor: Studier kring folklig diktning och musik*, edited by Eva Danielson, Sven-Bertil Jansson, Margareta Jersild, Märta Ramsten (Uddevalla: Bohusläningens Boktryckeri, 1990), 15-42; and Dag Strombäck, "Some notes on the Nix in older Nordic tradition, " in *Medieval literature and folklore studies: essays in honor of Francis Lee Utley*, edited by Jerome Mandel and Bruce A. Rosenberg (New Brunswick, New Jersey: Rutgers University Press, 1970), 245-56.
[65] af Klintberg, *Types of the Swedish folk legend*, 122-4.
[66] Lund, LUF 601:3 p. 145, quoted in af Klintberg, *Svenska folksägner*, 105.

yellow horse came up to them, and it was so friendly that some of the children tried to pet it. It laid down, and the children set themselves on his back, and the more of them got on his back, the longer he became. Then one of them shouted "my God, what a long horse!" Then it threw them all off of him and ran into the brook. The children were so terrified that they ran home and told everyone what had happened. And this is a true story, because my mother has shown me the spot many times.

There is, evidently, a handful of examples of this legend type in Scotland, although in Ireland the type is practically unknown.[67]

While in the Riding-Horse legend the horse appears as an aggressive force who attempts to lure humans to their death, the Work-Horse legends

---

[67] I have, unfortunately, not yet been able to visit the School of Scottish Studies in Edinburgh to consult the relevant materials, but Donald Archie MacDonald noted the existence of ten versions of the legend classified as F68 "Children Carried Off into Loch when they Ride on Water-horse." On the basis of the summary given by MacDonald, it would appear that the experience is typically fatal for Scottish children, and more drastic measures (such as chopping off a finger) are required to escape the each uisge. Donald Archie MacDonald, "Migratory legends of the supernatural in Scotland: a survey," *Béaloideas* 62/63 (1994/1995): 29-78, at 50. "As to Grown-ups' Ride on the Water-Horse, there are Scottish legends that correspond more or less to the Nordic pattern, but they appear to be few in number and sometimes confused." Almqvist, "Waterhorse legends," 109. There is an episode in the later medieval Fenian romance *Tóruigheacht an Ghiolla Dheacair* which provides a close parallel to the 'Children ride the Water-horse' legend, when the *Giolla Deacair*'s horse carries Conán Maol and another fourteen members of the *fianna* into the sea. Almqvist, "Upp flöt lever och lunga," 38-9. For the passage, see O'Grady, *Silva Gadelica*, i 259-63 (text), ii 294-7 (translation); see also Alan Bruford, *Gaelic Folk-tales and mediæval romance* (Dublin: Folklore of Ireland Society, 1969): 266. Natasha Sumner's Fionn Folklore Database lists sixteen modern versions of the story from Ireland: ten from the Main Manuscripts collection, four from the Schools collection, and two from printed sources (https://fionnfolklore.org/#/lays/gd). The episode with Conán and the horse figures in some, but not all of the accounts, which appear in manuscripts which have been digitized. I have not yet been able to visit the National Folklore Collection in Dublin to consult the remaining items.

are about a human attempting to gain control over a supernatural force and the consequences of failing to do so. In most Swedish examples, the farmer finds a strange horse near a body of water and puts a bridle, often containing iron, on the horse. The horse serves him well for a long time. Eventually the farmer takes the bridle off the horse, and the horse carries him into the lake and drowns him. A version of this legend appears as early as the thirteenth century in the Sturlubók recension of the Icelandic *Landnámabók* where it is told about Audun stoti, son of Vali the strong, a Hebridean, who discovers a grey stallion near Hjardarvatn.[68] Audun yoked the stallion to a plough, and it served him well, but when he kept the horse working after sunset it broke free and returned to the lake, never to be seen again.

The Work-Horse legend is well-represented in Ireland, although there are some noteworthy differences in how it is told. In continental Scandinavia, the horse rebels as soon as the owner relinquishes control. The Irish material, on the other hand, seemingly focuses on the mistreatment of the horse.[69] As in Peig Judge's story, the man may provoke the water-horse's anger by striking it with the bridle or a switch or, as in the *Landnámabók* account, by overworking the beast. The water-horse may be used as a racing animal rather than a beast of burden, and the rider's eagerness to win a particular race may provoke his mistreatment of the animal and the deadly consequences thereof. A striking motif found in the Irish material is the dismemberment of the rider: the liver, lungs, or heart may float to the surface, sometimes explained by the fact that the horse does not eat these things. As in Peig Judge's story, this may serve as an onomastic episode: *Loch an Chroí* 'Lake of the Heart' derives its name from the gory spectacle of the farmer's demise.

There are many earlier Irish literary reflexes of these narratives. In *Imthechta Tuaithe Luchra ocus Aided Fergusa*, the leprechauns employ a diminutive *ech uisce* 'water horse' to convey the dwarf Aodh across the sea to their land.[70] Although Aodh is originally terrified of this creature (which

---

[68] Finnur Jónsson, *Landnámabók I-III: Hauksbók, Sturlubók, Melabók m.m.* (København: Kongelige Nordiske Oldskriftselskab, 1900), 30 (Hausbók recension), 151 (Sturlubók recension). An English translation of the passage appears in Almqvist, "Waterhorse legends," 118.
[69] Ibid., 8-9.
[70] London, British Library, MS Egerton 1782, f. 31va; cf. O'Grady, *Silva Gadelica,* i 242 (text), ii 275 (translation).

he initially mistakes for a *míl muighi* 'hare'), there is no sense that it may drown its rider. Similarly benign water-horses appear in an episode in *Immram Brain*, which this text may be parodying.[71] In both *Fled Bricrenn* and *Aided Con Culainn*, Cú Chulainn's two horses, Liath Macha and Dub Sainglend, are presented in way which betrays familiarity with 'the Water-Horse as Racing-Horse' legend.[72] Unlike in the contemporary legends, Cú Chulainn is able to successfully tame these water-horses, yet another sign of his exceptional and heroic status. 'The Water-Horse as Racing-Horse'serves as a vehicle for a saint's curse in a number of texts, the earliest of which is the late Middle Irish *Aided Diarmada meic Cherbaill*. After Saint Ruadán curses Diarmait, thirty grey horses appear from the sea and are raced against Diarmait's own horses; they prove faster, but quickly return to the sea, drowning their riders.[73] The same episode appears in Mícheál Ó Cléirigh's life of Ruadán as well as his life of Brendan of Clonfert (where Brendan, rather than Ruadán, curses Diarmait).[74] A similar episode appears in the second recension of *Aided Diarmada*, where Brendan provides Ruadán with fifty horses in order to aid him in a dispute with Áed Gúaire; Áed accepts the horses as restitution and when men of his household race the horses on the green of Tara, the riders strike them with goads and are predictably driven into

---

[71] Kuno Meyer (ed. and trans.), *The voyage of Bran, son of Febal, to the land of the living* (London: David Nutt, 1895), 16-21.

[72] See note 13 above.

[73] O'Grady, *Silva Gadelica*, i 78 (text), ii 83 (translation). After I delivered this keynote, Jesse Harrington was kind enough to share a forthcoming chapter about this text. He suggested in private communication that this episode, which occurs at a pivotal point within the text, may serve as an allegory for "the appropriate, mutually supporting roles of king for cleric and cleric for king that has been compromised in the preceding exchange by the protagonists of the death-tale: i.e., as the respective vehicles necessary to get the other where they need to go." (Jesse Harrington, e-mail to author, October 12, 2023). If this legend has its origins in an ecclesiastical context, or at least was strongly associated with hagiography in the Middle Ages, that could go some way to explaining the pious streak in twentieth-century accounts which Almqvist noticed.

[74] Charles Plummer (ed.), *Bethada Náem nÉrenn: Lives of Irish Saints* (Oxford, Clarendon Press, 1922), i 88-9 (text, Brendan), i 325 (text, Ruadán), ii 85-6 (translation, Brendan), ii 317 (translation, Ruadán).

the sea.[75] The latter text adds a further detail: both horses and riders were transformed into seals upon entering the sea, perhaps echoing a widespread Northern European etiology for the common seal as the transubstantiated souls of the drowned.[76]

At first glance, these Gaelic and Nordic water-horse traditions would seem obviously connected, but the actual overlap of narrative traditions is fairly marginal. Both Gaelic and Nordic traditions contain narrative types not found in the other: 'the Water-Horse as Riding-Horse' is nearly absent in the Gaelic-speaking world, and racing-horse legends of the Irish type are absent in Scandinavia and its diaspora. Only 'the Water-Horse as Work-Horse' can truly be said to have crossed the border and, while there are some stray motifs which seem like obvious borrowings (such as the horse returning to the lake after sunset in the *Landnámabók* account of Audun stoti, or the floating viscera also found in Faroese tradition), the Nordic and Gaelic oicotypes are quite distinct.[77]

When we ask ourselves where this legend may have come from, and what routes it may have taken, multiple potential answers present themselves. First, 'the Water-Horse as Work-Horse' has its origins in the Gaelic tradition, and was borrowed into Nordic tradition with subsequent development in both cultural areas (for instance, as Almqvist suggested, the emphasis on animal welfare in the Irish material may reflect the influence of other religious legends).[78] Alternately, the legend is a Nordic import. A different possibility is that beliefs (and therefore narratives) about aquatic horses, or beings that were sometimes horses, were already well-established in both areas by the time that prolonged cultural contact had occurred, with the effect that imported narratives and motifs had to compete with established indigenous ones.

---

[75] O'Grady, *Silva Gadelica*, i 67-8 (text), ii 72 (translation). O'Grady's title, *Stair ar Áed Baclámh*, was his own invention, and one which arguably places undue emphasis on a fairly minor character. See Eystein Thanisch, "The reception and use of Flann Mainistrech and his work in medieval Gaelic manuscript culture," (PhD diss., University of Edinburgh, 2015), 145 n661.
[76] See Puhvel, "The seal," 326-31.
[77] Jakob Jakobsen, *Færøske folkesagn og æventyr* (København: S. L. Møllers bogtryggeri, 1901), 198.
[78] Almqvist, "Waterhorse legends," 114.

HOW TO TRAIN YOUR *NÄCKEN*

Having a catchy title like this is something of a double-edged sword; while it does guarantee a crowd, the speaker then must live up to its promise. At the risk of disappointing, I suggest that my title not be understood as a promise of instructions, but a question I have been, and still am, asking myself: how to train such an unruly being as the näck. No less elusive and protean are the other beings we have discussed: in attempting to wrestle the marmennill or leprechaun, we find ourselves flung into the misty realms of the Celtic wildman with his three-fold death, and further afield into Talmudic scholia. Although I have spent the better part of this article problematizing the comparative method in legend research, I by no means think that it ought to be abandoned: I hope to have shown that such enquiries have the potential to take us on strange and far-reaching journeys, touching upon diverse domains of cultural production in the process.

Traditions, like humans, travel, and travel is always a risky business. Legends may die, as they are forgotten or fail to take root in their new environments, and like our unfortunate would-be equestrians, may find themselves dismembered and reconfigured in surprising combinations which deserve our careful attention. Legends often have didactic value, no less for collectors and scholars: if we focus too much on where we are going, rather than the horse which bears us there, or if we drive it too forcefully in pursuit of our pet theories, we risk being dragged violently far away from firm ground.

Acknowledgements

I am grateful to the organizers of the 42nd Harvard Celtic Colloquium for the invitation to speak, as well as to the audience for their time and attention; and in particular to Guy Beiner, Jesse Harrington, and Professor Joseph Nagy for their helpful comments. Thanks are also due to Tommy Kuusela for countless conversations, e-mails, and introductions, as well as to my other friends, colleagues, and students in Uppsala who have eagerly shared their culture and history with me. Any error, oversights, and omissions, of which there are no doubt many, are my own.

I am also grateful to the editorial team as a whole for their patience and kindness when the preparation of this manuscript was delayed by an unforeseen loss in the family.

GREGORY DARWIN

Ranna beaga bacacha á scríobh agam
    Ba mhaith liom breith ar eireaball spideoige
Ba mhaith liom sprid lucht glanta glún a dhíbirt,
    Ba mhaith liom triall go deireadh lae go brónach.

"his honour would remain forever...," A reassessment of the relationship between royalty and physical impairment in medieval Irish society

Dylan Bailey

One-eyedness is a frequent motif within the surviving medieval Irish sagas, saints' lives, and law texts, especially in connection to kingship. Some scholars have argued that a significant social *geis* or 'taboo' was aimed at kings with physical impairments in medieval Ireland.[1] Jacqueline Borsje and Amy Mulligan have both discussed how the king's body was understood to act as a proxy for the kingdom and its people, and that a physical blemish on the king could cause disruption to the social order.[2] The

---

[1] Fergus Kelly, *A Guide to Early Irish Law* (Dublin: Dublin Institute for Advanced Study (DIAS), 1988), 20. For a discussion on the distinction between 'impairment' and 'disability', and how these two concepts from disability studies can be applied to a medieval context, see Irina Metzler, *Disability in Medieval Europe: Thinking about Physical Impairment during the High Middle Ages, c. 1100–1400* (London and New York: Routledge, 2006) and Matthieu Boyd, "Modeling Impairment and Disability in Early Irish Literature," *Proceedings of the Harvard Celtic Colloquium,* 41 (2022): 35-82. The former applies to medieval studies in general, while the latter specifically discusses these themes in relation to medieval Irish studies. My sincere gratitude must be expressed to Matthieu Boyd for sharing his insights at the 42nd Harvard Celtic Colloquium. For a wider discussion of the themes and terminology surrounding this topic, see Cordula Nolte, Bianca Frohne, Uta Halle and Sonja Kerth, (eds.), *Dis/Ability History der Vormoderne: Ein Handbuch/ Pre-Modern Dis/Ability History: A Companion* (Affalterbach: Didymos-Verlag, 2017), especially the contributions from Irina Metzler (58-61), Bianca Frohne (61-63), Wendy J. Turner (63-67), and Edward Wheatley (67-68).

[2] Jacqueline Borsje, "Demonising the Enemy: a Study of Congal Cáech," in *Proceedings of the Eighth Symposium of Societas Celtologica Nordica* 7, ed. Jan Erik Rekdal and Ailbhe Ó Corráin (Uppsala: University of Uppsala, 2007), 21-38, at 22; Amy C. Eichhorn-Mulligan, "The Anatomy of Power and the Miracle of Kingship: the Female Body of Sovereignty in a Medieval Irish Kingship Tale," *Speculum* 81/4 (October 2006): 1014-1054, at 1020; Amy C. Eichhorn-Mulligan,

idea of the king's 'Body Politic' was not unique to medieval Ireland, and examples can be found in various forms throughout the medieval world.[3] However, medieval Ireland seems to have been particularly concerned with the social implications of a damaged royal body.[4] Concepts of honour and physical wholeness were closely linked within the early Irish language. This is evident in the Old Irish term *enech* (which means both 'face' and 'honour'), whilst words like *ainim* (blemish) and *on* (fault) convey both physical blemishes and metaphorical injuries to one's reputation.[5] The compensation for injury was termed *lóg n-enech* 'the price of his face.'[6] Some narrative episodes concerning royal figures indicate that physical injury to the face could lead to a loss of honour, and therefore disqualification from the kingship. For example, both Cormac mac Airt and Congal Cáech ('Congal the one-eyed') are portrayed as has having lost (or

---

"Togail Bruidne Da Derga and the Politics of Anatomy," *Cambrian Medieval Celtic Studies* 49 (Summer 2005): 1-19, at 12, 18-19.

[3] Ernst Hartwig Kantorowicz, *The King's Two Bodies: A Study in Mediaeval Political Theology*, second edition (Princeton: Princeton University Press, 1997); *The King's Two Bodies: A Study in Mediaeval Political Theology* (oclc.org), originally published in 1957, is a seminal work on the 'Body Politic' in the medieval world. For a more recent overview of the history of this idea, see Cary J. Nederman and Kate Langdon Forhan, *Medieval Political Theory: A Reader: The quest for the body politic, 1100-1400* (London: Routledge, 1993). Irina Metzler (*Disability in Medieval Europe*, 51-52) and Cory James Rushton ["Introduction: Punishment and Pity," in *Disability and Medieval Law: History, Literature, Society*, ed. Cory James Rushton (Cambridge: Cambridge Scholars Publishing, 2013), 7-8, 10] have both written on this subject in relation to disability studies. For some more recent work, see Marybeth Ruether-Wu, "Revel, Reiving, and Outlawry: Regulating the Body Politic in Late Medieval Popular Literature" (PhD diss., Cornell University, 2013) and Hülya Tafli Düzgün, "Boundaries of the Body Politics in Medieval Hagiographical Romance," *Cogito* 12, no. 4 (Dec 2020): 220-227.

[4] Patricia Skinner, *Living with Disfigurement in Early Medieval Europe* (Palgrave Macmillan, 2017), 51-52, 119, 122-123, Living with Disfigurement in Early Medieval Europe | SpringerLink, also makes this point.

[5] Kelly, *Guide to Early Irish Law*, 8-9, 43, n. 1 on 125, 126, 149; Skinner, *Disfigurement in Early Medieval Europe*, 51.

[6] Kelly, *Guide to Early Irish Law*, 8.

been threatened with losing) their kingship due to the loss of an eye.[7] This stigma for kings with ocular impairments in particular might be explained by this impairment's links with social liminality. Joseph Falaky Nagy has described the status of poets in medieval Irish society as liminal, and Patrick Ford has argued that a state of blindness, either simulated or real, was a common part of the rituals for poetic practices in Ireland.[8] Since kings were often portrayed symbolically as the physical embodiment of society, one might wonder whether injury to the eyes of such a figure were understood to render his whole kingdom as a liminal entity, causing a serious disturbance to the so-called 'natural' order.[9]

Despite the evidence for a stigma against royal impairments in medieval Irish society, there are some instances in the literature where ocular impairments may be an indication of good kingship. This article will offer one case study where impairment appears to imply a good moral character, and will consider whether the attitude towards physical impairment in medieval Irish society was more nuanced than has been previously argued.[10]

The story of King Eochaid and the druid Lobán appears to be a part of the twelfth-century Irish-language text *Betha Ruadháin* "The Life of Ruadán." Both are found in Mícheál Ó Cléirigh's seventeenth-century compilation, now known as Royal Library of Belgium 2324-40, in Brussels. However, the Eochaid/Lobán story is in a different part of the manuscript

---

[7] Siobhán Barrett, "Varia I. The King of Dál nAraidi's Salve," *Ériu* 69 (2019): 171-178, at 173 talks about Congal Cáech; Eichhorn-Mulligan, "Togail Bruidne Da Derga," 10, mentions Congal and Cormac mac Airt.

[8] Patrick K. Ford, "The Blind, the Dumb, and the Ugly: Aspects of Poets and their Craft in Early Ireland and Wales," *Cambridge Medieval Celtic Studies* 19 (Summer 1990): 27-40, at 27, 37-38; Joseph Falaky Nagy, "Liminality and Knowledge in Irish Tradition," *Studia Celtica* 16-17, University of Wales Press (1981-1982): 135-143, at 135-142.

[9] A similar idea is expressed in Eichhorn-Mulligan, "Togail Bruidne Da Derga," 16-19.

[10] Boyd, "Modeling Impairment,", remarks that literature and law-texts are "imperfect mirrors of society" and cannot always be relied on to draw historical conclusions. I think bringing in more 'historical' sources can provide a fuller insight into how much the beliefs expressed in the more 'narrative' sources, such as the sagas and saints' lives', reflect the wider attitudes of medieval Irish society.

to the rest of *Betha Ruadháin*. This tale is found in ff. 160-161, whereas the main body of the life is at ff. 193-202.[11] This different location is why the story is included in the appendix to Charles Plummer's edition, and why I am hesitant to say with absolute certainty that it forms part of the saint's life proper. However, as both sections feature Ruadán, and a later manuscript (now known as Dublin, Royal Irish Academy, MS A iv 1 (968)) incorporates an abridged version of the story into the saint's life itself, it is unsurprising that Plummer chose to include it in his collection.[12] *Betha Ruadháin* in its current form dates from the second quarter of the twelfth century, but is probably based on earlier Latin and Irish versions.[13] Richard Sharpe initially dated the collection, which contains the earliest extant Latin version of this *Life* (the O'Donohue group of saints' lives), to as early as 750 CE, but scholars now argue that, although some individual lives can be dated to that period, both extant forms of the Latin and Irish *Lives* concerning Ruadán probably belong to no earlier than the twelfth century.[14]

---

[11] Charles Plummer, ed., *Bethada Náem nÉrenn*, vol. 1 (Oxford: Clarendon Press, 1922), xl.

[12] Plummer, *Bethada Náem nÉrenn*, vol. 1, xl.

[13] These points are made in Pádraig Ó Riain, *A Dictionary of Irish Saints* (Dublin: Four Courts Press, 2011), 541-542. Plummer, *Bethada Náem nÉrenn*, vol. 1, xl also argued that *Betha Ruadháin* was based on a Latin original.

[14] Richard Sharpe, *Medieval Irish Saints' Lives: an Introduction to Vitae Sanctorum Hiberniae* (Oxford: Clarendon Press, 1991), 324, 329, 333, 334. For more information see Jesse Patrick Harrington, "Sinners, Saints, Psalms, and Curses in "Aided Diarmata meic Cerbaill"," in *Proceedings of Defining the Boundaries of Celtic Hagiography: Textual Sources Outside Lives and Martyrologies Conference, 25–26 May 2018*, edited by Sarah Waidler (Dublin: Dublin Institute for Advanced Studies, forthcoming). Harrington mentions John Carey's scepticism of Sharpe's dating (John Carey, "Medieval Irish Saints' Lives: An Introduction to Vitae Sanctorium Hiberniae. Richard Sharpe," review of *Medieval Irish Saints' Lives*, by Richard Sharpe, *Speculum*, Jan. 1993, Vol. 68, No. 1, 260-262) and discusses an article by Pádraig Ó Riain which re-affirms the twelfth-century provenance of *Betha Ruadháin* (Pádraig Ó Riain, "The O'Donohue Lives of the Salamancan Codex: the Earliest Collection of Irish saints' Lives?" In *Gablánach in Scélaigecht: Celtic Studies in honour of Ann Dooley*, edited by Sarah Sheehan, Joanne Findon, and Westley Follett, 38-52, at 38-39, 42. Dublin: Four Courts Press, 2013). Thank you to Jesse Harrington for

HIS HONOUR WOULD REMAIN FOREVER

Although this date could be applicable to the specific story of Eochaid and Lobán, a few points of interest should be noted before moving on. This basic story seems to have developed separately from the rest of *Betha Ruadháin*, and was not always part of the Ruadán hagiographical tradition. A few similar tales predate *Betha Ruadháin* but do not feature the saint. One of these (*Talland Étair*) can be dated back to at least the tenth century. These earlier tales most likely inspired the story found in the Brussels manuscript, and will be discussed in more detail later. For now, it could be tentatively argued that such stories indicate an earlier provenance. This theory might be supported by the fact the story is, as mentioned above, found independently from *Betha Ruadháin* in the Brussels 2324-40 manuscript. This might have no significance, but should be noted when considering whether to apply the twelfth-century dating of *Betha Ruadháin* to this specific story. I have not drawn any strong conclusions yet, and there is neither the time nor space in this article to discuss this matter at any great length. It should be noted, however, that this specific Eochaid story does not appear to feature in any of the extant Latin lives concerning Ruadán.[15]

---

providing me with these helpful insights into the dating of *Betha Ruadháin* at the 42nd Harvard Celtic Colloquium.

[15] I have been unable to find any version of this story in the Latin versions of the *Life of Ruadhán*, either from *Vita Sancti Ruadani*, in *Vitae Sanctorum Hiberniae, partim hactenus ineditae*, vol. 2, ed. Charles Plummer (Oxford: Clarendon Press, 1910), 240-252, or *Vita S. Ruadani Abbatis de Lothra*, in *Vitae Sanctorum Hiberniae: ex Codice olim Salmanticensi, nunc Bruxellensi. Lives of the Saints of Ireland, from the Salamanca manuscript now of Brussels*, ed. W.W. Heist (Subsidia Hagiographica, 28, Brussels: Société des Bollandistes, 1965): 160-167. For Richard Sharpe's discussion of the compilation of this manuscript, see Sharpe, *Medieval Irish Saints' Lives*, 231-243. Charles Plummer ed., *Vitae Sanctorum Hiberniae, partim hactenus ineditae*, Volume I (Oxford: Clarendon Press, 1910), LXXXVI-LXXXVII (especially n.1 on LXXXVII) implies the story only features in the Irish-language versions, those in Royal Library of Belgium 2324-40 and the later Dublin, Royal Irish Academy, MS A iv 1 (968) manuscript. In the same volume, Plummer does not mention this story in his discussion of royal circuits (CXXVIII) or secular stories being adapted into ecclesiastical settings (CXXXII) in the context of the Latin lives. These are key motifs in the Eochaid/Lobán story, so it would be unusual for this story not to be mentioned in the discussion if it had been included in the earlier Latin texts. Plummer links the

This suggests that, as it is the earliest known version of the story involving Ruadán, the twelfth-century dating prescribed for the rest of *Betha Ruadháin* could be applied to this version of the tale. These arguments for and against an earlier date for this specific Eochaid/Lobán story should be kept in mind when discussing its origins and motifs later on in this article.

Plummer edited and translated the tale of Eochaid and Lobán as follows:

> *Fechtus dia ndeachaid anti naomh Rúadan for cuairt cleircechta go righ Eoghanachta Caisil .i. Eochaidh mac Mailughra, is hisin aimser tainic araile drái d'feraib Alban for cuairt bíd go feraibh Eirenn cona trom-dhaimh lais, do breith einigh Erenn, no d'fagail gach neith no sirfedh for fíora Eirenn.*
>
> *Lobhan ainm an druagh; go ttainicc go hairm i mbói Eochaidh, co nar gabh aisccidh ele uada, acht an aon shuil bói ina chionn do tabairt dó, no a einech, ⁊ einech bfer nErenn, da breith lais ind Albain. O ro chuala an righ anni sin, ro raidh go mairfedh a bhladh do shir, ⁊ nach mairfedh an roscc. Lasodhain ro la a mhér fona shúil, go ro theilcc an roscc i nucht an druagh.*
>
> *O'tconairc antí naemh Rúadhan an ithche neimh-dligthich sin ro shir an dráoi, ro leicc for a ghluinibh é, ⁊ dorinne croisfighill dhe, ⁊ ro guidh Dia go duthrachtach go ndechdais di shuil an druagh Lobain i ccenn in righ Eochadha, do fhognamh dó i nait a ruiscc fodheisin; ⁊ ro fíradh anni sin, tre impidhe naomh Ruadhain.*
>
> *Ro sginnsiott di shuil an druagh asa chionn tre impidhe naomh Ruadhain, ⁊ tre cumhachtaibh Dé, go ndechsat I nacchaidh ⁊ i neinech a bhethadh no beith occa; go nabradh gach aon atchidh é: 'Suil Lobháin fil occa', conidh desin ro len Súillebhain de. O'tconnairc Eochaidh*

Eochaid/Lobán story to these two themes in Plummer, *Bethada Náem nÉrenn*, vol. 1, xl, and Charles Plummer, ed., *Bethada Náem nÉrenn*, vol. 2 (Oxford: Clarendon Press, 1922), 363. This, again, suggests that such a story did not form a part of the extant Latin versions of the *Life of Ruadan* which Plummer discusses.

HIS HONOUR WOULD REMAIN FOREVER

an mirbal sin, ro edhbair é féin cona shiol, ⁊ cona chlannmaicne | a mbith-dilsi do Dia ⁊ do Ruadhan; gur moradh ainm De ⁊ Ruadhain desin.

Once when St. Ruadan was on a clerical tour to the king of Eoganacht Caisil, Eochaid son of Maelugra, a certain druid of the men of Alba came on a guesting tour to the men of Erin with his burdensome company, resolved to carry off the honour of Erin, or to get everything he should ask of the men of Erin.

Loban was the name of the druid. He came to the place where Eochaid was; and he would accept no other boon of him, except that the one eye which he had in his head should be given to him; otherwise he would carry off with him to Alba his honour, and the honour of the men of Erin. When the king heard this he said that his honour would remain for ever, but his eye would not so remain. Thereupon he put his finger under his eye, and threw the eye into the druid's bosom.

When St. Ruadan perceived the unlawful demand made by the druid, he fell on his knees and prostrated himself in 'cross-vigil,' and prayed earnestly to God that the two eyes of the druid might go into the head of the king Eochaid, to serve him in the place of his own eye. And this was fulfilled through St. Ruadan's intercession.

The two eyes of the druid started out of his head through the intercession of St. Ruadan, and through the power of God, and went into the face and countenance of Eochaid, and served him, as if they had been his own eyes from his birth, so that all who saw him said: 'It is Loban's eye (Suil Lobáin) that he has'; and so the name of Suiblebain (Sullivan) stuck to him. When Eochaid saw this miracle he offered himself and his seed and descendants in perpetual possession to God and to St. Ruadan. And the name of God, &c.[16]

Plummer argued this story is an ecclesiastical adaptation of the eleventh-century *Talland Étair* (often translated as "The Siege of Howth").[17] This text was later adapted into a (potentially) Middle Irish *Dinnshenchas* narrative concerning Loch Dergderc.[18] *Talland Étair* recounts how the poet Aithirne Ailgesach (a precursor to Lobán, and a figure often portrayed in a negative light in medieval Irish literature)

---

[16] *Betha Ruadáin*, in *Bethada Náem nÉrenn*, vol. 1, ed. Charles Plummer (Oxford: Clarendon Press, 1922), 317-329, at 329; *Life of Ruadan*, in *Bethada Náem nÉrenn*, vol. 2, ed. and trans. Charles Plummer (Oxford: Clarendon Press, 1922), 308-320, at 319-320. Various spellings of name.

[17] Plummer, *Bethada Náem nÉrenn*, vol. 2, 363. Rudolf Thurneysen dated the earliest extant version of *Talland Étair* to eleventh century [as noted by John Carey, "Irish Parallels to the Myth of Odin's Eye," *Folklore* 94/2 (1983): 214-218, at 214, 218]; however, the language is datable to at least the second half of the Old Irish period, c. 600 to c. 900 [Caoimhín Ó Dónaill, *Talland Étair: a Critical Edition with Introduction, Translation, Textual Notes, Bibliography and Vocabulary* (Maynooth: NUI Maynooth, 2005), 6, 13-14, 26, 32, 39]. Whitley Stokes cited references to the story found in the works of figures like Cináed úa Artacáin, who died in 975, to suggest this text was composed before 975 [Ó Dónaill, *Talland Étair*, 30, 32; Whitley Stokes, "The Siege of Howth," *Revue Celtique* 8 (1887): 47-63, at 47].

[18] Caomhín Ó Dónaill argues Loch Dergderc is roughly linguistically contemporary with *Talland Étair*, and it is hard to say which influenced which (Ó Dónaill, *Talland Étair*, 6), assuming either is the case. Plummer and other past scholars seem to have been confident in placing *Talland Étair* in the Old Irish period and citing it as the primary source of inspiration for *Betha Ruadháin* (see above, n.17). Stokes [Whitley Stokes, "The prose tales in the Rennes dindshenchas," *Revue Celtique* 15 (1894): 272-336, 418-484, at 272] argued for a Middle Irish date for Loch Dergderc, while Edward Gwynn argued that the collection this text belongs to could not be dated to earlier than the end of the eleventh century [Edward J. Gwynn, ed., *The Metrical Dindshenchas*, vol. 5 (Dublin: Hodges, Figgis, 1935), 91-92, 94, 111, 113-114] and cited a Middle Irish provenance (VIII). In the same volume, Gwynn argued that Loch Dergderc "borrowed from" *Talland Étair*, which suggests he believed that the former was produced later than the latter (94-95, 98-99).

demands the eye of a king named Eochaid mac Luchta.[19] This story, like the one featured in *Betha Ruadháin*, also involves Eochaid plucking out his only eye and giving it to the poet. The king then puts his head in a nearby stream and subsequently receives two fully working eyes.[20] *Talland Étair* is almost certainly based on earlier material.[21] There are some notable parallels with early Norse mythology, specifically the story of Odin, the god who gave up his eye in exchange for the wisdom found in drinking from the well of Mímir.[22] Victoria Simmons has suggested these similarities may be a result of cross-cultural influences from the Norse presence in Ireland.[23] Eochaid's self-mutilation is also similar to a story recounted in two Irish-language saints' lives concerning St. Brigit, where the saint removes her eye to avoid marriage. In the Old Irish *Bethu Brigte*, when Brigit's brother Beccán claims her body will be the possession of a husband, the saint *La sodain statim ad-aig-si a m-mér fo a suil* (immediately thrusts her finger into her eye) and destroys it.[24] This episode of Brigit's life also features in

---

[19] Caoimhín Ó Dónaill discusses the negative portrayal of Aithirne Ailgesach in *Talland Étair*, and how this matches the portrayals found in other examples of medieval Irish literature (Ó Dónaill, *Talland Étair*, 11). Ó Dónaill also highlights the point which was made by Gwynn [Edward J. Gwynn, ed., *The Metrical Dindshenchas*, vol. 3 (Dublin: Hodges, Figgis, 1913), 539] that Aithirne Ailgesach is actually called Ferchertne mac Athgló in the Dinnshenchas about *Loch Dergderc* (Ó Dónaill, *Talland Étair*, 5).

[20] For the full story see *Talland Étair*, in *Talland Étair: a Critical Edition with Introduction, Translation, Textual Notes, Bibliography and Vocabulary*, ed. and trans. Caoimhín Ó Dónaill (Maynooth: National University of Ireland (NUI Maynooth), 2005), 43-62. Summarised and discussed in Carey, "Irish Parallels to the Myth of Odin's Eye," 214-215.

[21] See my discussion above.

[22] Victoria Simmons, "Saint Brigit and the Modular Eye," *Studi celtici: rivista internazionale di storia, linguistica e antropologia culturale* 3 (2004): 181-205, at 186. My thanks to Helen Williams (U.E.A., Norwich) for reminding me of the one-eyedness of Odin.

[23] Simmons, "Saint Brigit and the Modular Eye," 193.

[24] *Bethu Brigte*, in *Bethu Brigte*, ed. and trans. Donnchadh Ó hAodha (DIAS, 1978), 1-33, at 5, 23. For more information on the dating of this text, see Seán Connolly, "Some Palaeographical and Linguistic Features in Early Lives of Brigit," in *Irland und Europa: die Kirche im Frühmittelalter* (Ireland and Europe:

a Middle Irish "Life of Brigit".[25] The similarities between this and the story of Eochaid and Lobán indicates a level of imitation from the author of *Betha Ruadháin*, who might have been keen to evoke the example of one of Ireland's patron saints.

The story of Eochaid and Lobán not only features an example of a king with an impairment in a positive light, but also one who gains a greater impairment during the narrative and yet remains king. None of the texts that include this story criticise the king's monocularism. The Dinnshenchas concerning Loch Dergderc describes Eochaid as *ríg co ngus glan...clí co ndeochair chuchta cain* [...] *clú enig do Gáedelaib* (a king of pure strength . . . a prop of his people, notable for goodly shape (and) generosity among the Gaels).[26] In fact, even Eochaid's further self-impairment, which renders him completely blind, reads more as an act of self-sacrifice and defiance than a punishment or sign of low moral character. *Talland Étair* praises "[*In*] *féli móir do:rigni in rí*" (the great act of generosity which the king had performed) in giving his eye away.[27] Caomhín Ó Dónaill has also

---

the Early Church), ed. Próinséas Ní Chatháin and Michael Richter (Stuttgart: Klett-Cotta, 1984), 272-279, at 272; Seán Connolly, "Vita Prima Sanctae Brigitae: Background and Historical Value," *Journal of the Royal Society of Antiquaries of Ireland* 119 (1989): 5-49, at 6; Máire Johnson, "In the Bursting of an Eye: Blinding and Blindness in Ireland's Medieval Hagiography," in *Wounds and Wound Repair in Medieval Culture*, ed. Kelly DeVries and Larissa Tracy (Leiden and Boston: Brill, 2015), 448-471, at 460; Kim McCone, "An Introduction to Early Irish Saints' Lives," *The Maynooth review* 11 (December 1984): 27-51, at 34; M. A. O'Brien, "The Old Irish Life of St. Brigit: Part II. Introduction and Notes," *Irish Historical Studies*, Vol. 1, No. 4 (September 1939): 343-353, at 343, 345; Sharpe, *Medieval Irish Saints' Lives*, 20.

[25] *Betha Brigte*, in *Three Middle-Irish Homilies on the Lives of Saints Patrick, Brigit and Columba*, ed. and trans. Whitley Stokes (Calcutta: Privately Printed, First Edition, 1877): 50-87, at 64-65. A similar version of this tale is also found in an earlier Latin life commonly referred to as *Vita Prima Sanctae Brigitae* ('The First Life of St Brigit'), which dates to the mid-eighth century. For more detail on the provenance of *Vita Prima Sanctae Brigitae*, and its relationship with the later Irish language versions, see Connolly, "Vita Prima Sanctae Brigitae" 5-13.

[26] Loch Dergderc, in *The Metrical Dindshenchas*, vol. 3, ed. and trans. Edward J. Gwynn (Dublin Institute of Advanced Studies, 1906, reprint 1941), 338-347, at 338-341.

[27] *Talland Étair*, 43, 52.

commented on Eochaid's generous character, arguing that the king's uncomplaining preparedness to take his eye out contrasts with Mess Gegrai, a more selfish king featured in *Talland Étair* who refuses to share food with his servant and subsequently loses his arm.[28] The positive portrayal of Eochaid in this tale is echoed in a seventeenth-century poem which Osborn Bergin titled "A Priceless Gift", where Brian Ó Corcrán expresses thanks to his patron for gifting him with a pair of spectacles by invoking the precedent of Eochaid giving his eye to Aithirne:[29]

> *Eochaidh éachtach na n-arm nglan,*
> *ní thug acht éanshúil d'ollamh,*
> *giodh toirbheartus do thuair teann,*
> *le bhfuair oirdhearcus Éireann.*
>
> Valorous Eochaidh of the shining arms
> gave only one eye to an ollav,
> though that was a gift that boded hardship,
> whereby he won fame throughout Erin.[30]

This provides evidence that, in other cases within early Irish literature, regal impairments were seen as signs of bravery. One can also find other examples of both Irish and non-Irish royals acquiring an impairment and continuing in their duties with no loss of status.[31] This indicates that royal

---

[28] Ó Dónaill, *Talland Étair*, 8, 10.

[29] Osborn Bergin, ed., *Irish Bardic Poetry* (DIAS, 1970, reprint 1984), 63.

[30] "A Priceless Gift", in *Irish Bardic Poetry*, ed. and trans. Osborn Bergin (Dublin:DIAS, 1970, reprint 1984), 63-65, 239-240, at 64, 240. Thanks to Jasper Kaufhold for bringing this poem to my attention.

[31] *Annála na gCeithre Máistrí* records an incident in 1018 where Donnchadh, the son of Brian Bóruma, is attacked and has his arm struck off (*Annála na gCeithre Máistrí* ("Annals of the Four Masters"), in *Annala Rioghachta Eireann: Annals of the kingdom of Ireland by the Four Masters, from the earliest period to the year 1616. Edited from MSS in the Library of the Royal Irish Academy and of Trinity College Dublin with a translation and copious notes*, vol. 2, ed. and trans. John O'Donovan (Dublin: Hodges & Smith, First Edition, 1848-51), 792-795, s.a 1018, (§10)). Donnchadh was eventually deposed as King of Munster, but not until 1064 (*Annála na gCeithre Máistrí*, 886-887, s.a 1064, (§6)). The fact Donnchadh was not immediately deposed suggests the taboo against kings with physical

impairments could sometimes be seen in a more positive light, associated with bravery and honour.

This more positive attitude is made clear in *Betha Ruadháin*, where it is observed that *go mairfedh a bhladh do shir, 7 nach mairfedh an roscc* ([Eochaid's] honour would remain for ever, but his eye would not so remain). Here, the text seems to be making a distinction between the king's physical *rosc* or eye/vision, i.e., his physical wholeness, and his *blad* or renown/honour.[32] This implies that, even if there is a physical cost to the act of self-impairment, the spiritual/moral benefits to this act are even greater. Similar attitudes are expressed concerning St. Brigit's impairment. After removing her eye, Brigit is quoted as remarking to her brother Beccán how she doubts *"ni cunte nech cuccaib filiam cecam"* ("that anyone will ask you for a blind girl").[33] Here, the saint acknowledges the typical cost of physical impairment for women within medieval Irish society. Through her self-impairment, Brigit has rendered herself less eligible for marriage and made

---

impairments was not always followed (My thanks to Tiago de Oliveira Veloso Silva for bringing both entries to my attention). There are also some non-Irish examples of early medieval kings who acquire physical impairments but continue in their positions, such as the Frankish "Sigibert the Lame" (Irina Metzler, *A Social History of Disability in the Middle Ages: Cultural Considerations of Physical Impairment* (Routledge: London & New York, 2013), 37). Metzler discusses this topic again, even bringing in the Irish example of Fergus mac Léti, in Irina Metzler, "Impaired Medieval Rulers: Notions of Functioning, Theoretical Demands of Integrity, Acceptance of Leadership Abilities," in *Dis/Ability History der Vormoderne: Ein Handbuch/ Pre-Modern Dis/Ability History: A Companion*, ed. Cordula Nolte, Bianca Frohne, Uta Halle and Sonja Kerth (Affalterbach: Didymos-Verlag, 2017), 221-222.

[32] *Blad* is translated as "Fame, renown"–*Electronic Dictionary of the Irish Language* (*eDIL*), s.v. 1 blad, accessed 15/11/2023, dil.ie/6007. *Rosc* can be translated as "An eye; common in Mid.Ir., later confined to poetic or rhetorical style" and as "The faculty of sight, vision" – *Electronic Dictionary of the Irish Language* (*eDIL*), s.y. 1 rosc, accessed 15/11/2023, dil.ie/35559. The emphasis on vision in the *Betha Ruadháin* passage highlights that Eochaid is made completely blind; the more likely Middle Irish setting of the text suggests this refers to a physical eye, as distinct from the "renown" or "honour" Eochaid is retaining, and not a more rhetorical 'vision', although of course a double meaning cannot be ruled out.

[33] *Bethu B*rigte, 5, 23.

it harder to provide her family with the social and economic benefits of such a union. This was a legal reality in medieval Europe. The onset of blindness in an intended bride was cited as a reason to break off an engagement in Lombard law, whilst in Wales a facial blemish could lead to disinheritance.[34] Despite the negative worldly consequences for the saint and her family, Brigit (much like Eochaid) perceives this act of self-impairment as an honourable act, in her case because it allows her to devote her life to God.

Both stories are referencing a biblical passage from Matthew 18:9, where Jesus teaches his disciples to resist the temptations of sin. More specifically, Christ preaches "And if thy eye scandalize thee, pluck it out, and cast it from thee. It is better for thee having one eye to enter into life, than having two eyes to be cast into hell fire". Both of these medieval Irish texts thus act as a kind of 'narrativization' of such Christian teachings. Here, two morally virtuous characters impair themselves in the name of a greater cause—for Brigit, her service to God, and for Eochaid, the honour of his men. The image of Christ in Matthew 18, urging his disciples to remove their eye as a testament to their honour and humility, links these two figures together and underlines their devotion to such higher causes. Regardless of the problems impairment might cause for them in the material world, both characters adhere very literally to this specific Christian teaching. Both Brigit and Eochaid's stories thus provide some fascinating insights into how the ocular impairment of a king could be perceived as a positive attribute within medieval Irish society. Kim McCone has also noted the allusions to comparable biblical passages in select medieval Irish texts that portray physical impairment.[35] Victoria Simmons has cited Matthew 5:29 when discussing this story, a quote not dissimilar to Matthew 18—"And if thy right eye scandalize thee, pluck it out and cast it from thee. For it is

---

[34] Skinner, *Disfigurement in Early Medieval Europe*, 79-80.
[35] Kim McCone, "Mocking the Afflicted: Morals and Missing Body-parts in Scéla Muicce Meic Da Thó and Waltharius." *Zeitschrift für Celtische Philologie* 68 (2021): 197-248, at 232. McCone argues the texts he examines are referencing Mark 9:42-48 ("... And if thy eye scandalize thee, pluck it out. It is better for thee with one eye to enter into the kingdom of God, than having two eyes to be cast into the hell of fire..."). This verse is practically identical to the teachings of Matthew 18:9. Thank you to Joseph Falaky Nagy for making me aware of this article at the 42nd Harvard Celtic Colloquium.

expedient for thee that one of thy members should perish, rather than that thy whole body be cast into hell".[36] Such strong biblical allusions challenge the inherent link between physical appearance and honour found in Old Irish terms like enech, as argued in previous scholarship.[37]

Other medieval Irish kings experienced visual impairments that left them with an uncertain social status. For example, Congal Cáech was a king of Ulster and Tara who is mentioned in several medieval Irish sources. §§31-32 of the seventh-century law-tract on bee-keeping, Bechbretha, mentions Congal in its commentary as follows:

> *Air is sí cétnae breth inso ceta-rucad im chinta bech for Congail Cháech cáechsite beich.*
>
> *Ba-ch rí Temro conid-tubart assa flaith.*
>
> For this is the first judgement which was passed with regard to the offences of bees on Congal the One-eyed, whom bees blinded in one eye.
>
> And he was king of Tara until [this] put him from his kingship.[38]

Máire Johnson and Amy Mulligan have both cited this text as an example of how ocular impairments may disqualify a medieval Irish king from the throne.[39]

Congal is also likely to be the individual referenced in a sixteenth-century Irish medical remedy collection, where a recipe for an eye salve (possibly intended to treat a bee sting near the eye) is attributed to "The king of Dál nAraidi". Siobhán Barrett argues that the king mentioned in this eye salve is Congal Cáech, on the basis of the aforementioned reference in

---

[36] Simmons, "Saint Brigit and the Modular Eye," 183.

[37] As discussed above, see Kelly, *Guide to Early Irish Law*, 8-9, 43, n. 1 on 125, 126, 149, and Skinner, *Disfigurement in Early Medieval Europe*, 51.

[38] *Bechbretha*, in *Bechbretha: an Old Irish Law-tract on Bee-keeping*, ed. and trans. T. M. Charles-Edwards and Fergus Kelly (Early Irish Law Series, 1. Dublin Institute for Advanced Studies, 1983), 68-69, §§31-32. See Barrett, "The King of Dál nAraidi's Salve," 173-174 and Eichhorn-Mulligan, "The Anatomy of Power," n. 22 on 1021, for the dating of *Bechbretha*.

[39] Eichhorn-Mulligan, "Togail Bruidne Da Derga," 4-5; Johnson, "In the Bursting of an Eye," 453.

HIS HONOUR WOULD REMAIN FOREVER

Bechbretha and the fact Congal is mentioned in the genealogies as a king of the Dál nAraidi.[40] Congal is likewise mentioned in the tenth-century saga *Cath Maige Rath*, where the Ulstermen start a dispute with Domnhall mac Áeda, the over-king of the Uí Néill and owner of the bees, regarding compensation for Congal's impairment.[41] Jacqueline Borsje has pointed out that, in *Cath Maige Rath*, the kingship of Tara appears to have been taken from Congal and given to Domnhall.[42] The fact that the central conflict has its origins in Congal's impairment shows the significance of the king's blemishing. These references to Congal in various legal, literary, and medical texts suggest there was an awareness in medieval Irish society of the stigma connected to kings and visual impairment.

The fate of Congal Cáech makes the story of King Eochaid all the more fascinating. Both kings acquire an impairment in the eye, and yet only one is removed from his throne. Why is this? One significant difference is the level of autonomy. Eochaid's impairment is committed by his own hand, whilst Congal's bee-sting is entirely involuntary.[43] The Irish law texts appear to care more about the specific reasons for a regal impairment rather than the impairment itself.[44] Although Eochaid is placed in his situation by Lobán, the impairment itself can be read as an act of deliberate defiance: *Lasodhain ro la a mhér fona shúil, go ro theilcc an roscc i nucht an druagh* (Thereupon he put his finger under his eye, and threw the eye into the druid's bosom). This impairment is not an expression of weakness from Eochaid, but indicative of the king's refusal to accept Lobán's power over him and his people. St. Brigit's impairment can also be read as an active choice. The Middle Irish "Life of Brigit" writes *Do-rat Brigit indsin a mér fó a súil co nas-tall as a cind co m-bói for a gruad* (Brigit put her finger under her eye, and drew it out of her head until it was on her cheek). This is a direct expression of the Christian messages found in Bible quotes like those found in Matthew 18. Kim McCone has highlighted that warriors

---

[40] Barrett, "The King of Dál nAraidi's Salve," 171-173. Many thanks to Siobhán Barrett for sharing this research with me.
[41] Barrett, "The King of Dál nAraidi's Salve," 174.
[42] Borsje, "Demonising the Enemy," 23.
[43] My appreciation must be expressed to Aoife Slattery for first pointing this distinction out to me.
[44] Kelly, *Guide to Early Irish Law*, 19.

associated with ocular impairments in medieval Irish literature are sometimes framed through a satirical lens.[45] Many of these impairments are often the involuntary results of enemy action, and McCone argues they were created by medieval scribes to parody the martial traditions of pre-Christian Europe.[46] However, neither Eochaid nor Brigit is a pre-Christian warrior. The proactive way both Eochaid and Brigit bring about their impairments contrasts sharply with the involuntary injuries afflicted on such warriors, and is a deliberate imitation of the Christian teachings of Matthew 18. There is nothing humiliating about how Eochaid and Brigit are depicted in relation to their impairment. The proactive way Brigit and Eochaid bring about their own impairments reaffirms their commitment to the Christian way of life, unlike the more passive and satirical portrayal of pre-Christian warriors in other medieval texts. This autonomous adherence to Christian teachings potentially explains one of the key differences between Congal and Eochaid.

Congal Cáech's situation is not completely black and white. As mentioned, in *Cath Maige Rath* the Ulstermen demand compensation for Congal's eye injury from Domnhall mac Áeda, the over-king of the Uí Néill.[47] The Ulstermen are clearly still willing to fight for Congal, despite his impairment. This indicates that even a king with a passively acquired impairment like Congal could have still sometimes been considered worthy of the throne. Congal seems to have remained king of Ulster until his death in 637.[48] Furthermore, Bechbretha claims Congal was only removed as the king of Tara after his impairment, not as the king of Ulster; indeed, he is accorded this title in both *Cath Maige Rath* and the saga *Fled Dúin na nGéd*.[49] Some medieval Irish law-texts describe the geis for a blemished king as applying specifically to those who ruled Tara. *Bretha Étgid* ("Judgements of Inadvertence") writes that *ba geis rig co nainim do bit a Temraig* (it was a prohibited thing that one with a blemish should be king

---

[45] McCone, "Mocking the Afflicted" 233.
[46] McCone, "Mocking the Afflicted" 221, 233, 241.
[47] Barrett, "The King of Dál nAraidi's Salve," 174.
[48] Both Kelly, *Guide to Early Irish Law*, 19, 21-22 and Eichhorn-Mulligan, "The Anatomy of Power," n. 22 on 1021 have pointed this out.
[49] Barrett, "The King of Dál nAraidi's Salve," 174.

at Temhair).[50] This implies the *geis* against kings with physical impairments only applied to specific kingships, in specific circumstances. Congal is king of Ulster and Tara, whilst Eochaid is king of Eoganacht Caisil, based in the Munster province.[51] Perhaps, whilst Tara was considered a seat of such symbolic significance that the physical perfection of the king was always required, there was more flexibility for a kingship like Ulster or Eoganacht Caisil.[52]

This is suggestive of temporal or regional variations in how medieval Irish society perceived regal impairments. Medieval Ireland was not a single political entity for much of its history. F. J. Byrne once calculated there were at least 150 kings in Ireland at any given time between the fifth and twelfth centuries.[53] For Eoin Mac Neill the number varied but was never

---

[50] Kelly, *Guide to Early Irish Law*, 20. My quote comes from a version of the text found in the *Ancient Laws of Ireland* (*Lebar Aicle* "The Book of Aicill"), in *Ancient Laws of Ireland*, vol. 3, ed. and trans. W. Neilson Hancock, Thaddeus O'Mahony, Alexander George Richey, and Robert Atkinson (Stationery Office: Dublin, 1873), 82-547, at 84-85). The section discusses this matter specifically in the context of an eye impairment (82-85). In the same part of *Guide to Early Irish Law*, Kelly also cites an extract from Trinity College manuscript E3.5, as found in D. A. Binchy, ed. and trans., *Corpus Iuris Hibernici*, vol. 1 (Dublin Institute for Advanced Studies, 1978), 250. The extract reads as ₇ ba geis rig co nainim do bith a temraigh. Although *Lebar Aicle* is the term used in the *Ancient Laws of Ireland*, *Bretha Étgid* is now considered the more accurate name (Kelly, *Guide to Early Irish Law*, 272).

[51] Plummer, *Bethada Náem nÉrenn*, Volume II, 372.

[52] Eoin O'Flynn refers to Tara as "symbolic" ["Brian and the Uí Néill Kingship of Tara." In *Medieval Dublin XVI: Proceedings of Clontarf 1014–2014: National Conference Marking the Millennium of the Battle of Clontarf*, ed. Seán Duffy (Dublin: Four Courts Press, 2017), 92-102, at 92]. Edel Bhreathnach refers to the "sacred" and "ceremonial" position of Tara in early Irish society ["Tara and Cashel: Manifestations of the Centre of the Cosmos in the North and the South," in *Celtic cosmology: perspectives from Ireland and Scotland*, ed. Jacqueline Borsje, Ann Dooley, Séamus Mac Mathúna, and Gregory Toner (Toronto: Pontifical Institute of Mediaeval Studies, 2014), 165-185, at 165-167]. F. J. Byrne also discusses the "national" significance and "sacral" nature of Tara (*Irish Kings and High-kings*, (Dublin: Four Courts Press, 2001, 2second ed.), 58-64.

[53] As noted in Kelly, *Guide to Early Irish Law*, 3-4.

less than 80 or more than 100.[54] Although there was broad linguistic and cultural cohesion shared between these kingdoms, they were almost always politically independent from one another.[55] This implies that each kingdom's individual laws and customs (including those relating to kings and impairment) could have varied. Fergus Kelly has suggested that differences in local custom might be one explanation for why some of the medieval Irish law texts contradict one another.[56] This regional disparity might explain some of the differences in how Eochaid and Congal are depicted.

There is also a practical element to consider here. Would an otherwise competent king who lost an eye really be asked to step down, especially if there was no clear succession? Physical impairments would have been common in medieval Ireland, where a majority of the people bore the physical signs of disease, injury, and famine.[57] Famine was particularly frequent in Ireland from the late thirteenth and early fourteenth centuries, with four occurring in 1295, 1310, 1315, and 1330-1331.[58] Such famines would have caused life-long health problems for the survivors, including ocular impairments.[59] This point can be supported by the archaeological evidence. An excavation in Ninch, Co. Meath, uncovered eleven complete human crania and 180 crania fragments (dated to between the early-fifth to

---

[54] As noted in D. A. Binchy, *Celtic and Anglo-Saxon Kingship* [O'Donnell lectures 1967-1968] (Oxford: Clarendon, 1970), 5.

[55] See Binchy, *Celtic and Anglo-Saxon Kingship*, 5, 11, 15, 31-33, 43-44, and Clare Downham, *Medieval Ireland* (Cambridge: Cambridge University Press, 2018), 81-83, 91-107, 112-113, 238-241.

[56] Kelly, *Guide to Early Irish Law*, 1-2. Patricia Skinner has also commented on "the fluidity of taboos" in relation to impairment in medieval Ireland (*Disfigurement in Early Medieval Europe*, 119).

[57] William Sayers, "The Laconic Scar in Early Irish literature," in *Wounds and Wound Repair in Medieval Culture*, ed. Kelly DeVries and Larissa Tracy (Leiden and Boston: Brill, 2015), 473-495, at 494-495.

[58] Finbar Dwyer, *Life in Medieval Ireland* (New Island Books, 2013), 53. Although both case studies discussed in this article date from before the late thirteenth and early fourteenth centuries, I would argue that these historical records can still be helpful in indicating of the sort of society that these texts were produced in.

[59] Dwyer, *Life in Medieval Ireland*, 58.

mid-seventh centuries) with lesions on the eye orbits and the parietal bone, which could be evidence of *cribra orbitalia* and *porotic hypoplasia*, respectively. Erin A. Crowley-Champoux suggests that such conditions were a result of poor nutrition, particularly iron deficiency.[60] Kim McCone discusses this factor in the case of medieval Irish warriors. He argues that, as regular fighting naturally entailed an above-average risk of physical impairment, it would be impractical to shame every warrior who carried some sort of blemish.[61] This would be especially senseless if the impairment did not stop the warrior from fulfilling his martial duties. McCone further suggests that certain physical impairments would not always have inherently affected a warrior's ability to fight. The loss of a single hand or eye, for example, could still allow a warrior to continue engaging in combat to some degree.[62] This makes one wonder if the stigma surrounding impairment depicted in the textual sources would have always been followed in reality. One can imagine a scenario where an otherwise competent medieval Irish warrior loses an eye and, despite what the law and stories might say, would have been allowed to carry on working.

One could apply this logic to medieval Irish kingship. McCone cites an example from the medieval Irish saga *Cath Maige Tuired*, where King Núada loses his hand and abdicates the throne, but returns when fitted with a silver hand, and after his successor Bres is expelled for his unkingly meanness.[63] This example hints at some scenarios where a king with an impairment could continue in his role, especially if there was no suitable successor. Bres' poor kingship ultimately leads to Núada returning, and not the physical state of either king. Would medieval Irish people have preferred a good king with one hand, or a bad king with two hands? I would argue that the reality of life in medieval Ireland would have led to the former overruling the latter on at least some occasions.

---

[60] Erin A. Crowley-Champoux, "Cattle, Food, and the Rise of Early Ireland" (PhD diss., University of Minnesota, 2022), 271-273. Thank you to Jenna Devanney for making me aware of this archaeological material.

[61] McCone, "Mocking the Afflicted" 211.

[62] McCone, "Mocking the Afflicted" 211.

[63] McCone, "Mocking the Afflicted" 215; This example is found in *Cath Maige Tuired*, in *Cath Maige Tuired: The Second Battle of Mag Tuired*, ed. and trans. Elizabeth A. Gray (Irish Texts Society no. 52. Kildare, First Edition, 1982), 24-73, at 24-25, 26-27, 36-37, 38-39, §§10, 11, 14, 45, 46, 47, 48, 53.

It is entirely possible that legal texts like Bechbretha use Congal merely to illustrate a point of law, and do not reflect the brutal reality of medieval Irish politics. Fergus Kelly doubts Congal's story is entirely historically true, as the human eye-closing reflex is so fast a bee sting would be unlikely to penetrate the cornea, let alone remove sight from the eye.[64] Congal might have been stung in the eye by a bee, and this might have caused some sort of infection, but would this have rendered him blind and/or automatically removed him from the throne? Helen Oxenham has suggested that this stigma against kings with impairments was more of an "illustrative example" than an absolute law.[65] This, along with the case of Eochaid, indicates that the stigma against kings with impairments in medieval Ireland was not as strong or consistent as the examples of Congal Cáech and others initially imply.

The differences found in these medieval Irish depictions of ocular impairment could also be explained by the type of text being discussed. The more 'literary' texts, such as the saints' lives and saga literature, mostly use one-eyedness to entertain and instruct their audience about religious and moral lessons. The saints' lives are in particular, by their very nature, focused on promoting the cult of a specific saint.[66] This can be seen in *Betha Ruadháin*, where it is ultimately the saint that removes Lobán's eyes and gives them to Eochaid, implying that Ruadán/God's power is superior to that of the king. Hagiography's focus on the saint means such sources often set out to invert social norms in the name of promoting the cult of the saint. Physical impairment was just one of the many means towards achieving this goal.[67] In contrast, the more 'practical' texts, such as law and medical tracts,

---

[64] Kelly, *Guide to Early Irish Law*, 239.

[65] Oxenham, *Perceptions of Femininity in Early Irish Society* (Woodbridge: Boydell, 2016), 148.

[66] Donna Thornton discusses this matter within a medieval Irish context ("The Lives of St Carthage of Lismore" (PhD diss., University College Cork, 2002), 2, 6. Valerie J. Flint, "The Early Medieval 'Medicus', the Saint—and the Enchanter," *Social History of Medicine*, Volume 2, Issue 2 (August 1989): 127-145, at 128, 136, and Metzler, *Disability in Medieval Europe*, 151-152, 178, discuss it in the wider medieval context.

[67] Metzler, *Disability in Medieval Europe*, 187, notes this from a continental perspective. Boyd, "Modeling Impairment,", discusses this from a medieval Irish perspective.

HIS HONOUR WOULD REMAIN FOREVER

tend to focus on practical matters, such as compensation for those who face public ridicule as a result of their impairment.[68] Sometimes these rules are illustrated with examples from history and literature, but overall they tend to focus more on the consequences of physical impairment for the individual and society, rather than on the more explicit narrative, political, and moral agendas found in the literary material. This could help to explain some of the differences in the portrayal of Congal Cáech and Eochaid. Eochaid predominantly features in more 'narrative' sources, such as *Betha Ruadháin* and *Talland Étair*. Congal features in a variety of sources, but the more 'practical' texts like *Bechbretha* focus on what the impairment reveals about specific legal matters, rather than containing any real moral judgements. This challenges the dichotomy suggested by some past scholars between good kingship and physical impairment in medieval Ireland.

Even when all these nuances are considered, a king without an impairment still remains the overall ideal in mainstream medieval Irish society. All three Eochaid stories discussed in this article end with the king acquiring two working eyes. This is portrayed in each tale as being better than his initial one-eyedness. There is certainly a tolerance for Eochaid's monocularism, but this is conditional on the king being made 'whole' again by the end. Caomhín Ó Dónaill argues that the wrong done to Eochaid in *Talland Étair* is put right by a cosmic rebalancing when God gives him the two new eyes.[69] The stigma for kings with impairments still exists in the Eochaid stories, even if presented more subtly than in the case of Congal Cáech. Perhaps, when Eochaid claims in *Betha Ruadháin* that "his honour would remain for ever, but his eye would not so remain", this is meant to suggest his actions and motives (his honour) redeem his self-impairment (his eye), rather than implying a distinction between his physicality and honour. By taking matters into his own hands, and actively impairing

---

[68] *Bretha Déin Chécht* describes the correct level compensation to be paid to the victim of a facial injury (*Bretha Déin Chécht*, in D. A. Binchy, "Bretha Déin Chécht," *Ériu* 20 (1966): 1-66, at 40-41, §31). According to the law-text on sick-maintenance, *Bretha Crólige*, a significantly visible wound warranted higher compensation than a more easily concealable wound (*Bretha Crólige*, in D. A. Binchy, "Bretha Crólige," *Ériu* 12 (1938): 1-77, at 50-53, §31). Amy Mulligan (Eichhorn-Mulligan, "Togail Bruidne Da Derga," 4) also addresses this.
[69] Ó Dónaill, *Talland Étair*, 10.

himself, Eochaid proves himself a worthy king despite his impairment, rather than because of it. It is the self-sacrifice of the king's honour/vision that makes Eochaid brave, and such a reading only works if one accepts that some stigma exists for kings with impairments within *Betha Ruadháin*.

This theme of restoration to bodily 'wholeness' can also be seen in the case of St. Brigit. In the Middle Irish "Life of Brigit", Brigit *Do-rat iar sin a dernaind fria rosc co m-ba h-ógslan fo chétóir* (put her palm to her eye and it was quite whole at once).[70] In both the Brigit and Eochaid stories, impairment is treated as a mistake to be corrected, a reoccurring trope within medieval Irish hagiography.[71] In fact, not only do the two protagonists have their bodies restored to 'wholeness', but both antagonists also lose their eyesight. The evil druid Lobán loses his eyes to Eochaid at the end of *Betha Ruadháin*. This is similar to the Middle Irish "Life of Brigit", where Brigit's wicked brother Beccán is also blinded.[72] Victoria Simmons has argued that sight is an important metaphor for understanding the supremacy of God, and helps to explain Beccán's fate. For Simmons, Beccán is unwilling to accept the divine plan for Brigit, and is thus literally blinded to reflect his metaphorical 'blindness' to the will of God.[73] Ocular impairments are still a punishment and sign of immorality within these stories, even when linked to moral characters like Brigit and Eochaid. That only *Betha Ruadháin* features this happening to an antagonist of Eochaid is perhaps another attempt to imitate the example of St. Brigit. This further demonstrates that physical impairments are primarily used in the medieval Irish saints' lives to convey the power of the saints and promote their cults, rather than to convey a positive depiction of physical impairment.

There is certainly enough evidence in medieval Irish literature to suggest a stigma existed for kings with physical impairments. Plenty of kings lost their status, or were threatened with losing their status, due to a

---

[70] *Betha Brigte*, 64-65.

[71] For another example of this, see *Betha Máedóc Ferna* (II), in *Bethada Náem nÉrenn*, Volume I, ed. Charles Plummer (Oxford: Clarendon Press, 1922), 190-290, at 210; Life of Maedoc of Ferns (II), in *Bethada Náem nÉrenn*, Volume II, ed. and trans. Charles Plummer (Oxford: Clarendon Press, 1922), 184-281, at 204. Metzler, *A Social History of Disability*, 5-6, also discusses the "restitution narrative" and its relation to medieval saints' lives and Disability Studies.

[72] *Betha Brigte*, 64-65.

[73] Simmons, "Saint Brigit and the Modular Eye," 185.

visual impairment. But there is also evidence for a more complicated attitude towards impairment in medieval Ireland. There is the element of autonomy to consider, as well as how much the portrayal of the king adheres to Christian ideology. There are also regional and temporal factors to consider here, along with the realities of life in medieval Ireland. One must ponder how the difference in audience and the type of text being discussed could also have influenced how regal impairments are perceived in these sources. However, even when all these elements are considered, a king without an impairment remains the overall ideal for medieval Irish society. Some degree of reassessment is certainly required regarding the social attitudes towards impairment in medieval Ireland, and how these are expressed in the surviving literary material.

Acknowledgements

I would like to thank the editors for *PHCC* for accepting this article for publication. This research was produced as part of the *Language, Education and Medical Learning in the Premodern Gaelic World* (LEIGHEAS) project led by Deborah Hayden at Maynooth University, funded by the Irish Research Council (Project ID IRCLA/2022/2922). My appreciation goes out to my supervisor Deborah Hayden, Gregory Darwin for the insights he made about my research at the 42nd Harvard Celtic Colloquium, and the anonymous *PHCC* reviewer for the comments on an earlier draft of this article. Any remaining errors or shortcomings are my own.

Animal Studies Meets Medieval Studies Meets Celtic Studies: An Invitation

Matthieu Boyd

Medieval Celtic Studies teems with memorable animals: Pangur Bán; the bulls of the *Táin*; Cú Chulainn's namesake, the hound of Culann the Smith; its supposed litter-mates, Mac Da Thó's speckled dog Ailbe and Celtchar mac Uthechair's beetle-black Dáelchú; the birdman and his people from "The Destruction of Da Derga's Hostel"; the swan-maiden from "The Dream of Óengus"; the war-goddess as carrion crow or croaking raven, hornless cow, entwining eel; the white, red-eared hounds of Arawn of Annwfn; the horses and birds of Rhiannon; Branwen's starling; Cú Chulainn and Pryderi's cognate foals; the ancient animals of "Culhwch and Olwen"; the boar Twrch Trwyth and his ruinous offspring; the boar of Ben Bulben; the Salmon of Knowledge; and many more. These have been examined in some older studies,[1] leading to conclusions such as this by Miranda Green:

> [A] brief exploration of the realm of modern and early modern attitudes to animals serves to highlight the contrast between the so-called 'civilized' world and that of the pagan Celts, who shared with the American Indians the regard for a maintenance of harmony and balance with the natural world and its creatures. The belief that beasts and humans are close and essential associates, joint owners of the earth, does not preclude exploitation or meat-eating, which occurred widely in the Celtic world [. . .] What does seem to have existed, however, is respect, and this appears to have resulted from the close link perceived between the natural and supernatural worlds. The world of the Celts was less anthropocentric than either that of modern peoples or of classical societies. This meant that animals were

---

[1] For example, Gwyn Jones, *Kings, Beasts & Heroes* (Oxford University Press, 1972), and Miranda Green, *Animals in Celtic Life and Myth* (Routledge, 1992).

regarded as occupants of the landscape in their own right and were not there simply for the use of man. The strong ritual element in so many aspects of Celtic life involved with animals implies that beasts were valued and belonged to the gods. Activities such as hunting were only permissible if certain criteria were met, which included sacrifice and other ritual activities.[2]

Now, distinct from the ongoing interest in fables, allegory, and the bestiary tradition, for over fifteen years there has been a distinct trend or strand of scholarship that involves applying the lens of critical animal studies to medieval literature, with books by Karl Steel, Susan Crane, and

---

[2] Green, *Animals*, 241. She adds in the next paragraph that "[a]nthropocentricity and the notion of animals as existing for the gratification of humans tends to go hand in hand with monotheism."

others.[3] With rare exceptions (such as Crane on Pangur Bán,[4] Sharon Kinoshita on the birdman in Marie de France's *Yonec*,[5] Caroline Walker

---

[3] Karl Steel, "How to Make a Human," *Exemplaria* 20.1 (2008), 3–27, *How to Make a Human: Animals and Violence in the Middle Ages* (Columbus: The Ohio State University Press, 2011), and *How Not to Make a Human: Pets, Feral Children, Worms, Sky Burial, Oysters* (Minneapolis: University of Minnesota Press, 2019); Susan Crane, *Animal Encounters: Contacts and Concepts in Medieval Britain* (Philadelphia: University of Pennsylvania Press, 2013); Peggy McCracken, *In the Skin of a Beast: Sovereignty and Animality in Medieval France* (University of Chicago Press, 2017); Nigel Harris, *The Thirteenth-Century Animal Turn: Medieval and Twenty-First Century Perspectives* (Palgrave Macmillan, 2020); and various articles, as in postmedieval 2.1 (Spring 2011), special issue on "The Animal Turn" ed. Peggy McCracken and Karl Steel. Judging by his earlier work, Pierre-Olivier Dittmar's *L'invention de l'animal: Essai d'anthropologie médiévale* (see http://crh.ehess.fr/index.php?1178) will also be a major contribution. Earlier publications of interest include Francis Klingender, *Animals in Art and Thought to the End of the Middle Ages*, ed. Evelyn Antal and John Harthan (Cambridge, MA: The MIT Press, 1971); Joyce E. Salisbury, *The Beast Within: Animals in the Middle Ages* (Routledge, 1994); *Animals in the Middle Ages: A Book of Essays*, ed. Nona C. Flores (Routledge, 1996); and Dorothy Yamamoto, cited below. These kinds of studies with a literary or anthropological orientation can be distinguished from work more rooted in the history of philosophy, specifically scholastic philosophy, for example: Ian Wei, *Thinking about Animals in Thirteenth-Century Paris: Theologians on the Boundary between Humans and Animals* (Cambridge University Press, 2020); Juhana Toivanen, *The Political Animal in Medieval Philosophy: A Philosophical Study of the Commentary Tradition c.1260-c.1410* (Brill, 2021), and Anselm Oelze, *Animal Minds in Medieval Latin Philosophy: A Sourcebook from Augustine to Wodeham* (Springer, 2021).
[4] Crane, *Animal Encounters*, 12-23; compare Gregory Toner, "'Messe ocus Pangur Bán': structure and cosmology," *CMCS* [=*Cambrian Medieval Celtic Studies*, previously *Cambridge Medieval Celtic Studies*] 57 (2009), 1–22.
[5] Sharon Kinoshita, "Colonial possessions: Wales and the Anglo-Norman imaginary in the Lais of Marie de France," in *Discourses on Love, Marriage, and Transgression in Medieval and Early Modern Literature*, ed. Albrecht Classen (Tempe, AZ: Arizona Center for Medieval and Renaissance Studies, 2004), 147–162, reproduced as Chapter 4 of Kinoshita, *Medieval Boundaries: Rethinking Difference in Old French Literature* (Philadelphia: University of Pennsylvania

ANIMAL STUDIES

Bynum and Catherine Karkov on Gerald of Wales's Irish werewolves,[6] and Dominic Alexander on animal resurrection[7]), the primary materials and disciplinary research of Celtic Studies haven't been a part of these discussions. As one reviewer of Kathryn Kirkpatrick and Borbála Faragó's edited collection *Animals in Irish Literature and Culture* put it in 2016, "Despite the rich and complex possibilities for discursive analysis presented by Ireland's historical, political, and cultural negotiations of its relationship with nonhuman animals, Animal Studies has virtually no presence in the Irish academy."[8] Like Disability Studies,[9] this would seem to be another area where the medieval Celtic literatures and cultures would present interesting complications and adjustments to the prevailing paradigms for making sense of how 'the Middle Ages' thought about something.

There is now a vast literature on Animal Studies and the relationship of animals to the human, to monsters and the abject, and, indeed, to the

---

Press, 2006). Compare Matthieu Boyd, "Background to the element of heroic biography in Marie de France's *Yonec*," *Romance Quarterly* 55.3 (Summer 2008), 205–230.

[6] Caroline Walker Bynum, "Metamorphosis, or Gerald and the Werewolf," *Speculum* 73.4 (1998), 987–1013, rpt. in Bynum, *Metamorphosis and Identity* (New York: Zone Books, 2001), 77–111, and Catherine E. Karkov, "Tales of the Ancients: Colonial Werewolves and the Mapping of Postcolonial Ireland," in *Postcolonial Moves: Medieval through Modern*, ed. Patricia C. Ingham and Michelle R. Warren (New York: Palgrave Macmillan, 2003), 93–109. Compare Kim McCone, "Werewolves, Cyclopes, *díberga*, and *Fíanna*: Juvenile Delinquency in Early Ireland," *Cambridge Medieval Celtic Studies* (*CMCS*) 12 (Winter 1986), 1–22; John Carey, "Werewolves in Medieval Ireland," *CMCS* 44 (Winter 2002), 37–72; and Matthieu Boyd, "Melion and the wolves of Ireland," *Neophilologus* 93.4 (2009), 555–570, and "The Ancients' Savage Obscurity: the Etymology of *Bisclavret*," *Notes and Queries* 60.2 (2013), 199–202.

[7] Dominic Alexander, *Saints and Animals in the Middle Ages* (Woodbridge: The Boydell Press, 2008), esp. Chapter 4, "The Irish variant," 57–84.

[8] *Animals in Irish Literature and Culture*, ed. Kathryn Kirkpatrick and Borbála Faragó (Palgrave Macmillan, 2015), reviewed by Maureen O'Connor at https://breac.nd.edu/articles/giving-voice-to-the-voiceless/. But see now Corey Lee Wrenn, *Animals in Irish Society: Interspecies Oppression and Vegan Liberation in Britain's First Colony* (SUNY Press, 2021).

[9] See Matthieu Boyd, "Modeling impairment and disability in early Irish literature," *Proceedings of the Harvard Celtic Colloquium* 41(2022): 35–82.

posthuman, meaning cyborgs, androids, and various other kinds of artificial or composite intelligence.[10] The discourse here is very rich; it involves philosophers from Rousseau to Derrida (whose first posthumous publication was *The Animal that Therefore I Am*[11]). And it engages questions of policy, in works like Peter Singer's *Animal Liberation*,[12] as well as literature, in works like J. M. Coetzee's *The Lives of Animals*.[13] Animals, as Marjorie Garber says, quoting Lévi-Strauss, are "good to think with," and a lot of very interesting thinking is being done with them. Philosopher Kelly Oliver argues that animals, at least on the philosophical plane, "teach us to be human."[14]

Critical animal studies is often concerned with how we treat animals and justify our treatment of animals—do animals have rights? Which animals deserve which kind of rights? What is the relationship between human and animal on which this is based? Oliver describes a couple of the basic positions like this:

> *Biological continuism* is the position that humans and animals are fundamentally the same, that their differences are no more than degrees of the same kinds of things, whether it is consciousness, emotions, pain, or linguistic systems. (This is the position of many philosophers of animal rights and animal welfare.) *Metaphysical separationism* is the position that humans and animals are fundamentally different types of beings whose similarities

---

[10] Steel, *How to Make a Human*, 3, note 7, cites foundational publications in this area. For an updated, dynamic resource, see http://www.animalstudies.msu.edu/bibliography.php.

[11] Jacques Derrida, *The Animal That Therefore I Am*, ed. Marie-Louise Mallet and trans. David Wills (New York: Fordham University Press, 2008): but Steel, *How to Make a Human*, 19, refers to "[t]he punning title–*L'animal que donc je suis* (The Animal that Therefore I Am/Follow)."

[12] Peter Singer, *Animal Liberation: A New Ethics for Our Treatment of Animals* (Harper Collins, 1975); *Animal Liberation Now: The Definitive Classic Renewed* (Harper Collins, 2023).

[13] J.M. Coetzee, *The Lives of Animals*, ed. Amy Gutmann (Princeton University Press, 2016).

[14] Kelly Oliver, *Animal Lessons: How They Teach Us To Be Human* (New York: Columbia University Press, 2009).

are superficial at best or anthropomorphisms at worst. (This is the position of much of the history of philosophy that justifies man's dominion over animals).[15]

I don't think it is too reductive to say that the medieval worldview *in general* has been characterized as one of metaphysical separationism. Steel, for example, argues:

> that the human subjugation of animals [*subjugation* is a key term for Steel] played an essential role in the medieval concept of the human. In their works and habits, humans tried to distinguish themselves from other animals by claiming that humans alone among worldly creatures possess language, reason, culture, and, above all, an immortal soul and resurrectable body. Humans convinced themselves of this difference by observing that animals routinely suffer degradation at the hands of humans. Since the categories of human and animal were both a retroactive and relative effect of domination, no human could forgo his human privileges without abandoning himself.[16]

Whereas Joyce Salisbury suggested that Marie de France's "sympathetic portrayal" of a werewolf in her lay *Bisclavret* showed a twelfth-century tendency toward "more compassion for the animal part within us all," Steel responds that "there is no discrete 'animal part' in humans unless humans are understood to have a separate, secure 'human part' independent of the

---

[15] Oliver, *Animal Lessons*, 8–9.
[16] Synopsis of Steel, *How to Make a Human*, at https://ohiostatepress.org/books/titles/9780814211571.html; compare p. 21 in the book itself (I find the synopsis wording clearer). Oliver's broad distinction between metaphysical separationism and biological continuism is somewhat contested by Steel, who says that "like Derrida, I resist 'biologistic continuism,' which effaces the differences between all animals, including those between all humans. My objection is not with species per se, not with 'dogs,' or 'apes,' or 'humans,' but with the word 'animals,' especially when 'an animal' is understood as existing (rather than as being *produced*) in opposition to 'a human'" (*How to Make a Human*, 20).

very processes Salisbury tracks."[17] There is other scholarship, says Steel, that avoids this problem: he first cites Dorothy Yamamoto,[18] then says that:

> [s]ome of the most promising work on animals in the Middle Ages derives from the anti-foundational work of Deleuze and Guattari. In their insistence on a world in which animals, people, and things constantly recombine in unbounded becoming, they undermine conceptions of a world of stable, merely interrelating monads. In their system, animals do not need to be considered as a wan imitation of the human, because no secure animality or humanity, as such, exists; no creature or thing can be reduced to being only with and for itself.[19]

---

[17] Steel, *How to Make a Human*, 12. More recently, in *How Not to Make a Human*, which opens with a discussion of *Bisclavret* as a prelude to a chapter on medieval pets, he reiterates that "we ought to avoid interpreting *Bisclavret* as saying something about 'the beast within': the modern cliché is not a medieval one, and, at any rate, the idea that something primitive lurks in humans, that this primitive element is animal, that this element is violent, and that this violent, animal element is somehow 'truer' than our veneer of humanity–such beliefs, more than a little redolent of the gendered clichés of popular evolutionary psychology, are an invitation to depoliticized interpretations of the violence of the court and violence against women" (13). In his opinion, a politicized interpretation is the way to go: "[w]hat ultimately matters to Bisclavret is an interspecies homosocial aristocratic loyalty; what matters is less that Bisclavret *has* intelligence than that his actions receive royal legitimization. By the tale's end, human difference comes to register only as a slight and fading ripple in its narrative current. Any contemporary theologian would be scandalized" (3). Thus "Marie's story is definitively medieval, but not medieval in the expected ways, if we judge 'medieval' on the basis of its most influential, widespread texts and ideas" (13). The same could be said for our Celtic materials. (For my own take on *Bisclavret*, see "The Ancients' Savage Obscurity.")

[18] Dorothy Yamamoto, *The Boundaries of the Human in Medieval English Literature* (Oxford University Press, 2000); "Aquinas and Animals: Patrolling the Boundary," in *Animals on the Agenda: Questions about Animals for Theology and Ethics*, ed. Andrew Linzey and Dorothy Yamamoto (Urbana: University of Illinois Press, 1998), 80–89.

[19] Steel, "How to Make a Human," 7 (compare *How to Make a Human*, 12).

ANIMAL STUDIES

But if that is the nature of one's reality, and yet one is constantly killing or eating animals, Steel points out that this ties down animality and humanity in quite a definite way:

> Even if barriers between humans and animals became, as Salisbury argues, a ludic zone in the later Middle Ages, this change did not result in subjectivized animals, while the only "rights" protecting animals were the property rights of their owners. Humans never ceased to domesticate or eat animals or to refuse reciprocity for these actions: in late medieval law, any domestic pig that ate a human was executed, while no form of Christianity allowed its practitioners to deny the legitimacy of eating pigs without risking the suspicion of heresy.[20]

Of course, historically speaking, the early Irish *bóaire* purchases his qualifications by the property he possesses, including animals,[21] and the relative standing of Ailill and Medb in the Pillow-Talk has the same kind of animal foundation. But the imbalance between Medb's property and Ailill's, that gives rise to her quest for the Brown Bull of Ulster, is in fact created by the Connacht bull Finnbennach himself, because he objects to being in a woman's herd.[22] This is not the subjugated animal that Steel writes about; he is notionally "property," but gets to choose whose property he is, and his choice is considered legitimate by Medb, though she resents it. His subjectivity arguably follows from his backstory as an Otherworld pig-keeper who has been through many transformations.[23] Other examples

---

[20] Steel, "How to Make a Human," 7 (compare *How to Make a Human*, 13–14).
[21] The authoritative resource on the historical situation of animals in early Ireland is Fergus Kelly, *Early Irish Farming*, rev. ed. (Dublin: Dublin Institute for Advanced Studies, 2000). It could be argued that the way both a *cumal* ('enslaved woman') and livestock such as milch cows are reduced to units of value in early Irish law is itself a kind of biological continuism, albeit an oppressive one.
[22] *Táin bó Cúailnge from the Book of Leinster*, ed. and trans. Cecile O'Rahilly (Dublin: Dublin Institute for Advanced Studies, 1967), 139.
[23] "De Cophur in Dá Muccida", in *The Book of Leinster,* vol. 5, ed. R.I. Best and Osborn Bergin (Dublin: Dublin Institute for Advanced Studies, 1967), 1121–1124, reproduced at https://celt.ucc.ie//published/G800011E/text003.html; trans. by Kuno Meyer, "The begetting of the two swineherds," in Alfred Nutt, *The*

of biological continuism in Celtic-language texts are easy to think of: Túan mac Cairill, the ancestral witness to the layers of pseudohistorical occupation of Ireland becomes renewed as a stag, a boar, a hawk, a salmon, and finally a man again.[24] In the Fourth Branch of the *Mabinogi*,[25] not only are Gilfaethwy and Gwydion punished by being transformed into a series of animals that mate with each other, their offspring are transformed (or, since their parents were originally human, transformed *back*) into the human children Hyddwn, Hychdwn, and Bleiddwn: their associations with particular animals are suggestive of the *gessi* that some early Irish heroes have not to injure or eat particular animals.[26] Lleu Llaw Gyffes, struck with Gronw's spear in carefully contrived circumstances, turns into an eagle; Blodeuwedd turns into an owl. These transformations might seem characteristic of an archaic mythological mode, a primordial flux, akin to Ovid's *Metamorphoses* (more on this below),[27] but they are too prevalent

---

Celtic Doctrine of Re-birth (Volume 2 of Nutt and Meyer's *The Voyage of Bran Son of Febal to the Land of the Living*) (London: David Nutt, 1897), 58–66, as well as in *The Táin*, trans. Thomas Kinsella (Oxford University Press, 1970).
[24] John Carey, "Scél Tuain meic Chairill," *Ériu* 35 (1984), 92–111; also trans. John Carey in *The Celtic Heroic Age*, fourth ed., ed. John T. Koch with John Carey (Aberystwyth: Celtic Studies Publications, 2003), 223–225.
[25] Most recently edited by Ian Hughes, *Math uab Mathonwy: the Fourth Branch of the Mabinogi* (Dublin: Dublin Institute for Advanced Studies, 2013); trans. Sioned Davies, *The Mabinogion* (Oxford University Press, 2007), 47–64 at 52-54.
[26] Most famously, Cú Chulainn must not eat dog, Conaire must not kill birds, and, arguably, Lugaid Mac Con must not eat mice: on the first two, see Matthieu Boyd, "On not eating dog," in *Ollam: Studies in Gaelic and Related Traditions in Honor of Tomás Ó Cathasaigh,* ed. Matthieu Boyd (Madison, NJ: Fairleigh Dickinson University Press, 2016), 35–46, and on the third, John T. Koch, "A Swallowed Onomastic Tale in *Cath Maige Mucrama*?" in *Ildánach Ildírech: A Festschrift for Proinsias Mac Cana*, ed. John Carey, John T. Koch, and Pierre-Yves Lambert (Andover, MA and Aberystwyth: Celtic Studies Publications, 1999), 63–80.
[27] As an aside, talking animals are a great way to navigate C. Scott Littleton's "A Two-Dimensional Scheme for the Classification of Narratives," *The Journal of American Folklore* 78.307 (1965), 21–27. Are they hoaxes like Clever Hans, or biologically interesting specimens like African gray parrots? History. Are they miraculous, like Balaam's ass? Sacred history. Totally unremarkable ("Good

to easily dismiss: as has been pointed out about approaching the Four Branches as mythological debris, these stories were obviously meaningful for a medieval audience in their extant forms.

The key term for Steel, as I mentioned, is subjection; it's not the killing and eating of animals *per se* that creates the relationship, it's the ownership and lack of reciprocity. Compare factory farming with the kind of traditional hunting in which there are rituals to thank and honor the animal for giving its life. In the Western tradition, animals are largely used to define 'man'—both species and gender—as what Derrida calls a "carnophallogocentric" subject—that is, a carnivorous, virile, speaking subject. In "The Story of Mac Da Tho's Pig," this is precisely the effect of the pig: the warriors are in verbal contention to demonstrate the manly power that entitles them to divide and devour the meat. The phallic aspect is expressed in a more everyday way by the expression 'bring home the bacon,' which is traditionally what men have done, and which has traditionally been their basis for making pronouncements about how society, and gender relations in particular, should work.

If we take the carnophallogocentric relationship as our baseline, we see several variations that affirm it. When the young Cú Chulainn returns from killing the sons of Nechta Scéne, he asks the charioteer whether it would be more usual to bring back deer and swans to Emain Macha alive or dead.[28] Clearly the common thing would be to kill them; so Cú Chulainn brings them back alive, trading in some carnivorousness for extra virility and heroic status. This relates, I think, to the role of Cú Chulainn's *gessa* in controlling his hunger and ensuring prosocial interactions involving food.[29] Meanwhile, if we consider "The Dream of Óengus," eating, speaking, and virility are all taken from Óengus at the same time: when the swan-woman Caer first appears to him, he tries to pull her into bed with him; and when the sexual overture fails, he finds himself unable to eat or speak.

The Swan Maiden tale, as Robert Bringhurst points out in connection with some Haida narratives about goose maidens, is "more broadly, the

---

morning, Mr. Fox, how are you, I'm off to seek my fortune")? Folktale. Creative and obviously more powerful than humans? Myth. Creepy, uncanny, disturbing? Legend.

[28] See Cecile O'Rahilly, *Táin bó Cúailnge: Recension I* (Dublin Institute for Advanced Studies, 1976), 146.

[29] See Matthieu Boyd, "On not eating dog."

universal story of the hunter who sees, as in a vision, the beauty of his prey and falls in love with what he came to kill."[30] And at that point he gives up his carnophallogocentric attempt at control and enters into a negotiation with the animal. As Tomás Ó Cathasaigh has shown,[31] this negotiation for Óengus involves grappling with imbalances of knowledge and power that initially favor the swan-maiden or the magic that surrounds her. Exactly the same thing happens when the birds that Conaire pursues into Dublin Bay in "The Destruction of Da Derga's Hostel" "throw off their bird-skins and turn on him with spears and swords"[32]; he finds himself in a negotiation rather than a state of imposing his will, and the bird-people school him pretty thoroughly; his failure to take their instruction to heart in the case of his foster-brothers is another instance of negotiation with the animal, in this case the (figurative or literal) wolves that his foster-brothers become as a result of their raiding, famously referred to in the text as their being *oc fáelad*, 'wolfing,' in the province of Connacht.[33]

Cú Chulainn has similar troubling experiences with birds in the story of his wasting-sickness[34] and in the episode where his would-be lover Derbforgaill comes over from Scotland as a bird.[35] Not realizing it's her, he

---

[30] Robert Bringhurst, *A Story as Sharp as a Knife: The Classical Haida Mythtellers and Their World*, second ed. (Vancouver: Douglas & McIntyre, 2011), 33-49.
[31] Tomás Ó Cathasaigh, *Coire Sois, The Cauldron of Knowledge: A Companion to Early Irish Saga*, ed. Matthieu Boyd (University of Notre Dame Press, 2014), 165-172.
[32] The Irish is "Fo-fácbad na h-eóin a n-énchendcha & imda-suat fair co n-gaíb & claidbib": *Togail Bruidne Da Derga*, ed. Eleanor Knott (Dublin Institute for Advanced Studies, 1936), 5, trans. Gantz, *Early Irish Myths and Sagas*, 60–106, who in this case has "The birds left their feather hoods, then, and turned on him with spears and swords," 66.
[33] See McCone, "Werewolves, Cyclopes."
[34] *Serglige Con Culainn*, "The Wasting Sickness of Cú Chulainn," ed. Myles Dillon (Dublin Institute for Advanced Studies, 1953), trans. Gantz, *Early Irish Myths and Sagas*, 153-178.
[35] This is told in *Tochmarc Emire,* ed. A.G. Van Hamel, *Compert Cú Chulainn and Other Stories* (Dublin Institute for Advanced Studies, 1933), 16-68, at 62, and in *Aided Derbforgaill*, ed. and trans. Kicki Ingridsdottir, "*Aided Derbforgaill*, 'The violent death of Derbforgaill': a critical edition with introduction,

ANIMAL STUDIES

hits her with a sling-stone. She falls to the ground and changes into human form. Cú Chulainn sucks the stone out of her side and heals her, but when she asks to sleep with him, he responds that he "will not mate with flesh which he has sucked," as *Aided Derbforgaill* puts it, which is probably a generalization of the incest taboo, based on suckling breasts; *Tochmarc Emire* mentions instead his drinking of her blood, hence consanguinity. Either way, he starts off by firing a stone at a bird, and ends up in a state of kinship with it.

Gwyn Jones compares Twrch Trwyth and the boar that kills Diarmaid on Ben Bulben with Moby Dick and the bear in Faulkner's story "The Bear"—animals that go beyond the merely animal, and are imbued with a human or godlike intelligence.[36] Hence we might propose a triangle of this type:

Human, animal, and divine: a conceptual map with selected hybrids

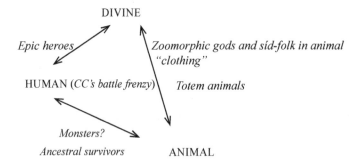

Think of zoomorphic gods or gods in animal form, Europa and the bull, the Morrígan in her multiplicity of animal forms when she attacks Cú Chulainn. For a warrior, the key difference is whether you butcher animals or *fight* them, which is another kind of negotiation. With Twrch Trwyth there is even *verbal* negotiation. In these cases the hero and the animal often share a fate: Diarmaid and the boar kill each other. Consider the death-tale

---

translation, and textual notes" (PhD dissertation, Uppsala, 2009): see Ingidsdottir, 21-22, for comparative discussion of the two versions.
[36] Jones, *Kings, Beasts*, 104-119.

of Celtchar mac Uthechair,[37] where Celtchar calls for his beloved Dáelchú in the presence of the Ulstermen, kills it with his spear as it comes when called, and dies as the dog's blood runs down his spear-shaft, along his arm, and penetrates his heart. Arguably, that scene is more moving that the one in which Cú Chulainn rather coldly kills his son; and Celtchar honors the animal even more, I think, than the human tribulation on the Ulstermen, Conganchnes mac Dedad, whom he kills without ceremony.

In these various examples, the animal often turns on the human who wants it for some particular purpose. Throughout her book, Kelly Oliver uses the image of Roy Horn, who was dragged offstage in Las Vegas by the white tiger he had lovingly trained—whenever philosophers want to use animals to advance certain arguments about the human condition, she says, the animals inevitably "bite back," or somehow manage to avoid the reductive purposes to which they are put. She writes, for example, of Derrida's acute embarrassment at standing naked in front of his cat, and finding himself in the animal gaze.

In learned Latin culture and the vernacular traditions proceeding from it, animals embody particular qualities or serve as religious exempla or allegorical figures: the genre of the animal fable, like Marie de France's *Fables*, and the bestiary tradition are two main examples. Thus the lion, whose cubs are supposedly born dead and who revives them with its breath, is a figure for Christ, as is the self-sacrificing pelican, which supposedly feeds its young by stabbing itself in the chest with its beak. If these animals "bite back," they do so subtly, on a philosophical level.[38] The animals in early Irish literature "bite back" more fiercely, because of their connection with supernatural power of one kind or another, primarily the power of the *síd* ('Otherworld'), but sometimes the power of the Christian God. The birds involved in the various negotiations that I mentioned are, of course, Otherworld people in bird form. Cormac mac Airt, in his famous judgment on the sheep that ate the queen's woad, could be said to appropriate the sheep and their *lommrad* or "stripping" of the woad easily enough, for his

---

[37] *Aided Cheltchair maic Uthechair*, ed. and trans. Kuno Meyer in *Death Tales of the Ulster Heroes* (Dublin: Hodges, Figgis, 1906), 24–31.

[38] Assuming the bestiary writer never finds himself in the jaws of a hungry lion. You know the joke: "Oh Lord, please make this lion a Christian!" And the lion settles down and solemnly says: "For what we are about to receive, may the Lord make us truly thankful . . . "

demonstration of *fír flathemon*, the truth and justice of a ruler; but of course, as Tomás Ó Cathasaigh has shown,[39] *lommrad* in the text *Cath Maige Mucrama* is at the center of a whole set of negotiations with the Otherworld, all of them involving animals: the horses that Ailill Ólomm sets to graze on Cnoc Áine, and the countless pigs that issue from the cave of Crúachu. These pigs are a wonderful example of the special irrepressibility of Celtic animals:

> 34. Now Mag Mucríma [was so called from] magic pigs that had come out of the cave of Crúachain. That is Ireland's gate to Hell. Out of it too came the swarm of three-headed creatures that laid Ireland waste until Amairgene father of Conall Cernach, fighting alone (?), destroyed it in the presence of all the Ulaid.
> 35. Out of it also had come the saffron-coloured(?) bird-flock and they withered up everything in Ireland that their breath touched until the Ulaid killed them with their slings.[40]
> 36. Out of it then had come these pigs. Whatever [land] they traversed no corn or grass or leaf grew on it until the end of seven years. Wherever they were being counted they would not stay there but would go into another territory. If the attempt to count them succeeded the counts did not agree, for example: 'There are three of them', said one man. 'There are more, seven of them', said another. 'There are nine of them', said another. 'Eleven pigs', 'thirteen pigs'. Thus it was impossible to count them. Nor were they able to slay them for when cast at they disappeared.
> 37. On one occasion Medb of Crúachu and Ailill [the human rulers of Connacht] went to Mag Mucríma to reckon them. They were counted by them then. Medb was in her chariot. One of the pigs jumped across the chariot. 'That pig is an extra one, Medb', said everyone. 'It won't be this one', said Medb, seizing the pig's

---

[39] Ó Cathasaigh, *Coire Sois*, 330–341.
[40] These are, or are akin to, the birds involved in Cú Chulainn's birth-tale. While *Compert Con Culainn* leaves it unclear whether they are *síd*-folk in bird form (the chains that link them are similar to the ones in "The Dream of Óengus") or merely birds from the *síd*, in *Feis Tige Becfholtaig*, ed. Kuno Meyer, *Zeitschrift für celtische Philologie* 5 (1905) 500–504, the birds are explained as fifty Ulster women who had been missing for three years and now appear in human form.

shank so that its skin split on its forehead and it left the skin in her hand along with the shank and it is not known where they went from that time onwards. It is from that Mag Mucríma is [named].[41]

The Otherworld has overstepped the bounds here, and it is for Ailill and Medb to set it right. The special Otherworldly character of pigs appears as well in the Fourth Branch of the *Mabinogi*, where their naming (*moch* or *hobau*, apparently a matter of innovation) is also an issue. Perhaps the hairless pinkness and unusual intelligence of pigs, and the ability of birds to navigate different elements (walking on the ground, flying in the air, and perhaps paddling in the water), makes these animals especially liminal, of special interest in connection with the liminality of the Otherworld that occupies a middle ground between settled humankind and raw nature.[42]

Tromhdámh Guaire[43] gives us another wonderful example of the irrepressible animal. Senchán Torpéist and his poetic retinue descend on King Guaire Aidne, who is famous for his hospitality, and are using the threat of satire to eat him out of house and home, as well as sending him on quests for exotic foods for which they have cravings. But Senchán makes two serious mistakes, both involving animals. First he satirizes the cats of Ireland for not keeping the mice under control, and is promptly carried off by Irusán, the king of the cats, who unlike Guaire and most other human kings, is not intimidated by satire. Irusán is about to eat Senchán when St. Ciarán of Clonmacnoise intervenes and saves him. But Senchán hasn't learned his lesson, and when he is back at Guaire's court, he forces Guaire's brother, the hermit Marbán—who has been supplying Guaire with the special food to meet all the poets' demands—to sacrifice his beloved white boar. And it is as a direct result of his destroying the deep friendship

---

[41] *Cath Maige Mucrama*, ed. and trans. Máirín O Daly (Dublin: Irish Texts Society, 1975). The spelling Mag Mucríma in this passage reflects the claimed etymology based on counting pigs (*muc* 'pig'; *rímid* 'counts'). On the larger dynamic, see Ó Cathasaigh, *Coire Sois*, 330–341.

[42] Later in the Fourth Branch, of course, it is a sow that helps Gwydion find and retrieve Llew Llaw Gyffes, transformed into a festering eagle after the attempt on his life; animals, as predators, prey, scavengers, and livestock, likewise play on the boundary between life and death.

[43] *Tromhdámh Guaire*, ed. Maud Joynt (Dublin: Stationery Office, 1931), https://celt.ucc.ie//published/G301041/index.html; trans. Patrick Ford in *The Celtic Poets* (Belmont, MA: Ford & Bailie, 1999), 77–111.

between Marbán and his boar that Marbán comes and brings Senchán's reign of imposition to an end. Like St. Íte and her stag beetle "fostering," which prepares her to nurse Jesus,[44] Marbán's friendship for the boar is coherent with his love of God, or is part of a progression towards it, as Bernard of Clairvaux's *On Loving God* says of loving other humans [true charity]: more biological continuism, really.

The ultimate irrepressible animal, if I can speak in the singular here, is in *Acallam na Senórach*, where we are told about Uaine, one of the unusual mistresses that Finn used to have: he didn't like her because she was always transforming into different animals.[45] We might wonder why it was that Finn objected, because he had other transforming lovers whom he liked: Oisín's mother, who was a deer half the time, or the lady who was alive by day and dead by night, so that Finn always smelled like a corpse.[46] The answer may lie in the multiplicity of her transformations. Finn's other lovers could be as liminal as he was, but their alternations were predictable. My first sense of Finn's objection to the woman who kept becoming different animals was an impression of how this might play out in his eyes: a sort of misogynistic excitement and post-coital disgust expressed in

---

[44] See Jenny C. Bledsoe, "St Ita of Killeedy and Spiritual Motherhood in the Irish Hagiographical Tradition," *PHCC* 32 (2012), 1–29; Thomas C. O'Donnell, "'It is no ordinary child I foster in my little cell': Fostering the Christ Child in Medieval Ireland," *Eolas* 10 (2017), 89–108. Bernard of Clairvaux, Four Degrees of Love, On Loving God, Ch. 12.

[45] 'Leannán sídh(e) do bói ac Find', ar Oissin .i. Uaine ingen Moduirnd, & tuc Find éra tochmairc furri ar a immat d' ilreachtaib a téiged sí, uair ní raibe bethadach na téighed sí 'na richt, Acallamh na Senórach I, ed. Whitley Stokes, in *Irische Texte*, ed. Whitley Stokes and Ernst Windisch, series 4, volume 1 (1900), 68, online at https://celt.ucc.ie//published/G303000/index.html: "A fairy sweetheart that Finn had, whom for the multiplicity of various shapes that she assumed (for there was not an animal but she would enter into its form) renounced her," trans. Standish Hayes O'Grady, The Colloquy with the Ancients, https://www.yorku.ca/inpar/colloquy_ogrady.pdf, 67.

[46] *Feis Tighe Chonáin*, ed. Maud Joynt (Dublin: Stationery Office, 1936), trans. N. O'Kearney, "Feis tighe Chonain Chinn-Shleibhe, or the festivities at the house of Conán of Ceann-Sleibhe in the country of Clare," *Transactions of the Ossianic Society* 2 (Dublin, 1855).

animal terms through the male gaze.[47] But the core of the problem could be what Joseph Nagy has written of as "a truth tested over and over again in Fenian narrative": "that transition is transcendence, that to pass from one category into another gives the passenger at least the momentary chance to be freed from categorization altogether."[48] Finn embodies this, but the lover he dislikes does so even more; and although Finn's career path, as a hunter and seer, requires him to negotiate with both the animal and the Otherworld, I think perhaps he liked to keep the upper hand in these negotiations: as evidenced by his role as the jealous pursuer of Diarmait and Gráinne or as a lover disgusted by infidelity,[49] Finn likes to be in control.

A few texts do propose a clear theoretical distinction between animals and humans. In *Fled Bricrenn* "Bricriu's Feast," the Ulster heroes travel to Connacht to be judged by Ailill and Medb.

> §57. One night when their meal was served, three cats from the Cave of Crúachu, i.e., three beasts of magic, were let loose to attack them. Conall and Lóegaire climbed into the rafters, leaving their food to the cats, and stayed there till morning. Cú Chulainn never fled from the beast that advanced on him, and whenever it stretched out its neck to eat, he swung his sword at its head—but the blow glanced off as if the cat were made of stone. Then the cat would fall back.[50] Under the circumstances, Cú Chulainn got no food or sleep till morning. By then the cats had vanished and the three heroes were found where they had spent the night.
> "Isn't that enough to judge you by?" asked Ailill.

---

[47] See my poem about this: Matthieu Boyd, "Circus," *The Malahat Review* 166 (Spring 2009), 70.
[48] Joseph Nagy, "Fenian Heroes and Their Rites of Passage," *Béaloideas* 54/55 (1986/1987), 161–182, at 167.
[49] See the story in Kuno Meyer, *Fianaigecht* (Dublin: Hodges, Figgis, 1910), xix–xx, trans. Patrick Ford, *The Celtic Poets*, 54–55.
[50] Here I follow Proinsias Mac Cana and Edgar Slotkin's unpublished edition and working translation at http://irishtextssociety.org/texts/fledbricrenn.html, in contrast to Henderson's "Then the cat set itself down."

ANIMAL STUDIES

"No," said Conall and Lóegaire, "we're not competing with animals, but with men."[51]

Conall and Lóegaire might seem to have a point, except that in "Bricriu's Feast," they are very obviously sore losers who reject every form of evidence that Cú Chulainn is better than they are.[52] This makes it hard to take them seriously, and their attempt at metaphysical separationism falters accordingly.

The oldest version of Cú Chulainn's death tale[53] likewise has this episode: Conall Cernach goes after Lugaid, son of Cú Roí mac Dáiri, to avenge Cú Chulainn's death. Lugaid demands fair play (*fír fer*) from Conall, which consists of having Conall fight him one-handed, since Cú Chulainn left Lugaid with only one hand. They fight for hours without resolution. Conall glances over at his horse, the *Derg Drúchtach* (Dripping Red), who is said to have a "dog's head" and to kill men in battle. She takes a bite out of Lugaid's abdomen, spilling his entrails. Lugaid protests that this is not fair play and Conall answers that "I only made you that guarantee on my own behalf. However, I didn't make any on behalf of animals and the legally incompetent" (my translation).[54] But this ethically questionable delegation to an animal partner is *not* clear evidence of metaphysical separationism, I would argue, since a warrior might resort to a human partner in the same way, as in *Mesca Ulad* when Cú Chulainn needs his charioteer Lóeg to kill a naked woman with a rock, an ignoble but necessary

---

[51] My translation for the *Broadview Anthology of British Literature* 3e website (2017), https://sites.broadviewpress.com/bablonline/wp-content/uploads/sites/27/2016/12/Fled-Bricrenn-Web-Concise-A-and-Med.pdf, from *Fled Bricrend, The Feast of Bricriu*, ed. and trans. George Henderson (London: Irish Texts Society, 1899), 72. The Irish for the last line is: "Na thó," or Conall ocus Loegaire, "ni fri biasta chathaigmit-ni, acht is fri dóini."
[52] I discuss this dynamic in Matthieu Boyd, "The Timeless Tale of *Bricriu's Feast*," *North American Journal of Celtic Studies* 1.2 (2017), 133–154.
[53] Bettina Kimpton, *The Death of Cú Chulainn: A Critical Edition of the Earliest Version of* Brislech Mór Maige Muirthemni *with Introduction, Translation, Notes, Bibliography and Vocabulary* (Maynooth: School of Celtic Studies, NUI Maynooth, 2009). Compare the translation by John Carey in *The Celtic Heroic Age*, 134–143.
[54] The Irish is: "Ni:tharddus-[s]a duit-siu [. . .] acht darmo chend féin. Ni:tharddus immurgu duit dar cend na robb & na n-écodnach" (Kimpton, 27).

action so that Cú Chulainn is able to defend himself against the warrior who is advancing on him.[55]

More broadly, Cú Chulainn's death-tale celebrates the affective bond between Cú Chulainn and the horse Liath Macha, which seems to have near-human intelligence. The horse shies away from the charioteer Lóeg, and weeps tears of blood at the prospect of going into battle with Cú Chulainn when the omens are against him. Lóeg, Liath Macha, and Cú Chulainn figure, *in that order* (i.e. the animal is not hit first), in the escalating sequence of spears enchanted to kill "kings" (but that turn out to strike first "the king of Ireland's charioteers" and "the king of Ireland's horses") that are hurled by Cú Chulainn's enemies. The wounded horse rampages to avenge Cú Chulainn and is the ultimate addressee of Emer's lament for her husband.

We can associate with other work in Animal Studies the various ways that animals give characters a chance to show their qualities. For example: The ducks of Lough Ennel give Cano of *Scéla Cano meic Gartnáin* the opportunity to demonstrate *ainmne* 'restraint,' a key theme of that saga.[56] In the First Branch of the *Mabinogi*, Arawn's dogs challenge Pwyll to demonstrate courtesy, and set him on a path to self-improvement when he falls short; the mice in the Third Branch are the final test of Manawydan's developing leadership.[57] Welsh poets can engage a bird as love-messenger (*llatai*).[58] The question is whether these examples tend to humanize or dehumanize the animals, or to subjugate them as opposed to engaging them as partners in character development or in the pursuit of significant goals.

---

[55] See Matthieu Boyd, "From King to Warrior in *Mesca Ulad*," *PHCC* 37 (2019, for calendar year 2017), 60–76, at 73–74.

[56] See Ó Cathasaigh, *Coire Sois*, 347.

[57] On the character arc of these two, see Catherine McKenna, "The Theme of Sovereignty in *Pwyll*," *Bulletin of the Board of Celtic Studies* 29 (1980–81), 35–52, and "Learning Lordship: the Education of Manawydan," in *Ildánach Ildírech: A Festschrift for Proinsias Mac Cana*, ed. John Carey, John T. Koch, and Pierre-Yves Lambert (Andover, MA and Aberystwyth: Celtic Studies Publications, 1999), 101-120.

[58] Most recently, see L. A. Brannelly, Jennifer Lopatin, and A. Joseph McMullen, "*Del cigne firent messager:* Swan as *llatai* in Marie de France's *Milun*," *Romance Notes* 62.3 (2022), 539-549.

ANIMAL STUDIES

This is an area where full engagement with the evolving[59] scholarship in Medieval Studies and Animal Studies will be valuable.

While a systematic reconsideration of Celtic animals might lead in many directions and seems likely to yield compelling results,[60] there are two specific lines of inquiry that suggest themselves to me at this stage.

First: The consensus is that the ancient Celts believed in the transmigration of souls—what Shakespeare, in *Twelfth Night* (IV.ii), calls "the opinion of Pythagoras concerning wild fowl," to which Malvolio replies: "That the soul of our grandam might haply inhabit a bird." In other words, Pythagoras, as Ovid tells us in *Metamorphoses* 15.60-142, thinks that people should be vegetarian, because any one of our relatives could have been reborn as the animal we contemplate having for lunch. This is the classic form of biological continuism. The Greek and Roman authors repeatedly say that the Celts and Pythagoras share this belief. Valerius Maximus, for example, says that the ancient Gauls "lend money repayable in the next world, so firm is their belief in the immortality of the soul. I would say that they are fools, except what these trouser-wearers believe is the same as the doctrine of toga-wearing Pythagoras."[61]

---

[59] For example, on the bird as love-messenger, compare Eliza Zingesser's booklength project *Lovebirds: Avian Erotic Entanglements in Medieval French and Occitan Literature*. https://ideasimagination.columbia.edu/fellows/ eliza-zingasser, accessed 12/2024.

[60] River Atwood Tabor's paper (unpublished) at the 2023 Harvard Celtic Colloquium, "Columba's Crane: An Exploration of Medieval Irish Ecological History," is exemplary as an inquiry into a single species. A further crane example involves the poet Athirne (see Ford, *The Celtic Poets*, 52): he gives "inhospitable" cranes to Midir of Brí Léith, and they stand outside the house and tell people not to visit, so no one does. The text doesn't say whether Midir appreciates these cranes, or whether he can't get rid of them because they were a gift. If he does like having them, they're like Conall's horse above: animal proxies that allow for an expedient but dishonorable outcome (sparing Midir the expense of entertaining guests) without their human (or *síd*-folk) principal being implicated in it, technically. If Midir *doesn't* like the cranes, they work the same way but on Athirne's behalf, setting back the cause of generosity and hospitality in Ireland while the misanthropic poet technically gets credit for being generous himself.

[61] Koch and Carey, *The Celtic Heroic Age*, 36; see also 12, 31, 35.

MATTHIEU BOYD

If we consider the transformations or transmigrations of Túan mac Cairill, Taliesin, and the pig-keepers who become the bulls of the *Táin*, the basis for a statement like that is obvious, and the way the texts are arranged in Koch and Carey's *The Celtic Heroic Age* clearly nudges us in that direction. But did the Gauls, or the early Irish, or the medieval Welsh, ever say the same? Did *they* know they shared this belief with Pythagoras, and if they did, were they interested in exploring the connection?

I think what I am really asking about here is the reception of Ovid's *Metamorphoses* in the medieval Celtic countries. Brent Miles and Paul Russell have looked into the reception of Ovid in Ireland and Wales respectively.[62] Miles finds that the Irish mined the *Metamorphoses* for what they could learn about the Theban cycle, and that's about it: where is the evidence that in the vast project of synthetic pseudohistory, or the impulse that led the Irish to (notionally, at least) discard the *Táin* in favor of Isidore of Seville's *Etymologies* and then to get it back, there was any place carved out for a synthetic treatment of Ovid's theme of "bodies changed into new forms"? Russell explicitly wonders "why Welsh poets would be fixated on Ovid as a love poet rather than as, for example, the composer of the *Metamorphoses,* a work which would have accorded well with accounts of shape-shifting and the like in native Welsh tales."[63] He suggests this might have been because the Welsh lacked access to the *Metamorphoses*, by contrast with the *Ars amatoria*. But another explanation suggests itself. In

---

[62] Brent Miles, *Riss in Mundtuirc*: The Tale of Harmonia's Necklace and the Study of the Theban Cycle in Medieval Ireland," *Ériu* 57 (2007), 67–112, and *Heroic Saga and Classical Epic in Medieval Ireland* (Cambridge: D.S. Brewer, 2011); Paul Russell, *Reading Ovid in Medieval Wales* (Columbus: The Ohio State University Press, 2017). The survey collection *Ovid in the Middle Ages*, ed. James Clark, Frank Coulson, and Kathryn McKinley (Cambridge University Press, 2011), mentions Ireland exactly once: "The earliest surviving manuscript of the *Metamorphoses* (London, BL, Add. MS 11967, s. $x^{ex.}$), was written in an Irish script and incorporates erroneous readings that are redolent of the Insular tradition," which could be taken as weak evidence for access to the *Metamorphoses* in Ireland. Ultimately there is also Eochaidh Ó hEodhasa's seventeenth-century *"Mór theasda dh'obair Óivid"* ("Much is wanting from Ovid's work"), which engages with the *Metamorphoses* as a political history of the world (the Four Ages in Book 1 and the history of Roman rulers in Books 14 and 15).

[63] Russell, *Reading Ovid*, 221.

ANIMAL STUDIES

a famous essay on the marvelous in the Middle Ages, Jacques Le Goff suggested that *mirabilia* (to be distinguished from white and black magic, and Christian *miracula*) were essentially derived from local paganism, not the Classical tradition.[64] It is difficult to argue from absence, but it could be that the idea of animal transformation was so securely attached to the native tradition in Ireland and Wales that they didn't want or need to bring Ovid into it.[65]

This puts a new complexion on the expansion of the category of the "Breton lay," Marie de France's signature form, in medieval French. Formally, this kind of lay (*lai*) is a short narrative poem in octosyllabic rhyming couplets.[66] One thing that characterizes the lay as a genre, besides the claim of Breton origin, is animal transformations: the hawk-knight in Marie's *Yonec*; the white deer or boar that turns into a lady bathing in a fountain. By the end of the thirteenth century, as evidenced by compilations like BNF fr. 2168,[67] the genre of the lay was admitting material that originally had no connection whatsoever to Brittany—including the Old French poems based on Ovid's *Metamorphoses*: *Narcisus* and *Piramus and Thisbe*.[68] The standard view of this development is that "[i]n some instances, [the word lai] seems to indicate nothing more than a brief verse narrative turning on a love-problem."[69] But I wonder if in the specific case of these Ovidian poems, the primary umbrella available at the time, at least

---

[64] "The Marvelous in the Medieval West," in Jacques Le Goff, *The Medieval Imagination*, trans. Arthur Goldhammer (University of Chicago Press, 1988), 27–46.

[65] "We have that already," as Jerry Hunter put it to me in conversation at the 2023 Colloquium.

[66] See Matthieu Boyd, "What is a lay? I: Celtic lays," *Le Cygne* (third series) 1 (2014), 22–26; "Breton lays in Britain," in *The Blackwell Encyclopedia of British Medieval Literature*, ed. Siân Echard and Robert Rouse (Wiley-Blackwell, 2017).

[67] Keith Busby, *Codex and Context: Reading Old French Verse Narrative in Manuscript*, Volume 2 (Amsterdam: Rodopi, 2002), 466.

[68] These have been edited and translated by Penny Eley: *Piramus et Tisbé* (Liverpool Online Texts Series, 2001: https://www.liverpool.ac.uk/media/livacuk/modern-languages-and-cultures/liverpoolon-line/piramus.pdf); *Narcisus et Dané* (Liverpool Online Texts Series, 2002: https://www.liverpool.ac.uk/media/livacuk/modern-languages-and-cultures/liverpoolonline/narcisus.pdf).

[69] Busby, *Codex and Context*, 466.

in the vernacular, for "bodies changed into new forms" was a notionally "Breton"—that is, Celtic—one.[70] In the fourteenth century, when the earlier Ovidian lays are subsumed into the enormous vernacular *Ovide moralisé*,[71] this changes, and all of Ovid's marvelous animal transformations are subjugated, to use Steel's word again, in the service of Christian truth.

A second major line of investigation would follow from Miranda Green's observation that the attitude to animals exemplifies how "the pagan Celts [...] shared with the American Indians the regard for a maintenance of harmony and balance with the natural world and its creatures."[72] Green has not been the only one to propose this kind of comparison,[73] and it might be time to consider seriously how appropriate and productive it would be to bring Celtic Studies into dialogue with Indigenous Studies (which is a separate question from how appropriate and productive it is to analyze the Celtic-speaking peoples themselves as 'indigenous'). It is already standard to consider the Celtic-speaking peoples as colonial and postcolonial subjects (who also become, within the British Empire and elsewhere, colonizers themselves). One of the things that may well be reflected in the redaction of Celtic literature in a colonial context—in the composition of

---

[70] Marie's own "Breton" lays had some degree of Ovidian influence: see "Roundtable: Marie and Ovid" (with contributions by Rupert Pickens, Dorothy Gilbert, Emanuel Mickel, and Susan Hopkirk), *Le Cygne* (third series) 5 (Fall 2018), 53–84. But that in no way undermines the point that this material came to be packaged as *lais de Bretaigne*, not as *lais d'Ovide* or *lais de muance* (lays of transformation/metamorphosis). And this was not because Ovid's corpus was broadly considered sacrosanct, so that no more material could be added to it: the Middle Ages were quite happy to credit Ovid with Latin material that he didn't write. See *Appendix Ovidiana: Latin Poems Ascribed to Ovid in the Middle Ages*, trans. Ralph Hexter, Laura Pfuntner, and Justin Haynes (Cambridge, MA: Harvard University Press, 2020).

[71] See *The Medieval French* Ovide moralisé*: An English Translation*, 3 volumes, trans. and ed. K. Sarah-Jane Murray and Matthieu Boyd (Cambridge: D.S. Brewer, 2023), 283–293 (Narcissus), 310–323 (Piramus and Thisbe), 493–515 (Philomena, attributed to Chrétien de Troyes).

[72] Green, *Animals*, 241.

[73] See Boyd, "On not eating dog," where I consider Dumézil's juxtaposition of Cú Chulainn's Boyhood Deeds with the *hamatsa* dance among the Kwakwa̱ka̱'wakw (an Indigenous culture of the Pacific Northwest, in what is now British Columbia).

ANIMAL STUDIES

Acallam na Senórach, and the writing of the *Mabinogion* tales in their present form, and the quasi-ethnographic descriptions of birdmen and werewolves discussed by Kinoshita, Bynum, and Karkov—is a consciousness of preserving a relationship to animals that is more fraught and intimate than the mainstream European relationship that scholars like Steel (in *How to Make a Human*) describe. This is not merely the stereotype about Celts living in harmony with nature: negotiations with the irrepressible animals in our texts are very often *not* harmonious, but they are complex and sometimes deeply respectful. Any efforts along these lines would need to balance their attempts at productive generalizations with attention to local detail and specific communities. The dangers of simplistically stereotyping 'pagan Celts' (or any 'Celts') will be familiar to us; the dangers of stereotyping Native Americans (and other Indigenous people), in all their diversity of languages and cultures, should be correspondingly obvious.

In calling for a renewed and systematic evaluation of animals in Celtic texts within larger theoretical frameworks, this paper has necessarily only scratched the surface of the topic. The invitation to Celtic scholars is to engage with the theoretical frameworks and the generalizations from outside the field; the invitation to everyone else is to consider the Celtic texts, to see how those might complicate their thinking;[74] the invitation to both groups is to be in dialogue with one another. There are dozens of interesting animal examples in the literature that I haven't mentioned, and we may find that there are important differences in outlook across different texts or different types of texts in our traditions.[75] Legal material, and any

---

[74] I am grateful to the anonymous reviewer for *PHCC* for comments on this paper, and appreciated their paraphrase of my argument, i.e. "Taking up this material should [. . .] afford opportunities to complicate some of the claims of critical animal studies, e.g., its frequent swipes at 'western epistemologies' (etc.), which take the worldwide colonial era as paradigmatically 'western,' and also to free critical animal studies from its entanglements with modern philosophy." Of course, any outside engagement with Celtic-language sources should involve due consideration of the specialist research on those sources and their cultural context.

[75] Especially since so many medieval Celtic-language works are anonymous, the presumption has often been a commonality of outlook: "the public of early narrative did not seek to discover the unique world-view of a particular author,

other evidence we have for the historical rather than literary treatment of animals, should plainly factor into our thinking too.[76] But I hope I've been able to offer a convincing sense that, in the face of a thriving zone of theoretical discourse and some attempts to generalize about its application to the Middle Ages, there is an opportunity for Celtic Studies to 'bite back.'

---

but rather, sought recognition of familiar codes and conventions shared from one work to another" (Máire Herbert, "*Fled Dúin na nGéd*: a Reappraisal," *Cambridge Medieval Celtic Studies* 18 [1989], 75–87, at 75). But it seems clear that even if that was the case, different texts adopt particular slants or attitudes to their material.

[76] Again, Kelly, *Early Irish Farming*, is exemplary; see also J.P. Mallory, *In Search of the Irish Dreamtime: Archaeology and Early Irish Literature* (London: Thames & Hudson, 2016), 101–132. For some engaging cases of animals in Welsh law, see Nerys Patterson, "Honour and Shame in Medieval Welsh Society: A study of the role of burlesque in the Welsh laws," *Studia Celtica* 16 (1981), and Robin Chapman Stacey, *Law and the Imagination in Medieval Wales* (University of Pennsylvania Press, 2018).

Women's libraries in medieval Brittany, thirteenth through the fifteenth centuries

Yves Coativy

Medieval libraries have been at the heart of research for many years, both in France and in the English-speaking world. After making an inventory of the surviving medieval books and then describing the libraries, historiography has evolved towards studies more focused on social groups or gender.[1] While kingdoms and a few important families have been studied, smaller regions that evolved in parallel with–but not on the margins of–kingdoms have received less attention from researchers. Brittany is one such area.[2] The duchy has benefited from several highly erudite studies, but the place of women has been neglected. A medieval library is a collection of books–not necessarily numerous, but often luxurious and costly. The sources are fairly numerous but uneven. We have identified 21 libraries or sets of books, ranging from a few to a hundred, for a total of around 277 books.[3] The archives contain several old inventories, often wills or post-mortem inventories. We also have many books that have come down to us, but they overrepresent books of hours, books on parchment, and illuminated books. It is difficult to include printed books because incunabula are few, difficult to attribute, and not designated as such in inventories. However, we know that books have been printed in Brittany since the 1470s.[4] What survives is therefore only the tip of the iceberg.

---

[1] A summary bibliography of the main works concerning Europe is available here: http://theleme.enc.sorbonne.fr/bibliographies/codicologie/bibliotheques_medievales

[2] The main works concerning Breton appear below in the footnotes.

[3] Approximately 277, as it is sometimes difficult to separate single books from collections of books in one volume. The inventory is based on lists published by Diane E. Booton, *Manuscripts, Market and the Transition to Print in Late Medieval Brittany* (London: Ashgate, 2009), appendix B, 249-362, then completed using the bibliography.

[4] Malcolm Walsby, *The Printed Book in Brittany, 1484-1600* (Leiden: Brill, 2011), 17-43. The titles of books printed in Brittany before 1500 are not found in

A striking example of all these difficulties is found in the library of Marie de Bretagne, abbess of Fontevrault (†1477),[5] whose library inventory contains 92 titles, of which only one book of hours is currently known to survive.[6] Almost half of its contents were on paper (47), although the vast majority of all extant books are on parchment. The same holds for every library known only from documents. The data are also limited by the destruction of books early on and the centuries-old sorting of bibliophiles, who have selected the finest books.[7] Medieval inventories go some way to compensating for this problem, but the number of works currently in our possession pales in comparison with medieval production. The inquiry suffers from another documentary bias: the over-representation of aristocratic owners, which certainly corresponds somewhat to medieval reality, but leaves us in the dark about the bourgeoisie. Despite all these difficulties and limitations, we can nonetheless draw some interesting conclusions while waiting for a historian to take up the subject for a systematic study.

Book owners and library composition

Unsurprisingly, the social group which most concerns this investigation is princesses and aristocrats.[8] This is a group restricted to the social elite, the ducal family and families of the Breton high aristocracy. Bourgeois women seem to be absent, but it is difficult to say whether they did not own books or just did not feel the need to mark their possession. There are very few books in bourgeois wills and post-mortem inventories with the rare exception of the usual book of hours. The same applies to the lesser and middle nobility, who also seem to possess, at most, only a book of hours. Most of these were also lay people, but there were at least two

---

women's libraries, except for Ludolf de Saxe, *La vie de Jésus Christ*, printed in Bréhan-Loudéac in 1485 and present in the libraries of Marie de Bretagne (two copies of *La vie du Christ*) and Jeanne de Raguenel.

[5] Only death dates are given, as the birth years of these women are generally poorly recorded or unknown. The situation is similar for the men of this period.

[6] It is kept in New York, Brooklyn Museum Ms 19.78.

[7] Yves Coativy, "The Destruction of Archives in Brittany," *Proceedings of the Harvard Celtic Colloquium*, 40 (2021), 169-183.

[8] Indeed, it's telling that one of the most serious websites on the subject is called https://booksofduchesses.com/.

nuns: Marguerite de Rohan (†1496) and Marie de Bretagne (who owned the largest library, but its contents are known only from an inventory), not to mention Françoise d'Amboise, a duchess who died in 1485 in the odor of sanctity.

According to a variety of disparate sources, the size of these libraries varied from a few books to several dozen. This undoubtedly depended on wealth, but also on whether their owners' interest was in reading itself or books as objects of art as some women towards the end of the period collected books, such as Catherine de Coëtivy (†1529) or her cousin Jeanne de Raguenel (†1501). These women's libraries have several common features. They contain almost exclusively French books, except for a few rare Latin titles, and there are no books in Breton. This was the norm at the time, as Breton was the language of the people in Lower Brittany, while French was the daily language for the elites, and Latin was used by the men and women of the Church. The very first printed book in Breton was a Breton/Latin/French dictionary printed in 1499 for the use of the clergy.[9] Antoine Dufour, author of *Vies de femmes célèbres* ("Lives of Famous Women"), makes the same observation about Latin: "Most of the noble ladies of France do not hear Latin . . . but their mother tongue."[10]

The composition of these libraries corresponds to what we know of medieval libraries more generally, with books on piety and religion accounting for around 71 percent of the total, including iconic works, such as the book of hours used to keep track of daily prayers. Next come medieval history and books on morality (11.5 percent), almost on par with books by classical authors (10 percent). Novels, which are rare, account for 5 percent of the sample and the remainder is made up of a few little-known poetry titles and practical objects such as world maps. However, these figures must be treated with caution as they are distorted by the over-representation of fine books (illuminated and on parchment) at the expense of books on paper–most of which have been lost or cannot be attributed– and by the over-representation in the corpus of the essentially religious library of Marie de Bretagne, the abbess of Fontevraud.

Two major intellectual trends in the late Middle Ages and the Early Modern Period had profound impacts on medieval Breton libraries: a

---

[9] Jehan Lagadeuc, *Le catholicon* (Tréguier: Jehan Calvez, 1499).
[10] Antoine Dufour, *Les vies des femmes célèbres* (Genève-Paris: Droz, 1970), 1.

culture of the macabre, and the Renaissance spirit. The culture of the macabre developed from the second half of the fifteenth century onwards, due to the recurrence of epidemics, wars and the revival of religious thought with the *Devotio moderna* among other factors. In Brittany, several significant medieval events can be linked to it including the macabre dances of Kermaria an Iskuit (Ploubazlanec, Côtes d'Armor) and Kernascléden (Morbihan), the appearance of the Ankou, a character unique to Brittany who is frequently depicted on the walls of religious buildings as death's servant,[11] and the burial of all social classes in churches. This current of thought is reflected by several works kept in the libraries under investigation such as Jean Gerson's *Science de mourir ou livre de sapience* (Science of Dying or Book of Wisdom) and René d'Anjou's *Mortifiement de vaine plaisance* (Mortification of Vain Pleasure). One also finds several religious works on the theme of death and hell, such as *Joies de paradis et peines de l'enfer* (The Joys of Heaven and the Pains of Hell), *Traité des peines de l'enfer* (Treatise on the Punishments of Hell), *Douze périls d'enfer* (Twelve Perils of Hell), *Office de la mort* (Office of Death), Pierre de Nesson's *Leçons des vigiles des morts* (Lessons from the Vigil of the Dead) and Jean Le Fèvre's *Le répit de la mort* (Respite from Death). This atmosphere also appears in the form of images. The wound in Christ's side, for example, is depicted very realistically in a book of hours by Isabeau Stuart (†1494).[12] A motto found in Catherine de Coëtivy's copy of *La légende dorée* (The Golden Legend) by Jacques de Voragine may also be linked to this state of mind, "*Nespoir. Ne. Peur*" (no hope, no fear).[13]

Towards the end of our period, from the fourteenth-century onwards in Italy, and in the course of the following century in France, there was a

---

[11] For the culture of the macabre in Brittany, see Cristina Bogdan, Ilona Hans-Collas, Yves Coativy and Didier Jugan (dir.), *Hirie dime, varchoas dide. La mort et ses représentations* (Brest: Centre de recherche bretonne et celtique, 2023). On the Ankou as a specifically Low-Breton character, Daniel Giraudon, *Croyances et légendes de la mort en Bretagne et pays celtiques. Sur les chemins de l'Ankou* (Fouesnant: Yoran Embanner, 2012).

[12] BnF Ms Latin 1369, folio 410, verso. The preservation in Paris of the tip of the Longinus spear since its purchase by Louis IX gives the size of the wound.

[13] BnF Fr 244-245, folio 1, recto. See François Avril & Nicole Reynaud, *Les manuscrits à peintures en France 1430-1515* (Paris Bibliothèque nationale de France, 1998), 258-259.

renewed interest in ancient authors (for which the original text is now preferred to compilations), the appearance or rediscovery of Greek classics (especially after 1453), the development of a new literature focused on man, and increased separation between religion and the secular world. These trends are reflected by the appearance of books by Classical or Italian Humanist authors in Catherine de Coëtivy's library, which is clearly 'renaissante.' Alongside the usual religious books, we find such works as Vegetius' *Art militaire* (Military Art translated by de Jean de Meun), Cicero's *La rhétorique* (The Rhetoric translated by Jean d'Antioche), Livy's *Les trois décades* (The Three Decades translated by Pierre Bersuire) and *Livre de la première guerre punique* (The First Punic War translated by Jean Le Bègue), Josephus's *La guerre des Juifs* (The Jewish War translated by Guillaume Coquillart) and *Le livre des Cas des nobles hommes et femmes de Boccace* (Boccaccio's On the Fates of Illustrious Men and Women translated by Laurent de Premierfait).[14] We also find works by Boccaccio, as well as a volume by Petrarch, *Des remèdes de l'une et l'autre fortune* (Remedies for Both Fortunes), in the libraries of Jeanne de Laval (†1498) and Jeanne de Raguenel.[15] This 'renaissante' evolution is not unique to women's libraries, and can also be found in contemporary male Breton libraries, such as that of Catherine's uncle, Prégent de Coëtivy (†1450), or in the rest of France.[16] Finally, it is no surprise to see an increase

---

[14] About this humanist translator who worked mainly for the French aristocracy, Anne D. Hedeman, *Translating the past : Laurent de Premierfait and Boccaccio's De Casibus* (Los Angeles: The Paul Getty Museum, 2008) and A. Hedeman, "Translating Power for the Princes of the Blood: Laurent de Premierfait's Des cas des nobles hommes et femmes" in *Textual and Visual Representations of Power and Justice in Medieval France*, R. Brown-Grant, B. Ribémont, and A. Hedeman eds. (London: Ashgate, 2015), 15-41.

[15] *La patience de Griselidis* also by Petrarch was printed in Bréhan-Loudéac in 1485 (NS). Walsby, *The Printed Book in Brittany*, 266.

[16] Jacques Verger, "Manuscrits et auteurs italiens dans les bibliothèques universitaires françaises à la fin du Moyen Âge," *Libri, lettori e biblioteche dell'Italia medievale (secoli IX-XV). Fonti, testi, utilizziazione del libro / Livres, lecteurs et bibliothèques de l'Italie médiévale (IXe-XVe). Sources, textes et usages.* Actes de la table ronde italo-française (Rome, 7-8 mars 1997), Documents, études et répertoires de l'Institut de Recherche et d'Histoire des Textes 64 (Aubervilliers: Institut de Recherche et d'Histoire des Textes (IRHT), 2001), 131-145, especially 137 and 141.

in the number of books which an individual owns and perhaps (though this is not easy to demonstrate for lack of documentation) the move towards a 'secularization' of themes, with more novels, ancient authors, philosophy and morals (Boethius), and less religion, other characteristic elements of the Renaissance in Europe.

Libraries are built up in a variety of ways including purchases, patronage, and commissions. Several manuscripts seem to have passed from one library to another through purchase. In Catherine de Coëtivy's library, for example, we find a fifteenth-century composite copy of Saint Augustine's *La Cité de Dieu* (The City of God).[17] These are two volumes brought together to complete the text. Originally owned by Jehan, Duc de Berry, only the first volume bears the arms of Antoine de Chourses and Catherine de Coëtivy, who subsequently acquired it. The copy of *Cas des nobles hommes et femmes* from the same collection belonged to Prégent de Coëtivy before passing into his niece's collection. Louise de Coëtivy (†1553) also spent 5 s 6 d on the purchase in 1540 "d'une paire d'heures pour madame de Taillebourg" ("of a pair of hours for Mme. De Taillebourg").[18]

Several examples of commissions are well documented. For example, in 1456, Dom Armel Guilleron of Sainte-Claire de Nantes received £b 6 and 10s for writing a book for the duchess Françoise d'Amboise. Payment was made "du commandement de la duchesse" ("at the duchess' command") for the writing salary, which amounted to £b 3 13s 4d[19]. In the same vein, Isabel Stuart, wife of Duke François I of Brittany (r. 1442-1450), inscribed, or had inscribed, in a volume of the *Somme le Roi* (The King's Sum): "Isabel, daughter of the King of Scotland, Duchess of Brittany, Countess of Montfort and Richemont, commissioned this book. Whoever finds it will return it to her; and had it written for her devotion by the hand

---

[17] Chantilly, Musée Condé, Ms no. 122-123 (322-323); Alexandre Laborde, *Les manuscrits à peintures de la Cité de Dieu* (Paris: Rahir, 1909), tome I, second half, 464-468.

[18] Louis de La Trémoille, *Inventaire de François de La Trémoille 1542* (Nantes: Emile Grimaud, 1887), 133.

[19] Jean-Luc Deuffic, *Le livre d'heures enluminé en Bretagne. Car sans heures ne puys Dieu prier* (Turnhout: Brepols, 2020), 87. The rest of the money was used to pay for supplies. The Breton pound (£b) did not have the same value as the French pound (tournois) and was worth 20% more.

of Jehan Hubert in the year one thousand four hundred and sixty-four. *Explicit Deo gracias.*"[20] Likewise, Louise de Laval (†1468) commissioned two works about Gregory the Great–*Les dialogues* (*Dialogorum libri quattuor de vita et miraculis partum italicorum et de aeternitate animorum*) and the *Vie de saint Grégoire* ("Life of Saint Gregory") by Jean Le Diacre– in one volume produced by Antoine Simonet, "ad instantiam illustrissime domine comitissa Penthevria" (At the request of the most illustrious lady, Countess Penthevria).[21]

Patronage is another way of enriching a collection. *Le livre de grâce* (The Book of Grace) by Pierre Fontaine "*est dédié à la reverence de tres noble et tres excellente dame Madame Jehanne d'Orléans, cousinne germaine du roy Louys, douzième de ce nom et comtesse de Tailhebourg*" (is dedicated to the reverence of the very noble and excellent Madame Jehanne d'Orléans, first cousin of King Louys, twelfth of this name and Countess of Tailhebourg).[22] Pierre Le Baud dedicated his *Généalogie des ducs de Bretagne* (Genealogy of the Dukes of Brittany) to Duchess Marguerite de Foix (†1486), who owned two copies,[23] and the poet Jean Meschinot dedicated a ballad to her. Patronage was a well-known phenomenon at the end of the Middle Ages for women and men alike and queens such as Jeanne d'Évreux (†1371) and Anne de Bretagne (†1514) practiced it extensively.

This raises a difficult question as these objects are both books and works of art. Which was more important in the case of large, illuminated books on vellum, the quality of the text or that of the illustrations? Catherine de Coëtivy and Jeanne de Raguenel, who accumulated fine books, were certainly more interested in books as objects of value than in the texts themselves. Other cases are less clear cut, even if collecting books was part of a wider practice of accumulating ostentatious luxury objects by members of the aristocracy.

---

[20] Deuffic, *Le livre d'heures enluminé en Bretagne*, 9.
[21] Booton, *Manuscripts, Market and the Transition to Print in Late Medieval Brittany*, 316.
[22] Musée Condé, Ms 160 (778) late fifteenth/early sixteenth century.
[23] BnF Ms Fr 6011 and Bib. Genève Ms Fr 131.

YVES COATIVY

Is there such a thing as a 'woman's' library?

It is hard to say what typified a woman's library as opposed to a man's in the late Middle Ages. The first thing to consider is whether the owner is a woman, which is the starting point of this work. But we can also look in the inventories to see whether female authors are represented, and whether certain themes appear to be more specifically feminine than others. We can cautiously point to a few elements that may shed some light on the subject. First, in addition to the great 'classics' of the period, characteristics of specifically feminine literature can also be discerned. The first characteristic is the presence of several works by female writers, such as Christine de Pizan (c. 1363-c. 1430), a rare female author in a world of men, whose works are found in the homes of Gilette de Derval (†1487) and Abbess Marie de Bretagne (*La cité des dames*); Catherine de Coëtivy (*Le livre du corps de policie*) and Marguerite de Bourgogne (†1441) (*Le livre des trois vertus*). Christine de Pizan's books were widespread in medieval libraries, and Brittany was no exception to the phenomenon, but even if women were reading her work (Isabeau of Bavaria, Queen of France, or the Dauphine Marguerite of Burgundy, for example), this is no guarantee of their approbation since many copies are found in the libraries of male clerics who regarded her very poorly, more out of a misogynistic reflex than anything else. Another female author is Agnès d'Harcourt whose *Vie de madame Isabeau de France* (The life of Madame Isabeau de France) was in the library of Marie de Bretagne.

Second, there are titles that seem to be aimed directly at women, such as the two *livres d'heures de la Vierge* (books of hours of the Virgin) owned by Marie de Rieux (†1465) or the *livres d'heures de Notre-Dame* (book of hours of Our Lady) owned by Marie de Bretagne and by Jeanne de Navarre. In the same vein, we find volumes such as Durand de Champagne's *Miroir de dames* (Ladies' mirror) in the libraries of Jeanne de Navarre and Jeanne de Laval, *Les Vertus que les dames doivent avoir* (Virtues That Ladies Should Have) and *La belle dame sans merci* (The Beautiful Lady without Mercy) in the library of Marguerite de Bretagne, decorated with her coat of arms, Alain Chartier's *Le livre des quatre dames* (The Book of Four Ladies) in the library of Jeanne de Laval, and Guillaume de Saint-Cloud's *Le calendrier de la reine* (The Queen's calendar) and Durand de Champagne's *Mes dames et mes demoiselles* (My ladies and girls) in the library of Marie de Bretagne. Although these books are also found on occasion in men's libraries of the same period, they are much rarer.

The representations of the owners in their books as well as the mottos and other formulas found in them are a reminder of how personal these objects are. The last books that Catherine de Coëtivy had decorated bear the motto "*La demeure*" (i.e. "*Là je demeure*", in my books I remain). She was a widow at the time and had lost her only son.[24] This sentiment is reinforced by other marks, such as the personal prayer for the birth of a son in a book of hours by Marguerite de Foix. In the case of remarkable personalities, the mark of ownership elevates the object to the rank of relic and contemporaries certainly understood this well in the case of Françoise d'Amboise's book of hours, which is preserved as a relic in the Nazareth community she founded.[25]

When they are present or have not been subsequently replaced, the marks of ownership are familiar–coats of arms, signatures, ex-libris, initials, small texts, etc.–sometimes with a touch of humor, as in this rhyming poem:

> *Ces matines (heures) sont à Isabeau du Pontbriand*
> *Qui les trouvera s'il les range sans les garder longuement*
> *et il aura sans faille*
> *une bonne trouvaille*
> *d'un pot de vin*
> *ou de cervoise*
> *et sera à bien*
> *lieu bien aise.*

> These matins (hours) belong to Isabeau du Pontbriand († 1449)
> Who will find them if he puts them away without keeping them for a long time
> and he will have without fail
> a good find
> of a pot of wine
> or cervoise

---

[24] R. Claerr and M.-P. Dion, *La Collection Chourses-Coëtivy: Une librairie médiévale à l'aube de la Renaissance* (Chantilly: Musée Condé, 2019), 11.
[25] Deuffic, *Le livre d'heures enluminé en Bretagne*, 87.

and will be at [a] good comfortable place.[26]

In the same vein, "*C'est livre est à Nicole de Bretaigne. Qui le trouvera cy le rende et elle poyra bien le vin*" (This book belongs to Nicole de Bretaigne. Whoever finds it will give it back and she will pay the wine).[27] Similarly, Jeanne de Raguenel writes in her copy of the *Débat de Fortune et Vertu devant Raison* (Fortune and Virtue Debate before Reason): "ce livre [est] a Madame la Viscomtesse de la Bellière, dame de Regnac" (This book belongs to Madame la Viscomtesse de la Bellière, dame de Regnac).[28]

We also get a glimpse of the family ties that bind these women together. Catherine de Coëtivy, for example, was fostered by her aunt Jeanne de Raguenel, who shared an interest in collecting books with her husband Tanguy du Chastel. It may even have been Jeanne de Raguenel who taught Catherine de Coëtivy to read. As an adult, she assembled a remarkable library with her husband, Antoine de Chourses.[29] She may also have been influenced by the example of two bibliophile uncles, Prigent VII and Alain de Coëtivy (†1474). The two sisters of the de Laval family, Jeanne and Louise, clearly shared the same cultural heritage and taste for books.

Finally, there are clear examples of the transmission of works between women. For example, Jeanne Porchere, abbess of the church of Longchamp from 1467 to 1484, acknowledged on September 14, 1467, that she had received from the nun Colette Tirande a copy of the *Hours for the use of Rome* bearing the arms of Marguerite d'Orléans, countess of Etampes and Vertus, lady of Clisson, which had been sent by Marie de Bretagne, abbess

---

[26] Deuffic, *Le livre d'heures enluminé en Bretagne*, 150.
[27] Booton, *Manuscripts, Market and the Transition to Print in Late Medieval Brittany*, 330.
[28] BNF, Ms Fr 12781, folio 114, verso.
[29] Roselyne Claerr, "Un couple de bibliophiles bretons du XVe siècle: Tanguy (IV) du Chastel et Jeanne Raguenel de Malestroit," in *Le Trémazan des Du Chastel, du château fort à la ruine, actes du colloque de Brest, 10, 11 et 12 juin 2004*, ed. Yves Coativy (Brest: Centre de recherche bretonne et celtique, 2006), 176.

of Fontevrault.[30] In the same spirit, Isabeau de Pontbriand gave her *hours* to Jacquette Berthelot, her niece.[31]

The uses of books

The first use was undoubtedly for personal reading. By the end of the Middle Ages, many women knew how to read, and a book like Guillaume Merlin's *Petite instruction et manière de vivre pour une femme séculière* (A Little Instruction and a Way of Life for a Secular Woman) which was printed in Paris in 1553, but written by a woman in the late fifteenth or early sixteenth century, is a reminder of the need to read prayer books at the very least.[32] It includes advice such as: "read at least one or two pages of a devotional book to nourish your soul" and "keep yourself busy reading beautiful books." This advice also applies to nuns. In a text from the second half of the fourteenth century attributed to Cardinal Pierre de Luxembourg (1369-1387) the following advice appears for after a meal: "When you have said grace, go to your room and study some good writing that is beneficial to the soul." As for Jean Gerson, in *La Montagne de contemplation* (Mountain of Contemplation, 1400), he recommends daily religious reading to pious laypeople. This book was present in Marie de Bretagne's library, as was "a small book by Pierre de Luxembourg", the nature of which is unfortunately unknown.

In 1398, Queen Isabeau commissioned the *Hours of Notre-Dame* in shaped letters illuminated in gold and azure (the colors of the Capetians) for her daughter Jeanne, then aged seven and future Duchess of Brittany, to help her learn to read. She also ordered various items: a bookmark, gilded silver clasps and fabric to make a purse "to hold the hours."[33] This type of object can be found in the inventory of Marguerite de Rohan's possessions, a book of hours with two gold clasps kept in the upper room in an iron-

---

[30] Deuffic, *Le livre d'heures enluminé en Bretagne*, 104.

[31] Deuffic, *Le livre d'heures enluminé en Bretagne*, 150.

[32] Margriet Hoogvliet, "Une petite instruction pour femme séculière: lectures religieuses des femmes et bibliothèques à la fin du Moyen Âge et au 16ᵉ siècle," *La revue de la Bibliothèque nationale et universitaire de Strasbourg*, 14, 2016, 36-43. Unfortunately, we do not know if this book was known in Brittany at the time.

[33] Deuffic, *Le livre d'heures enluminé en Bretagne*, 110.

bound leather chest,[34] while the books of Marie de Bretagne, abbess of Sainte-Madeleine d'Orléans, were kept in a chest in the chapel of her lodging.[35]

Catherine de Coëtivy learned to read from a book of hours, as a letter from her mother Marie de Valois about the *"heures pour [ses] petits enfants qui vont a l'ecole"* (Hours for [her] grandchildren going to school) indicates.[36] Jeanne de Raguenel also took care of the child's education, implying that the education of girls was entrusted to women. Later, Catherine de Coëtivy's library contained Geoffroi de La Tour Landry's book, *Pour l'enseignement des filles* (For Girls' Education).[37] It is both a book of memories and a collection of anecdotes and *exempla* of various origins intended for the education of little girls. Lastly, based on its title, *Les Heures aux petites filles* (The Hours for Little Girls), found in the library of Jeanne de Derval, may be for little girls either because of its ornamentation or because it was designed to teach them to read.

It is hard to measure the extent to which an illuminated or non-illuminated book is an *objet d'art* or a collector's item, or the pleasure their owners derived from leafing through them as though they were. However, it is important to bear in mind that, in the Middle Ages, paintings were first displayed in books, before moving them out and onto easels or canvases in the fifteenth-century.[38] It is probable that some libraries (Catherine de

---

[34] Deuffic, *Le livre d'heures enluminé en Bretagne*, 128; Booton, *Manuscripts, Market and the Transition to Print in Late Medieval Brittany*, 322.

[35] Deuffic, *Le livre d'heures enluminé en Bretagne*, 75-76.

[36] *Lettres de Marie de Valois, fille de Charles VII et d'Agnès Sorel, à Olivier de Coëtivy, seigneur de Taillebourg, son mari (1458-1472)*, ed. Paul Marchegay (Les Roches-Baritaud: L. Gast 1875), 28, no. 32 (from the Annuaire départemental de la Société d'émulation de la Vendée, 1874).

[37] Chantilly, Musée Condé Ms 293 (726), fifteenth century; Michel Zink, *Introduction à la littérature française du Moyen Âge* (Paris: Le livre de poche, 1993), 144.

[38] Painting can also be seen in stained glass windows in churches and on the walls of castles and churches. This subject, which was virtually dormant in 20th-century Brittany, was thoroughly revitalized at a seminal symposium held in Rennes on October 6, 7 and 8, 2016. It gave rise to a highly documented book, *Peintures monumentales de Bretagne. Nouvelles images, nouveaux regards du*

WOMEN'S LIBRARIES

Coëtivy, Jeanne de Raguenel) were first and foremost collections of *objets d'art*, which does not preclude them from having been read. The exceptional preservation of the most beautiful objects indicates that they must have been opened with great care from the very beginning, and the marks of ownership indicate the pride that their owners took in these magnificent *objets d'art*.

Finally, these women lent books to each other. This practice is attested by the inventory of Marie de Bretagne's library, in which several books are mentioned as being on loan, some of which were even given away or lost.[39]

*

This study sheds light on the nature of women's libraries in Brittany at the end of the Middle Ages. First, the chronology is later for women than for men, both individuals and monastic communities. In the case of men, mention of books began to multiply as early as the thirteenth century, and we know of some fine monastic libraries (in Quimper in the 1270s, for example), whereas in the case of women, we had to wait until the end of the fourteenth century, more than 100 years later, which suggests a delay in the spread of reading among women. After that, the evolutionary process is the same: we find the influence of the culture of the macabre, and witness the introduction of Renaissance texts. Investigated in their full context, these women's libraries display particular characteristics as opposed to those of men. Female authors such as Christine de Pizan have a prominent role in such collections, and we can see the contemporary transfer of books from woman to woman. This latter phenomenon deserves to be better studied, but it would require a time-consuming, almost genealogical approach to books. Finally, there were women bibliophiles in Brittany at the end of the Middle Ages, some of whom, like Catherine de Coëtivy and Jeanne de Raguenel, rose to the top of the French and even European rankings thanks

---

Moyen Âge à nos jours, eds. Christian Davy, Christine Jablonski, Didier Jugan Didier, Cécile Oulhen and Christine Leduc-Gueye Christine (Rennes : Presses universitaires de Rennes, 2021).

[39] "Item presté à frère Jehan Jolles, La montaigne de contamplacion, qu'il a perdue" ("Item lent to frère Jehan Jolles, La montagne de contemplation, which he lost"). Booton, *Manuscripts, Market and the Transition to Print in Late Medieval Brittany*, 327.

to the quality of their libraries, and who are undoubtedly another manifestation of the Renaissance spirit. This work is only an outline, and many aspects of the question could be developed, such as marks of ownership, the transmission of books, the weight of commissions and patronage, etc. We can only hope that someone will go beyond this outline and take up this subject again in depth.

Acknowledgements

Many thanks to Sam Puopolo for his help in proofreading this text.

The Gaelicisation of Two Medieval Irish Romances: *Beathadh Sir Gui o Bharbhuic* and *Bethadh Bibuis o Hamtuir*

Benedetta D'Antuono

From the mid-fifteenth to the early sixteenth centuries, Ireland witnessed a period of extensive translation efforts that has been called the 'second phase' of Irish translation, where various Latin, English, and French works were rendered into Early Modern Irish.[1] Significantly, the manuscript tradition indicates the considerable popularity of the 'romance' genre, with no fewer than eight extant romance translations.[2]

The surviving corpus of romance translations includes *Beathadh Sir Gui o Bharbhuic* and *Bethadh Bibuis o Hamtuir*, dating from the last quarter of the fifteenth century.[3] These texts represent the Early Modern Irish versions of the Middle English romances *Guy of Warwick* and *Bevis of Hampton*, which were first written in the fourteenth century and are themselves renditions of Anglo-Norman redactions from the mid-thirteenth century.[4] While various recensions of both romances exist, the core narratives remain essentially the same as in the Anglo-Norman sources. In

---

[1] Aisling Byrne, *Translating Europe: Imported Narratives and Irish Readers at the End of the Middle Ages*. (Maynooth: School of Celtic Studies, 2019), 3. There survive translations of Guy of Warwick, Bevis of Hampton, La Queste de Saint Graal, Fierabras, Caxton's Recuyell of the Historyes of Troye, William of Palerne, the Seven Sages of Rome, and Octavian.

[2] Aisling Byrne, "The Circulation of Romances from England in Late-Medieval Ireland," in *Medieval Romance and Material Culture*, ed. Nicholas Perkins (Cambridge: D. S. Brewer, 2015), 183-198, at 183.

[3] Based on the manuscript context of the two adaptations and on the timeframe of their translator's activity, the *terminus post quem* is the year 1474 and the *terminus ante quem* is *c.*1490 (Byrne 2019, 10).

[4] Alison Wiggins (2007) "The Manuscripts and Texts of the Middle English *Guy of Warwick*," in *Guy of Warwick: Icon and Ancestor*, eds. Alison Wiggins and Rosalind Field (Cambridge: Boydell & Brewer, 2007), 61-80, 65. Ronald B. Herzman et al., "Bevis of Hampton", in *Four Romances of England: King Horn, Havelok the Dane, Bevis of Hampton, Athelston*, eds. Ronald B. Herzman et al. (Kalamazoo: Medieval Institute Publications, 1997), 187-340, 187.

Guy of Warwick, the knight Guy fights overseas to prove himself worthy of marrying Felice, the Earl of Warwick's daughter. However, regretting his violent actions, he leaves her to embark on an atonement pilgrimage. In *Bevis of Hampton*, Bevis escapes his mother's attempts to murder him by leaving England and reaching the kingdom of Armenia, where he marries Princess Josian, who helps him restore his position in his motherland. Among the various recensions, this article explores the Early Modern Irish adaptations of these narratives in relation to their corresponding Middle English sources, with a specific focus on the translation process.

The Irish translations of these popular romances are exclusively transmitted in the second, fifteenth-century section of the composite manuscript TCD MS 1298 (*olim* H 2.7). The codex was in all likelihood commissioned by the Fitzgerald of Allen, a minor branch of the Fitzgerald Earls of Kildare, and entirely written by Uilleam Mac an Leagha.[5] This scribal figure, a member of the contemporary Mac an Leagha family of medical scribes and translators, has also been identified as the translator of both romances.[6] The exact source texts he employed are still unidentified and probably lost; however, linguistic and content clues suggest that they were English rather than Anglo-Norman.[7]

As was common practice for medieval renditions of narrative texts, the English sources underwent an intensive adaptation process. This process prioritised acceptability to the recipients over faithfulness to the source, to the point that translations should be referred to as adaptations and

---

[5] Aisling Byrne, "Cultural Intersections in Trinity College Dublin MS 1298," in *Adapting Texts and Styles in a Celtic Context: Interdisciplinary Perspectives on Processes of Literary Transfer in the Middle Ages: Studies in Honour of Erich Poppe*, eds Axel Harlos and Neele Harlos (Münster: Nodus Publikationen, 2016), 289-304, at 289-295, 298-301.

[6] Aisling Byrne, "Writing Westwards: Medieval English Romances and their Early Modern Irish Audiences," in *Medieval into Renaissance: Essays for Helen Cooper*, eds Andrew King and Matthew Woodcock (Cambridge, MA: Boydell & Brewer, 2016), 73-90, at 78.

[7] Fred Norris Robinson (ed. and tr.) "The Irish Lives of Guy of Warwick and Bevis of Hampton," *in Zeitschrift für Celtische Philologie 6* (Halle: Max Niemeyer, 1908), 9-180, 273-338, at 12-13, 18-19.

translators as redactors.[8] This tendency was particularly true of the Irish context, where foreign stories were adapted to suit Irish taste in a striking manner.[9] The Irish versions of *Guy of Warwick* and *Bevis of Hampton* are no exception to this. Previous studies on the adaptation process of *Beathadh Sir Gui o Bharbhuic* and *Bethadh Bibuis o Hamtuir* by Erich Poppe, Velma Bourgeois Richmond, and this author have evidenced the substitution of Middle English structural and stylistic features with Irish ones, and an increased emphasis on the ideas of piety, codes of conduct, and chivalry.[10]

Significantly, the adaptation process of the two romances involved a sustained Gaelicisation effort, which ensured that the target texts reflected the late-medieval Irish social, legal, and historical context and literary trends. The Gaelicisation of *Beathadh Sir Gui o Bharbhuic* and *Bethadh Bibuis o Hamtuir* has thus far been subject to little scholarly attention, the topic having been most notably addressed by Poppe in relation to *Bethadh Bibuis o Hamtuir*, with occasional references to *Beathadh Sir Gui o Bharbhuic* as a secondary point of comparison.[11]

Poppe's findings reveal that the Gaelicisation process of *Bethadh Bibuis o Hamtuir* entailed incorporating key legal and social concepts. To

---

[8] Ivana Djordjević, "Mapping Medieval Translation," in *Medieval Insular Romance: Translation and Innovation*, eds Judith Weiss et al. (Cambridge: Boydell and Brewer, 2000), 7-23, at 9.
[9] Nessa Ní Shéaghdha, "Translations and adaptations into Irish", in *Celtica 16* (Dublin: Dublin Institute for Advanced Studies, 1984),107-124, at 109.
[10] Benedetta D'Antuono, *Beathadh Sir Gui o Bharbhuic: A Medieval Irish Romance* (Venezia: Università Ca' Foscari Venezia, 2022). Erich Poppe, "The Early Modern Irish Version of *Beves of Hamtoun*," in *Cambrian Medieval Celtic Studies 23* (Cambridge: Cambridge University Press, 1992), 77–98, at 90-93. Erich Poppe, "Narrative structure of medieval Irish adaptations: the case of Guy and Beues," in *Medieval Celtic Literature and Society*, ed. Helen Fulton (Dublin: Four Courts, 2005), 205–229. Erich Poppe, "Cultural transfer and textual migration: Sir Bevis comes to Ireland," in *Hiberno-Continental cultural and literary interactions in the Middle Ages*, eds Wolfram R. Keller and Dagmar Schlüter (Münster: Nodus Publikationen, 2017), 205–220; Velma Bourgeois Richmond, "A Celtic *Guy of Warwick*," in *The Legend of Guy of Warwick* (New York: Garland Publishing, 1996), 145-152.
[11] Erich Poppe, "The Early Modern Irish Version of *Beves of Hamtoun*," in *Cambrian Medieval Celtic Studies 23* (Cambridge: Cambridge University Press, 1992), 77–98, at 90-93.

begin with, the close relationship between characters is defined in terms of fosterage, a fundamental social institution of Irish society. Moreover, the main female character in the tale, princess Josian, is given the faculty to choose her spouse, possibly hinting at the contemporary social standing of noblewomen. Last, as shall be discussed in further detail, the modification of an episode emphasises the practice of hospitality, deeply rooted in Irish legal sources and literary tradition.[12] Poppe's noteworthy observations on *Bethadh Bibuis o Hamtuir*, however, have not yet been followed by a comprehensive examination of the Gaelicisation process in *both* romances. In response to this lacuna, this study intends to extend the analysis to both *Beathadh Sir Gui o Bharbhuic* and *Bethadh Bibuis o Hamtuir*.

The convenience of exploring these romances together arises from their strong interconnection in both their Middle English and Early Modern Irish versions. The Middle English romances *Guy of Warwick* and *Bevis of Hampton* are more similar to each other than to any other stories in the Matter of England.[13] These romances exhibit a highly episodic nature, largely based on the theme of exile and return, and they share a similar plot depicting " . . . young English heroes who travel great distances, win the love of beautiful ladies, and fight Muslim enemies."[14] Additionally, they are deeply intertwined through pious crusading overtones, as they both celebrate crusader knights.[15] The romances retain this prominent similarity within the Irish context. To start with, they still feature parallel plots, comparable structural traits, and shared thematic choices. Moreover, their proximity is further reinforced by their sequential arrangement in TCD MS 1298. Recent studies on the compositional strategies behind miscellaneous manuscripts indicate that their juxtaposition was guided by their similarity and meant to foster a unified interpretation effort.[16]

---

[12] Poppe, "The Early Modern Irish Version of *Beves of Hamtoun*," 90-93.
[13] Leslie Jean Campbell, *The Matter Of England In Middle English Romance* (Jackson, MS: The University of Mississippi, 1983), 110.
[14] Byrne, *Translating Europe*, 3.
[15] Byrne, *Translating Europe*, 18.
[16] For an exploration of the mechanisms behind the compilation of composite manuscripts and on the hermeneutical consequences of textual disposition see Karen Pratt et al., *The Dynamics of the Medieval Manuscript: Text Collections from a European Perspective* (Göttingen: Göttingen University Press, 2017). For

TWO MEDIEVAL IRISH ROMANCES

In its study of the Gaelicisation of *Beathadh Sir Gui o Bharbhuic* and *Bethadh Bibuis o Hamtuir*, this paper seeks to introduce a novel perspective on the topic. In particular, it substitutes the approach of comparative literary studies with that of modern translation theory. The theoretical framework and methodologies of modern translation theory provide the instruments to acquire a deep understanding of the translation process and, consequently, of its Gaelicisation component. However, there is no agreement on the opportunity to employ modern translation theory for the study of medieval translations. Two main objections have been raised against this choice. The first objection emphasises that applying translation theories to medieval texts is anachronistic, given the lack of evidence for medieval translators viewing translation as a separate literary genre. The second objection questions the very necessity of using the "impenetrable language of theory."[17] Scholars have been conducting research on medieval translated texts without explicitly citing or employing translation theory, despite knowingly or unknowingly applying its principles and approaches.

Nonetheless, there are effective ways to address these two objections. First, the idea that using translation theory for medieval translated texts is anachronistic is undermined by the principle that the absence of evidence does not serve as evidence itself. Indeed, as Diana Luft notes, "the fact that translators do not discuss the mechanisms at work in their translations does not mean that they are unaware of the operation of those mechanisms, or that they are producing less sophisticated renderings because of it."[18] Second, the decision to locate a study in a specific theoretical framework and utilise its specialised terminology presents advantages for academic discussion. As Luft acknowledges, "while the vocabulary of theory can be specialised, that specialisation means that it can also be more specific. This

---

a discussion on the relevance of manuscript context in relation to the study and interpretation of Old French verse narratives, see Keith Busby, *Codex and Context: Reading Old French Verse Narrative in Manuscript* (Amsterdam-New York: Editions Rodopi B.V., 2002).

[17] Diana Luft, "Translation Theory and Medieval Translation," in *Translations from Classical Literature: Imtheachta Æniasa and Stair Ercuil ocus a Bás*, ed. Kevin Murray (London: Irish Texts Society, 2006), 83-100, at 83.

[18] Luft, "Translation Theory and Medieval Translation," 86.

specificity can serve not just to hone our language when we talk about translation, but to hone our thinking about translation as well."[19]

Within the field of medieval studies, there is a lack of consensus concerning the most suitable theory for the intended purpose. Specifically, when implementing modern translation theory in the analysis of translated texts, the choice typically falls between a normative or descriptive approach. In the 1960s and 1970s, early translation theory largely employed the normative approach. This perspective regards the source text as the sole determinant of meaning in the translation process. As a result, it focuses on assessing the degree of equivalence between the texts by identifying which elements from the source were or were not represented in the final product without considering the reception context.[20] The descriptive approach was introduced during the late 1970s and early 1980s by the school of Descriptive Translation Studies, founded by Gideon Toury.[21] This method views the target text as the primary determinant of meaning and its goal is to comprehend the translation process rather than prescribing a fixed set of norms for achieving a perfect translation.[22] Consequently, this approach involves the formulation of a descriptive comparison between the source and target text with the purpose of elucidating the rationale behind the distinctive characteristics observed in the target text. Given the nature of medieval translated narratives as purposeful rewrites crafted within a specific *milieu* that governs the translator's choices, Descriptive Translation Studies appears to be the most effective approach to examining this body of texts.

In consideration of the peculiarities of medieval textual production, primarily the *mouvance* characterising manuscript witnesses, the application of Descriptive Translation Studies to medieval translated texts must be combined with philology. It is important to note that, in this

---

[19] Luft, "Translation Theory and Medieval Translation," 100.
[20] Massimiliano Bampi, "Translating and Rewriting in the Middle Ages: A Philological Approach," in *Philology Matters! Essays on the Art of Reading Slowly*, ed. Harry Lönnroth (Leiden: Brill, 2017), 164-181, at 164.
[21] For an in-depth presentation of the method of Descriptive Translation Studies and exploration of the move from a normative to a descriptive approach, see Gideon Toury, *Descriptive Translation Studies and Beyond* (Amsterdam: John Benjamins Publishing, 1995).
[22] Susan Bassnett, *Translation Studies* (London: Routledge, 2002), 37-38.

context, the term 'philology' is not being used in the sense of historical linguistics but in that of *Textwissenschaft*, or 'the science of text', a discipline focused on restoring and interpreting texts within their production and reception context.[23] As Massimiliano Bampi observes, integrating philology with Descriptive Translation Studies in the study of medieval translated texts is beneficial from at least two points of view. First, philology regulates the application of translation theory to texts that are distant in both time and space. Specifically, it traces the boundaries of theoretical speculation within the material evidence found in manuscripts, and it emphasises the limitations of using critical editions, which are based on reconstructive principles. Second, philology vastly broadens the comprehension of the text being studied. The thorough attention given to the production and reception of texts yields valuable information about the specific context in which they are received.[24] This necessary synthesis of philology and Descriptive Translation Studies is facilitated by their mutual utilisation of the close reading method and their use of language as a means to attain a more profound comprehension of the text rather than as the focal point of analysis.[25]

In light of these considerations, this study investigates *Beathadh Sir Gui o Bharbhuic* and *Bethadh Bibuis o Hamtuir* by integrating Descriptive Translation Studies with a philological approach. More specifically, it pursues a descriptive comparison between the current critical editions of the relevant works. As for *Beathadh Sir Gui o Bharbhuic* and *Bethadh Bibuis o Hamtuir*, this study follows Fred Norris Robinson's critical editions (1908) of the only extant copies. As for *Guy of Warwick*, it employs Julius Zupitza's critical edition (1883) of the recensions of the couplet *Guy* and stanzaic *Guy* preserved in Edinburgh, National Library of Scotland, Advocates' MS 19.2.1 (henceforth: Auchinleck); however, if need be, it also considers Alison Wiggins's edition (2004) of the same recension of the stanzaic *Guy*. As for *Bevis of Hampton*, this analysis adopts the critical

---

[23] Bampi, "Translating and Rewriting in the Middle Ages: A Philological Approach," 168.
[24] Bampi, "Translating and Rewriting in the Middle Ages: A Philological Approach," 168.
[25] Harry Lönnroth and Nestori Siponkoski, "The Philology of Translation," in *Philology Matters! Essays on the Art of Reading Slowly*, ed. Harry Lönnroth (Leiden: Brill, 2017), 136-163, at 137.

edition by Ronald Herzman, Graham Drake, and Eve Salisbury (1997), primarily based on the Auchinleck redaction of the romance.Still, in consideration of the limitations of the *restitutio textus*, the comparison resorts to the primary manuscript sources of all works as a second point of comparison when necessary.[26]

Before proceeding any further, however, an important methodological caveat rooted in philological considerations must be foregrounded. The uncertainty around the exact source text means that any conclusions regarding the redactor's Gaelicisation endeavour must be considered as somewhat speculative. Nonetheless, as the following discussion hopes to show, substantial evidence exists for ascribing an effort of Gaelicisation to the redactor. In particular, the descriptive comparison between source and target text suggests that Uilliam Mac an Leagha pursued a Gaelicisation strategy by emphasising the concepts of hospitality, clothing, and music. The next sections discuss textual passages that showcase the stronger presence of these themes in the Irish version; they also offer specific reasons for attributing this increased emphasis to the translator's Gaelicisation effort.

Hospitality

The first aspect in consideration is the adaptations' heightened focus on hospitality. Both *Beathadh Sir Gui o Bharbhuic* and *Bethadh Bibuis o Hamtuir* present additional or extended references to this social custom. In *Beathadh Sir Gui o Bharbhuic*, this difference is visible in the description of the welcome given by the Greek emperor to Guy and his retinue, who had come to protect Constantinople from the Saracens.

---

[26] Fred Norris Robinson (ed. and tr.), "The Irish Lives of Guy of Warwick and Bevis of Hampton," in *Zeitschrift für Celtische Philologie 6* (Halle: Max Niemeyer, 1908), 9-180, 273-338. Julius Zupitza (ed.), *The Romance of Guy of Warwick, the 1st or 14th-Century Version, ed. from the Auchinleck Ms. and from Ms. 107 in Caius College, Cambridge* (London: Early English Text Society, 1883). Alison Wiggins (ed.), *Stanzaic Guy of Warwick* (Kalamazoo: Medieval Institute Publications, 2004). Ronald B. Herzman et al., "Bevis of Hampton", in *Four Romances of England: King Horn, Havelok the Dane, Bevis of Hampton, Athelston*, eds. Ronald B. Herzman et al. (Kalamazoo: Medieval Institute Publications, 1997), 187-340.

TWO MEDIEVAL IRISH ROMANCES

I)   Guy of Warwick

Ac when þemper̲our wist atte frome / þat Gij of Warwike was y-come, / **Tvay erls he dede after him go, / & loueliche he bad hem com hi*m* to**. */ & sir Gij hi*m* goþ to þemperour fre: /* **'Welcome, sir Gij**,*' þan seyd he. /* '*Of þine help gret nede haue we. / Michel ich haue herd speke of þe.*'

When the emperor was informed that Guy had arrived in Constantinople, **he sent two earls to meet him and he instructed them to welcome him warmly**. Then Sir Guy himself promptly rode to the emperor, who said: '**Welcome, Sir Guy**. We are in great need for your help. I heard a lot [of stories] about you.'[27]

I)   Beathadh Sir Gui o Bharbhuic

₇ **rothoirbir** *in t-imper* **teora póg** *co dil, dichra, dethtairisi dó,* ₇ *rogabh* **ar laim** *e,* ₇ *docuir* **an lámh ele fona braigid,** ₇ *is mur-sin doruc in t-imper* **leis é isin palas rigdha**, ₇ *docuir an t-imper Sir Gyi* **ara gualaind budhéin do caithem a coda**. *Roordaigh in t-imper iarom* **seomra uasal** *do derugudh do* **Sir Gyi cona muindtir**, [₇] **gach aenní da n-íarfaidis** *do tabairt doib.*

And the emperor **kissed him three times** fondly, fervently, and faithfully, and took him **by the hand**, and put **his other hand about his neck**, and it is thus that the emperor took Guy **with him into the royal palace**, and the emperor placed Sir Guy **at his side to eat his food**. Then the emperor ordered a **high chamber** to be made ready for **Guy and his followers** *and* **everything** to be given to them **that they might ask for**.[28]

In the English version, the emperor dispatches two earls to greet Guy and engages in a brief conversation with him. In the Irish adaptation, the

---

[27] Zupitza, *The Romance of Guy of Warwick*, 166, ll. 2869-2876. Unless otherwise stated, all translations from Middle English in this article are mine. Underlining in the text indicates expansions. The use of runic letters in ME is too common to need additional comment.

[28] Robinson, "The Irish Lives," 52. Translation at 132.

emperor welcomes Guy affectionately, accompanies him to his majestic palace, and bestows numerous honours upon him and his entourage. To start with, the emperor grants Guy the privilege of dining beside him and sharing his food. Additionally, he requests that arrangements for sleeping be made for Guy and his retinue and expects their every need to be met. Therefore, the emperor's generosity is greater in the adaptation than in the English version.

An equally illustrative instance of *Beathadh Sir Gui o Bharbhuic*'s emphasis on hospitality appears later in the tale. The day before engaging in a duel with his main antagonist, the Duke of Lombardy, Guy is cast into the ocean by the duke's followers while asleep. When he wakes up, he prays to God to save him, and a passing fisherman happens to find and rescue him.

I)   Guy of Warwick

Now herkeneþ a litel striif, / Hou he saued þe pilgrims liif / Iesu, þat sitt in trone, / Wiþ a fischer þat was comand, / In þe se fische takeand / Bi himself al-on. / He seþ þat bed floter him by: / 'On godes half,' he gan to cri, / 'What artow? say me son.' / þe pilgrim his heued vp pliȝt, / & crid to him anon riȝt, / & made wel reweli mon. // 'Gode man,' þan seyd he, / 'Y leue on god in trinite: / þe soþe þou schalt now sen. / Vnderstode þou ouȝt of þe batayl hard / Bitven þe pilgrim & sir Berard, / Hou þai fouȝten bitven?' / þe fischer seyd, 'y seiȝe þe fiȝt / Fro þe morwe to þe niȝt: / For noþing wald þai flen. / þemperour comand þo / þai schuld be kept boþe tvo, / Tomorwe bring hem oȝen.' // 'Icham,' he seyd 'þe pilgrim / þat fauȝt wiþ þe douke Berardin / For Tirri, þe hendi kniȝt. / Ȝistreuen we wer deled ato; / In a chaumber y was do / Wiþ seriaunce wise & wiȝt: / Hou ich com her no wot y nouȝt. / For his loue þat þis warld haþ wrouȝt, / Saue me ȝif þou miȝt.' / **þe fischer tok him into his bot anon, / & to his hous he ladde him hom,** */ & saued his liif þat niȝt.*

Now listen to the story of how Jesus, who sits on the heavenly throne, saved the pilgrim's life thanks to a fisherman who was out fishing alone. The fisherman saw the bed where Guy was lying floating by him: 'For God's sake,' he shouted, 'Who are you? Tell me, son.' The pilgrim lifted his head and immediately shouted back and made great lamentation. 'Good man,' he said, 'I believe in God and the Trinity: you shall now learn about my true identity. Have you heard of the harsh fight between the pilgrim and sir Berard, how they fought bravely against each other?' The fisherman said: 'I saw the fight from morning to night: neither showed signs of retreat. The emperor guarded both of them and established that they may resume their fight tomorrow.' 'I am,' said he, 'the pilgrim that fought with Duke Berard for Tirri, the brave knight. Yesterday evening, we were separated; I was in a chamber with strong guards. I do not know how I came hither. For the love of he who has created this world, save me if you can.' **The fisherman immediately took him into his boat, took him to his house,** and saved his life that night. [29]

I)   Beathadh Sir Gui o Bharbhuic

Dala Sir Gyi iarum, rofuadaighedh a n-aigein e, ⁊ roduisigh sé asa colludh, ⁊ roeirigh na suidhi ara lebaidh, ⁊ rofhech osa cinn, ⁊ roataigh Dia co dichra da furtacht. ⁊ Adubairt: 'A tigerna,' ar-se, 'ata a fis agud nach do chinn luaighechta ⁊ nach d'fagail airim docuadus do comrug, acht d'furtacht mo carud on ecoir doronad air; ⁊ a thigerna, gab agum,' ar-se. Is ann-sin doconuic Sir Gyi an luingin iascaid ina docum, ⁊ fochtuid scela de. Adubairt Gyi: 'An cualabur,' ar-sé, 'luagh aran duine mbocht dorinde comrucc aniug a cathraigh an imper?' 'Docualamar,' ar-siad, '⁊ robo maith a maisi dó é.' 'Is misi doroine sin,' ar Gyi, '⁊ rofelladh orum am cholludh ⁊ ni fedur cinnus docuiredh ann-so me, ⁊ a n-anoir Dia tabraidh cabuir orum.' Dorug in t-iasgaire Sir Gyi isin luing leis, ⁊ dorug da tigh fein hé annsa [ca]thraigh, ⁊ **dorinne**

---

[29] Zupitza, *The Romance of Guy of Warwick*, 548, stanzas 198-200.

BENEDETTA D'ANTUONO

fothrugudh fair, ⁊ tucc biadh ⁊ deoch dó, ⁊ tuc air suan ⁊ sircolladh do denum ar imdhaidh uasail, oiredha.

As for Sir Guy, then, he was carried away into the ocean, and awoke from his sleep, and sat up on his bed and looked above him and prayed to God fervently for help. And he said: 'O Lord,' said he, 'thou knowest that it was not for the sake of reward nor to achieve fame that I went to battle, but to save my friend from the injustice that had been done him; and O Lord, forgive me,' said he. Then Sir Guy saw a little fishing boat approaching him, and he asked tidings of it. Guy said: 'Have you heard any mention of the poor man who fought a battle today in the city of emperor?' 'We have,' said they, 'and that was well done of him.' 'It was I who did it,' said Guy, 'and I was betrayed in my sleep, and I do not know how I was put here, and in God's honor give me help!' The fisherman took Sir Guy into the boat with him, and took him to his own house in the city, **and gave him a bath and food and drink, and put him to sleep and long slumber on a high, stately bed.**[30]

In the English version, the fisherman limits himself to taking Guy to his house. By contrast, in the Irish adaptation, he is more considerate towards Guy: indeed, not only does he bring him to his house, but he also gives him a bath and food and drink, and he prepares a stately bed for his rest.

As mentioned, Poppe previously considered *Bethadh Bibuis o Hamtuir*'s emphasis on hospitality in reference to a specific episode in the narrative, when, after escaping from the prison of the king of Damascus, Bevis comes across a castle where he hopes to find temporary shelter.[31]

I) Bevis of Hampton

Beves to the castel gate rit / And spak to hire, above him sit: / 'Dame,' a seide, 'that sit above, / For that ilche lordes love, / On wham thin herte is on iset: / Yeve me today a meles met!' / The levedi answerde him tho: / 'Boute thow fro the gate go, / Thee wer beter elleswhar than her; / Go,

---

[30] Robinson, "The Irish Lives," 94-95. Translation at 162.
[31] Poppe, "The Early Modern Irish Version of *Beves*," 90-93.

or the tit an evel diner! / Me lord,' she seide, 'is a geaunt / And leveth on Mahoun and Tervagaunt / And felleth Cristene men to grounde, / For he hateth hem ase hounde . . . !' . . . Unto the geaunt ful swithe he ran /And kedde that he was doughti man, / And smot ato his nekke bon: / The geaunt fel to grounde anon. / Beves wente in at castel gate, / The levedi a mette ther-ate. / 'Dame!' a seide, 'go, yeve me mete, / That ever have thow Cristes hete!' / The levedi, sore adrad with alle, / Ladde Beves in to the halle, / And of everiche sonde, / That him com to honde, / A dede hire ete al ther ferst, / That she ne dede him no berst, / And drinke ferst of the win, / that no poisoun was ther-in.

Bevis rode to the gate of the castle and said to [the woman] who was standing on top [of the tower]: **'O lady,' said Bevis, 'standing at the top [of the tower], for the love of the Lord, who created the world, give me some food today!'** The lady answered him: **'Get away from the gates; you are better off elsewhere than here; go, or else you will be served a deadly dinner!** My lord' said she, 'is a giant who believes in Mohammed and Termagaunt, and he kills Christians as he hates them so much that he treats them like hounds . . . !' [During the fight] Bevis rushed against the giant and fought him valiantly until he struck off his head and **made him fall to the ground. [Once he had killed the giant], Bevis went [back] to the castle gates and said to the lady: 'O lady, go and fetch me some food . . . ! ' The lady escorted Bevis to the hall and served him every dish that he requested** without harming him, and she served him wine that was not poisoned.[32]

I) Bethadh Bibuis o Hamtuir

. . . ₇ ar rochtain doruis na cathrach [Bibus] do docunnuicc in righan rathmur, rouasul ar barr in tuir os cinn doruis na cathrach, ₇ **robennaigh Bibus di, ₇ roiar biadh uirre anoir an Athar Neamda. Adubairt in righan: 'Tarra**

---

[32] Herzman et al., "*Bevis of Hampton*," 250-252, ll. 1835-1848, 1917-1932.

astegh,' ar-si, '₇ dogebuir do lordaethain bidh ₇ digi.'
Docuaidh Bibus astegh iar-sin, ₇ dotuirrling Bibus isin halla
riga, ₇ **dosuidh ar bord,** ₇ **docuiredh biadh ina fiadhnuse.**
₇ Nír cian dó mur-sin co facaidh in fomoir feramail,
fírgranna . . .

. . . On reaching the gate of the city, [Bevis] saw a lady,
gracious and noble, on the top of the tower over the gate of
the city; **and Bevis greeted her and asked her for food in
honor of the Heavenly Father.** The lady said: **'Come in,'
said she, 'and thou shalt have thy fill of food and drink.'**
Then Bevis went in, and dismounted in the royal hall, and
**sat at table, and food was put in his presence. And it was
not long before he saw a bold, horrible gian. . .** [33]

In both versions, upon arriving at the castle gates, Bevis encounters a lady and, following his admission, engages in a successful duel against the castle's owner. Nonetheless, there is a difference in the hospitality the lady offers to Bevis. In the English version, she does not display a hospitable demeanour. To begin with, she ignores Bevis's request for food and strongly urges him to abandon the castle, as its current owner, a pagan giant, holds a deep hatred for Christians. Moreover, once Bevis is let into the castle, she does not provide him with any food or drink until the fight against the giant is over and she is asked to do so by Bevis himself. Conversely, in the Irish adaptation, the lady cordially welcomes Bevis and grants his request for food and drink prior to his confrontation with the castle owner, who is depicted as a giant seeking revenge on Bevis for killing his brother.

A case where hospitality is more prominent in the Irish adaptation can also be found at an earlier stage in the tale, namely when Bevis is imprisoned by the king of Damascus.

    I)   Bevis of Hampton

Thanne seide Brademond to twenti king, / That were that dai at is gistning, / A spak with tresoun and with gile: / 'Ariseth up,' he sede 'a while, / Everich of yow fro the bord, / And wolcometh your kende lord!' / Alle hii gonnen up

---

[33] Robinson, "The Irish Lives," 188. Translation at 311.

right stonde, / And Brademond tok Beves be the honed / And held him faste at that sake, / That he ne scholde is swerd out take, / And cride, alse he hadde be wod, / To hem alle, aboute him stod: / 'Ase ye me loven at this stounde, / Bringeth this man swithe to grounde!'

Then Brademond turned to the twenty knights at his banquet that day and **said treacherously: 'Stand up,' he said, 'each of you, leave your table and welcome your gentle lord.'** All the knights immediately stood up, **and Brademond took Bevis by the hand and held him fast enough not to let him unsheathe his sword.** Then, as if mad, he shouted to all the knights around him: **'If ye really love and respect me at this moment, quickly bring this man to the ground!'** [34]

I) Bethadh Bibuis o Hamtuir

Tainic in ri co lathair, ⁊ rothuirrling Bibus aran fod a fiadhnuse in righ, ⁊ dorinde umla do, ⁊ tug in litir ina laim, ⁊ roleigh Bramon litir. ⁊ Adubairt: 'Doden-sa gach ni adeir in sgribenn-so,' ar-sé, 'uair is tu-sa Bibus o Hamtuir, ⁊ is tu rogab misi, ⁊ romarb mo muindtir, ⁊ roben fhuasgailt asum, ⁊ tug orum freagra ⁊ umla do thabairt do duine fa mesa na me fein.' ⁊ Adubairt Bramon: **'Tabur biadh do Bibus,' ar-se, 'uair ni cubaidh oglach tigerna maith gan anoir do denum do.' Dorughadh Bibus do halla in righ, ⁊ tucadh biadh do, ⁊ robadur aga fiarfaige diaroil créd in bas doberdis dó.** *Adubairt drong dib a losgadh co lanaibeil; adubradar drong ele a crochadh co congairech; adubradar drong ele a tarraing a ndiaig ech; adubradar drong ele a cur a prisun da pianad.* **Adubairt Bibus:** *'Is nar sin', ar-se, 'i. in nech dothiucfadh le techtairecht do cur cum bais, ⁊ is amlaidh is maith dibh misi do cur tar an cathraigh amach, ⁊ trealam catha do tabairt damh, ⁊ sluaigh na cathrach uili do beth ina trealam catha am timchell, ⁊ a mbeth uili gum ledrad ⁊ gum lanbualadh ar*

---

[34] Herzman et al., "*Bevis of Hampton*," 238-239, ll. 1395-1406.

aenslighi, ₇ is lugha d'adhbur gotha dibh-si misi do marbadh mur sin na mo marbadh ann-so'. **Adubairt aroile dona sluaghaibh***: 'In uair fa fuaruis-[s]e sinne roime-so ar fairsinge na feronn docuris ár ar muindtire; ₇ dodenta in cetna anois, da faghtha ₇ amuigh sinn'.* **Is annsin** *doluigedh an laachradh láncalma ar muin Bibus conar ba luaithi saithchi brighmur bech os bechlusaib naid sluaigh dana, dimsacha na Damaisci a cengal ₇ a cuibrech an curadh crodha, ceimdighaind. ₇ Docuiredur Bibus* **iar-sin** *ina cime crapaillti a prisun peannuidech da pianad, ₇ dorug Bibus bata bunnremur leis isin prisn . . . .*

The king came to the place, and Bevis dismounted on the ground in the king's presence, and made him an obeisance, and gave the letter into his hand; and Bramon read the letter. And he said: 'I will do everything that this writing says,' said he, 'for thou art Bevis of Hampton, and it is thou who took me captive, and killed my followers, and got ransom from me, and imposed it upon me to give homage and tribute to a man who was lower than myself.' And Bramon said: **'Give Bevis food,' said he, 'for it is not fitting to treat the retainer of a noble lord with dishonor.' Bevis was taken to the king's hall, and food was given him;** and **they were asking each other** what death they should inflict upon him. Some of them said to burn him at once; others said to crucify him with acclaim; others said to drag him after a horse; others to put him in poison for his punishment. **Bevis said**: 'That is shameful', said he, 'to put to death one who comes in with a message; and it is this it would be well for you to do, to set me outside the city, and to give me equipment of battle, and all the hosts of the city to be in battle equipment around me, and all of them to be attacking me and smiting me together; and it is less cause of shame to you to kill me like that than to kill me here.' **One of the companies said**: 'At the time when thou haddest us before in the breadth of the land, thou didst slay our army; and thou wouldst do the same now, if thou shouldst get us out in the field.' **Then** a group of bold warriors fell on Bevis's back so that swarms of eager bees would not be quicker at the honey-flowers than were the bold, proud hosts of Damascus at binding and fettering the brave, firm-stepping warrior. **And after that** they put Bevis as a fettered captive in a cruel prison for his punishmet . . . .[35]

In the English version, the king of Damascus orders his followers to rise and greet Bevis, with the intention of having them help him to physically apprehend the knight. Besides limiting himself to a gesture of hospitality as modest as a greeting, the king deliberately employs it to carry out a sort of ambush on Bevis. In the Irish rendition, the king cordially receives Bevis by presenting him with food; afterwards, the king and his lords disclose their plan to kill Bevis. Specifically, they deliberate on the most appropriate way to carry out his execution, and Bevis himself participates in the conversation to emphasize their disregard towards the codes of conduct. It is only after the debate is over that the king's soldiers take action to attack and imprison the knight. Thus, in contrast to the English version, the king's welcoming gesture towards Bevis is not only more lavish, but also not directly aimed at his capture, which occurs at a later point in time.

The insertion of more or less extended references to hospitable behaviour in the Irish adaptations appears to have been an invention of the redactor rather than something reproduced from his English models. This is primarily suggested by cumulative evidence, in that hospitality is consistently emphasised in multiple instances throughout both tales. Furthermore, the custom of hospitality seems to have been deeply rooted in the Irish social, legal, and literary context. The role of hospitality in medieval Ireland has been extensively studied by Catherine Marie O'Sullivan, who maintains that hospitality was integral to late-medieval Irish society as it formed " . . . the nexus of people's most important relationships."[36]

The Irish Annal tradition places high emphasis on the social value of hospitality: chroniclers dedicated considerable attention to distinguished

---

[35] Robinson, "The Irish Lives," 185. Translation at 208-209.
[36] Catherine Marie O'Sullivan, *Hospitality in medieval Ireland, 900–1500* (Dublin: Four Courts Press, 2004), 14.

men and women revered for their generosity. Usually, these people were placed in three categories: guesthouse keepers, pious individuals, and members of the powerful elite.[37] The relevance of hospitality to the last group is also evidenced in bardic poetry; the patrons' hospitality, deemed to confirm their true nobility and righteousness to dominate, was one of the stock themes of praise poems.[38]

The medieval Irish legal system provides further evidence of the prominence of hospitality. Notably, this practice was discussed in law texts spanning from the early to the late Middle Ages. Several Old Irish law tracts address this ubiquitous social custom, specifically *Críth Gablach*, *Uraicecht Becc*, and *Bretha Nemed Toísech*.[39] In particular, they sanctioned the general duty of all householders to provide hospitality, the amount and mode of hospitality associated with a given social rank, and the payment of the full honour-price for refusing hospitality (*etech*) or driving away a person seeking hospitality (*esáin*).[40] Late-medieval legal glosses and parliamentary ordinances adapted early Irish principles to respond to contemporary concerns and tackled the phenomenon of forced hospitality (*coinnmheadh*), where lords and their attendants exacted lodging and free entertainment from various churches and inhabitants of the land.[41] These ordinances were specifically designed to revise the principle of Early Irish Law that entitled Irish kings and, later, their armies to receive maintenance and entertainment, called *cáe* (guesting) and *congbáil* (entertainment).

---

[37] O'Sullivan, *Hospitality in medieval Ireland*, 18.
[38] Claire Downham, *Medieval Ireland* (Cambridge: Cambridge University Press, 2017), 313.
[39] O'Sullivan, *Hospitality in medieval Ireland*, 18.
[40] Fergus Kelly, *A Guide to Early Irish Law* (Dublin: Institute for Advanced Studies, 1988), 139.
[41] O'Sullivan, *Hospitality in medieval Ireland*, 19. For further insight into the custom of coinnmed, see Adrian Empey and Katharine Simms, "The Ordinances of the White Earl and the Problem of Coign in the Later Middle Ages," in *Proceedings of the Royal Irish Academy: Archaeology, Culture, History, Literature* (Dublin: Royal Irish Academy, 1975), pp. 161-187. I wish to extend my thanks to Graham O' Toole for recommending this article.

TWO MEDIEVAL IRISH ROMANCES

Their promulgation occurred in both Anglo-Norman and Gaelic territories, where they were tailored to address the concerns of specific lordships.[42]

Finally, hospitality had a long-standing tradition in medieval Irish literature. To begin with, texts from the extant body of gnomic literature, such as *Tecosca Cormaic* and *Audacht Morainn*, provide evidence for collective beliefs on the appropriate ways to present or reciprocate hospitality. Additionally, the idea of hospitality is also emphasised in various *scéla* (tales). The stories in the Ulster cycle, such as *Fled Bricrend* and *Scéla Muicce Meic Dathó*, revolve around the distribution of the *curadmír*, a magical piece of pork meat destined for the bravest hero at the feast. Other stories like *Bruidne Da Chocae*, *Togail Bruidne Dá Derga*, and *Aided Guill ocus Gairbh* provide further evidence of Irish guesthouses and their keepers.[43] The practice of hospitality is also featured in Saints' Lives dating to the Middle and Early Modern Irish periods. Hagiographies provide evidence on various aspects of religious hospitality: its customs and the types of buildings dedicated to this practice, such as the *tech n-oíged* (guesthouse), which were prominent in monastic settings.[44]

The redactor's increased attention towards the custom of hospitality likely derives from his attempt to accommodate the expectations of his audience; Mac an Leagha was translating for the Fitzgeralds of Allen, a family of the Hiberno-Norman aristocracy, who would presumably have been aware of the vital role played by hospitality in reinforcing their social standing. Furthermore, and more significantly to the purpose of this discussion, the redactor might have placed more emphasis on hospitality to Gaelicise his source text; by inserting copious and detailed references to hospitality, Mac an Leagha would have infused his adaptations with an element deeply rooted in the contemporary social, legal, and literary context.

---

[42] Canon Adrian Empey and Katharine Simms, "The Ordinances of the White Earl and the Problem of Coign in the Later Middle Ages," in *Proceedings of the Royal Irish Academy: Archaeology, Culture, History, Literature* (Dublin: Royal Irish Academy, 1975), pp. 161-187, 162, 178.

[43] O'Sullivan, *Hospitality in medieval Ireland*, 24.

[44] O'Sullivan, *Hospitality in medieval Ireland*, 26.

BENEDETTA D'ANTUONO

Clothing

An increased emphasis on clothing supports an argument for the Gaelicisation effort. Both *Beathadh Sir Gui o Bharbhuic* and *Bethadh Bibuis o Hamtuir* diverge from their sources by featuring additional or extended descriptions of garments. *Beathadh Sir Gui o Bharbhuic* presents various instances of this trend; when the character's appearance is briefly mentioned in the English source text, the Irish target text distinguishes itself by adding various details. This difference is apparent in the early stages of the tale, specifically when Guy is attending to Felice and her maids.

1.) Guy of Warwick

In a kirtel of silk he gan him schrede, / Into chaumber wel sone he ȝede. / Þe kirtel bicom him swiþe wel, / To Amenden þer on was neuer a del.
He wore a tunic of silk, and he immediately reached for her chamber; **the tunic suited him perfectly and did not need any alterations.** [45]

2.) Beathadh Sir Gui o Bharbhuic

*Dala Gyi immorro docuir sé **léine sremnaighi sroill re grian a geilchnis**, ⁊ inar ingnathach orsnaith ⁊ gúdna sgiamach sgarloide air amuigh anechtair. ⁊ Docuaidh roime fon maisi-sin co grianan na h-ingine.*

As for Guy, then, he put **a shirt of thin satin next the brightness of his white skin** and **a wonderful tunic of gold thread and a fine, scarlet gown outside of it**; and in that splendour, he went to the maiden's bower.[46]

In the English version, Guy's attire merely consists of a tunic of silk which perfectly suits his figure. In the Irish adaptation, instead, Guy's clothing is more opulent: he is wearing a shirt of thin satin, a wonderful tunic of gold thread, and a fine, scarlet gown. Notably, the decoration of the tunic, the shirt and gown, and the judgments of value are absent in the English version.

---

[45] Zupitza, *The Romance of Guy of Warwick*, 14, ll. 211-214.
[46] Robinson, "The Irish Lives," 25. Translation at 106.

TWO MEDIEVAL IRISH ROMANCES

Beathadh Sir Gui o Bharbhuic's emphasis on clothing is also present later in the tale, in the description of the Duke of Louvain's appearance as he asks the emperor to forgive him for having killed his brother, Sir Sadon.

1.) Guy of Warwick

*Than he threwe **his mantell** of / Many man had grete rewthe therof. / **In his sherte** he stode allone / For him was made mikell mone.*

Then he took off **his mantle**, and many men wept at this gesture of his. He stood [in front of the emperor] with **his shirt** alone, and there was great lamentation for him.⁴⁷

(I)   Beathadh Sir Gui o Bharbhuic

₇ *docuaidh co hurrlum,* ₇ *roben* **na hédaighi romaisecha sida de acht amain aenleine shremnaigi sroill re grian a geilcnis** ₇ *dochuaidhitir . . . a fiadnuse an imper,* ₇ *rolig a glún des* ₇ *clé fai,* ₇ *rocrum a fiadhnuse an imperi.*

And [the duke] went readily, and took off **his splendid, silk garments, all except one fine silk shirt next the brightness of his white skin**, and he went . . . into the presence of the emperor and bent his right and left knees beneath him, and knelt in the emperor's presence.⁴⁸

While in this instance the source text does not specify any attribute of either the duke's mantle or his shirt, the target text features specifications of material and judgments of value for both the duke's garments and his shirt; the former are splendid and made of silk, the latter is fine and made of silk, too.

The same tendency to emphasise details of clothing is featured in *Bethadh Bibuis o Hamtuir*. An illustrative example of this is found when Sisian's chamberlain asks Bevis to consider forgiving the princess, who had angrily ordered him to leave her kingdom as he would not marry her.

---

⁴⁷ Zupitza, *The Romance of Guy of Warwick*, 153, ll. 2611-2614. Due to missing folia in the Auchinleck MS, Zupitza edited this portion of the text from Cambridge, Gonville and Caius College, MS 107/176.
⁴⁸ Robinson, "The Irish Lives," 48. Translation at 129.

BENEDETTA D'ANTUONO

(I)   Bevis of Hampton

Ac for thow bringest fro hire mesage, / I schel thee yeve to the wage / **A mantel whit so melk***: /* **The broider is of Tuli selk***, /* **Beten abouten with rede golde***.*

And to thank you for bringing her message, I shall give you **a mantle white as milk** as a reward: **it is made of silk from Toulouse, embroidered with red gold.** [49]

(I)   Bethadh Bibuis o Hamtuir

₇ Robui **bratt uasal do sida glegel, glangresach** *fa Bibus, ₇* **ilimud do [tinlaice?] oir** *₇* **do legaib lanmaisecha loghmura ar na cengal** *₇* **ar na cumdach furan caemetach-sin,** *₇ tug Bibus do Bonufas e arson a aisdir.*

And Bevis had a **noble garment of shining, bright-embroidered silk,** and **many fine bars (?) of gold and splendid precious stones attached and fastened to that beautiful garment,** and Bevis gave it to Boniface to reward him for his errand.[50]

In the English version, Bevis expresses his gratitude to Boniface by presenting him with a white mantle crafted from Toulouse silk and adorned with intricate red gold embroidery. The Irish adaptation, instead, provides a more sophisticated depiction of the same clothing item, highlighting its grandeur and beauty. The fabric is intricately embroidered and adorned with exquisite gold bars and rare gemstones.[51] The English version is deficient in both descriptive details and expressions of appreciation, and the clothing item itself is inferior because it does not have gold bars or precious stones.

Another episode that demonstrates *Bethadh Bibuis o Hamtuir*'s increased attention to clothing features Princess Josian, who is about to be forcefully given in marriage to King Ybor, wearing a special object to protect her virginity in the name of her loyalty to Bevis.

---

[49] Herzman et al., "*Bevis of Hampton*," 232, ll. 1155-1159.
[50] Robinson, "The Irish Lives," 182. Translation at 306.
[51] In this paper, I endorse Robinson's interpretation of *tinlaice oir* as 'bars of gold'.

TWO MEDIEVAL IRISH ROMANCES

(I)   Bevis of Hampton

*"Ac for the love, that was so gode, / That I lovede ase min hertte blode, / Ichave," she seide, "**a ring** on, / That of swiche vertu is the ston: / While ichave on that ilche ring, / To me schel no man have welling, / And Beves!" she seide, "be God above, / I schel it weren for thee love!"*

"And for the love [I had for Bevis] that was so strong that it felt like my heart was bleeding, I have **a ring** on," said she, "whose gem is of special virtue: while I am wearing that ring, no man shall have my virginity. And Bevis!" said she, "by God who is in heaven, I shall wear it for your love!"[52]

(I)   Bethadh Bibuis o Hamtuir

*Iarna clos-sin do t-[S]isian, dorindi **si cris alainn orsnaith ₇ do sida somaisech**, ₇ docuir si annsa cris co glicc, gaesmur leisin glicus nGregach nach fedfaidis flr in talman a buain asa hoghacht in cein do beth in cris tairsdi.*

When Sisian heard this, she made a **beautiful girdle of gold thread and of resplendent silk**, and wisely and skilfully, by the wisdom of the Greeks, she put into that girdle power to prevent any man in the world from destroying her virginity so long as that girdle should be upon her.[53]

In the English version, the princess is wearing a magical ring, a common element in Middle English romances, whereas in the Irish adaptation she is wearing a magical girdle. The adaptation's increased emphasis on clothing results from two main factors. First, the text substitutes an accessory, the ring, with a piece of clothing, the girdle. Second, the passage includes details on the girdle fabric, made from a blend of gold and silk threads, and the complimentary comments praising its beauty and the radiance of the silk fabric.

---

[52] Herzman et al., "*Bevis of Hampton*," 240, ll. 1467-1474.
[53] Robinson, "The Irish Lives," 290. Translation at 313.

The ornamented descriptions of prized garments likely resulted from the redactor's intervention. This is not only indicated by the consistent presence of this feature, but also by the extensive evidence in historical, legal, and literary sources that demonstrate a considerable level of interest and reflection regarding clothing in early- and late-medieval Ireland. There was a significant increase in textile and leather production in late-medieval Ireland, and different types of fabrics and colours were associated with a specific social status.[54] The correlation between rank and clothing is attested to by the Annals of the Four Masters in the regulations promoted by King Eochaidh Eadghadhach:

> This was the first year of Eochaidh Eadghadhach, as king over Ireland. He was called Eochaidh Eadghadhach because it was by him the variety of colour was first put on clothes in Ireland, to distinguish the honour of each by his raiment, from the lowest to the highest. Thus was the distinction made between them: one colour in the clothes of slaves; two in the clothes of soldiers; three in the clothes of goodly heroes, or young lords of territories; six in the clothes of ollavs; seven in the clothes of kings and queens.[55]

Clothing was also an important part of Irish jurisprudence, as it was the subject matter of various law texts throughout the Middle Ages. In Early Medieval Ireland, an illustrative case in point is a tract from the eighth-century legal compilation *Senchas Már*, *Cáin Íarraith* ('The Law of the Fosterage Fee'), surviving in fragments interspersed with commentary. Specifically, the text in question discusses which clothes the foster children ought to wear, as well as the connection between the foster children's social extraction and their attire.[56] In Late Medieval Ireland, the legal codification

---

[54] Downham, *Medieval Ireland*, 195. Amy Mulligan, "*Togail Bruidne Dá Derga* and the Politics of Anatomy", in *Cambrian Medieval Celtic Studies 49* (Cambridge: Cambridge University Press, 2005), 1-19, at 8.

[55] John O'Donovan, *Annala Rioghachta Eireann: Annals of the Kingdom of Ireland, by the Four Masters, from the earliest period to the year 1616*, 7 vols, vol. 1 (Dublin: Hodges, Smith & Co., 1856), 43, 45.

[56] William Neilson Hancock et al. (ed. and tr.), *Ancient laws of Ireland*, 6 vols, vol. 2: *Senchus Mor* (Dublin: Stationery Office, 1869), 146-149.

of clothing is represented by the sumptuary laws that began to be promulgated after the Anglo-Norman invasion. These sought to ensure ethnic differentiation by distinguishing English and Irish dress.[57] The most notorious example in this sense appears in clause III of the Statutes of Kilkenny (1366), which read: "it is ordained and established . . . that every Englishman use the English custom, fashion, mode of riding and apparel, according to his estate . . . ."[58] The jurisprudential interest in ethnic differentiation continued throughout the final stages of the late medieval period, the mid- to late fifteenth century, when the adaptations of *Guy of Warwick* and *Bevis of Hampton* were produced.[59]

Lastly, from a literary point of view, detailed descriptions of characters' clothing appear in many medieval Irish *scéla*. Earlier in the Irish literary tradition, an illustrative case is represented by the portrayal of the high-king Conaire Mór in the sequence of *tableaux* characterising the final section of the tenth-century tale *Togail Bruidne Dá Derga*, which tells the story of Conaire's ascension to kingship and tragic fall.

> *At-chíu ardroth n-imnaisi ima chend cocoirse, conid fultu frithechrus. fordath n-órda n-ollmaise. fallire h-úasa berrad buidechas.* **At-chíu a brat n-derg n-ildathach nóthech siric srethchise. sluind ar delbthar n-dennaisi.** *di annor aurrdreic ailbeand alathúaith n-dronaicdi. At-chíu delg n-and olladbul. de ór uili indtlaisi. lasaid ar lúth lánésci. lainne a chúairt chorcairgemach. caera creithir comraicthi. con-gaib ar dreich n-dennmaisi. iter a dá coro gelgúalaind.* **At-chíu a léne lígdae línidi. conid ven sreband sirechtach. scáthderc sceo deilb illdathaig.** *ingelt súili sochaidi. cotgaib ar méit muinenchor. saerthus ar neim imdénum óir fri siric srethchisi. ó adbrond co urgúalaind nó co aurglúne.*

---

[57] Sparky Booker, "Moustaches, Mantles, and Saffron Shirts: What Motivated Sumptuary Law in Medieval English Ireland?" in *Speculum 96, 3* (Chicago: University of Chicago Press, 2021), 726-770, at 741.

[58] John Hardiman (tr.), "A Statute of the Fortieth Year of King Edward III, enacted in a Parliament held in Kilkenny, A.D. 1367, before Lionel Duke of Clarence, Lord Lieutenant of Ireland," in *Tracts relating to Ireland, 2* (Dublin: Graisberry and Gill for the Irish Archaeological Society, 1843), 3-121, at 11-13.

[59] Booker, "Moustaches, Mantles, and Saffron Shirts," 742-745.

BENEDETTA D'ANTUONO

At-chíu a chlaideb n-órduirn n-indtlaise.' . . . 'Nícon fil locht and isind fir sin eter cruth ₇ deilb ₇ decelt . . .

I see the diadem of a fair prince, proper to the dignity of a ruling lord. I see a crown encircling his head, the colour of beautiful gold over his yellow, curly hair. **I see his cloak red, multihued, of excellent braided silk.** I see a huge brooch, ornamented with gold, that shines with the vigour of the full moon. I see a circle of crimson gems in a bowl-like cluster . . . **I see a tunic of splendid linen, silken its sheen, refracted and many-coloured its hue** . . . I see his sword, its hilt ornamented with gold, in its scabbard of white silver; the latter, with its five concentric circles, retains its excellence. I see his bright, lime-whitened shield overhead; it scorns throngs of enemies. His spear of sparkling gold would illumine a feast, and his shaft is of ornamented gold.' . . . 'There is no flaw in him, not as to form or shape or clothing . . . '[60]

This passage exhibits a high degree of attention to garments. The pieces of clothing are assigned a colour, a material, and a judgment of value; the cloak, made of the finest braided silk, is colourful, and the tunic, made of linen, is also multicoloured and has a silky shimmer.

The strong and well-evidenced significance of clothing in medieval Irish social, legal, and literary contexts indicates that the redactor's deliberate focus on garments and jewelry was driven by an intention to Gaelicise the text. Through additional or extended references to the characters' attire, Uilleam Mac an Leagha appealed to his target audience, who lived in a society where clothing had a prominent place. Moreover, he facilitated the integration of his text into the target literary tradition, which frequently featured elaborate descriptions of clothing.

Music

The final aspect investigated is the increased focus on music. This feature emerges in *Beathadh Sir Gui o Bharbhuic*, in the episode relating

---

[60] Eleanor Knott (ed.), *Togail Bruidne Dá Derga* (Dublin: Dublin Institute for Advanced Studies, 1936), 30-32. Translation by Jeffrey Gantz, *Early Irish Myths and Sagas* (London: Penguin Books, 1981), 90-91.

TWO MEDIEVAL IRISH ROMANCES

the procession arranged by the Emperor of Constantinople to welcome Guy and his followers. The event is described as follows:

> ₇ *Adubairt an t-imper re lucht na cathrach dul a prosesiam a n-arrthaisc Sir Gyi. Is ann-sin tángadur lucht gacha heglusa don cathraigh co tapraibh ₇ co priceduibh ₇ co lampaib lansoillsi, co cloguibh, co mbachlaibh, co minnuib; ₇ sluaigh na cathrach co n-ethaigib somaisecha sidha ₇ orshnaith, ₇ an rí co coroin cengailti, clochbuadhaigh cumdaigh fura cenn, ₇* **aes ciuil na cathrach a comseinm itir orgán ₇ gitart ₇ galltrumpa ₇ tabur ₇ fhedan ₇ cruiti ₇ clairsigh ₇ na huili ceol archena**.

And the emperor bade the people of the city go in procession to meet Sir Guy. Then came the men of every church in the city with tapers and with (*priceduibh*) and with bright lamps, with bells and with staves and with relics; and the people of the city with splendid garments of silk and of gold thread, and the king with his crown on his head, tightly bound, set with jewels and adorned, and the **musicians of the city playing the organ, and the guitar (?), and the trumpet, and the tabor and the pipes and the fiddle and the harp, and all the other instruments besides**.[61]

Together with providing further proof for the adaptation's emphasis on clothing and accessories, this episode assigns a key role to music, as the scene features musicians playing the organ, the guitar, the trumpet, the tabor, the pipes, the fiddle, and the harp. The procession and, accordingly, the reference to musicians and their instruments, is absent from the English version.

The procession scene, which normally features some kind of musical entertainment, was a typical element in the structure of Middle English romances.[62] Therefore, the possibility that this passage was already included in Mac an Leagha's source text must be conceded. Nevertheless, I

---

[61] Robinson, "The Irish Lives," 52. Translation at 132.
[62] Susan Wittig, *Stylistic and Narrative Structures in the Middle English Romances* (Austin: University of Texas Press, 1978), 62.

would propose that the inclusion of this rather lengthy musical reference is likely due to the translator's intervention. To start with, this is suggested by the fact that the redactor consistently retains or adds musical details throughout the adaptation. For instance, the musical entertainment characterising Guy and Felice's wedding in the English version is retained in the Irish, which reads: *₇ dob imdha céol ₇ eladhna aran mbanais-sin* ("and there was much music and minstrelsy at that wedding").[63] Furthermore, the interest in music and musicians is firmly rooted in the Irish literary tradition, legal tracts, and society. Of particular significance is the fact that sources from these three realms focus on several of the instruments mentioned in *Beathadh Sir Gui o Bharbhuic*, specifically the trumpets, harps, pipes, and fiddles.

As far as the Irish literary tradition is concerned, descriptions of musicians and musical instruments are found in both place-name lore and in various scéla. One example may be found in the Dindshenchas poem on the fair (*óenach*) at *Carmun*, a poem that belongs to the Dindshenchas Érenn corpus, a compilation of prose or verse compositions on the lore surrounding prominent places of Ireland. The poem showcases a variety of musical instruments being played at the fair honouring the goddess Carmun:

> *Is iat a ada olla / stuic, cruitti, cuirn chróes-tholla, /*
> *cúisig, timpaig cen tríamna, / filid, ocus fáen-chlíara. //*
> *... Pípai, fidli, fir cengail, / cnámfhir ocus cuslennaig, /*
> *...*
>
> These are the Fair's great privileges: / trumpets, harps,
> hollow-throated horns / pipers, timpanists
> unwearied, / poets and meek musicians. // ...
> Pipes, fiddles, gleemen / bones-players and bagpipers, /
> ...[64]

As for the scéla, a vivid portrayal of music and musicians is witnessed in the tale *Togail Bruidne Dá Derga*. The final sequence of *tableaux* describing the characters visible in the hostel presents extensive references to pipes and pipers, as well as harps and harpers.

---

[63] Robinson, "The Irish Lives," 82. Translation at 152.
[64] Edward Gwynn, *The Metrical Dindsenchas*, Todd Lecture Series, 10 (Dublin: Hodges & Figgis, 1913), 18, 20. Translation at 19, 21.

TWO MEDIEVAL IRISH ROMANCES

(I) Pipes and pipers:

At-chonnarc and imdae ₇ nónbor inti . . . **"Nónbor cuisleannach** *inn sin do-róchtatar co Conaire ara airsceláib a Síd Breg. It é a n-anmand: Bind. Robind. Rianbind. Nibe. Dibe. Deichrind. h-Umal. Cumal. Cíalgrinn.* **It é cuisleandaich ata dech fil isin domun.** *Do-thaedsad .ix. n-deichenbor ₇ rl. ₇ maídfid cach fear díb búaid ríg ₇rl. ₇ ima-ricfa élúd doib íarum, ar bid imguin fri scáth imguin friu. Génait ₇ ní génaither, úair is a síd doib."*

I saw an apartment with nine men in it . . . 'Those are the **nine pipers** that came to Conare from Síd Breg because of the famous tales about him; their names are Bind, Robind, Ríanbind, Nibe, Dibe, Dechrind, Umal, Cumal, and Cíalgrind. **They are the best pipers in the world**. They will match the performance of anyone in the hostel; each of them will boast of victories over kings and royal heirs and plundering chieftains, and they will escape afterwards, for combat with them is combat with a shadow. They will slay and will not be slain, for they are of the Side.'[65]

(I) Harps and harpers:

Atcondarc nónbur n-aile friu anair. Nói monga cráebacha cassa foraib. Nói mbroit glassa luascaig impu. Nói ndelce óir ina mbrataib. Nói failge glano immá láma. Ordnasc óir im ordain cach ae. Auchuimriuch n-óir 'm o chach fir. Muince aircit im brágit cach ae. Nói mbuilc co n-inchaib órdaib uasib hi fraig .i. nói flesca findarcit inna lamaib . . . **Nói crutiri ind rig insin** *[₇ a nói cruite úasaib, Eg.]. Side ₇ Dide, Dulothe ₇ Deichrinni, Caumul ₇ Cellgen, Ól ₇ Ólene ₇ Olchói. Atbela fer cach ae leo.*

To the east of them I beheld another ennead. Nine branchy, curly manes upon them. Nine grey, floating (?) mantles about them: nine pins of gold in their mantles. Nine rings

---

[65] Knott, *Togail Bruidne Dá Derga*, 23. Translation by Gantz, *Early Irish Myths and Sagas*, 82.

of crystal round their arms. A thumbring of gold round each man's thumb; an ear-tie of gold round each man's ear; a torque of silver round each man's throat. Nine bags with golden faces above them on the wall. Nine rods of white silver in their hands ... They are the king's **nine harpers, [with their nine harps above them** (from MS Egerton 92)]: Side and Dide, Dulothe and Deichrinne, Caumul and Cellgen, Ól and Ólene and Olchói. A man will perish by each of them.[66]

In both excerpts, the musicians are presented as richly dressed and ornamented, as indomitable warriors, and, in the case of the pipers, as members of the Otherworldly people of the *Síd*. Together with further substantiating the importance of clothing in medieval Irish culture, these representations suggest that musicians were assigned a high position in the hierarchical Irish society, strengthening the case for the relevance of music in the target context.

From a legal standpoint, the topic of music appears in several Irish legal texts from the earliest stages of the medieval period. For instance, the Old Irish law-tracts on status dedicate considerable attention to musicians; more specifically, various tracts address their honour-price. Thus *Uraicecht Becc* sanctions that the only entertainer with independent legal status (*soíre*) is the harpist (*cruit*), who has an honour-price of 5 *séts*.[67] *Bretha Nemed Déidenach*, however, includes pipers among those professionals who have their own honour-price (*eneclann*), aligning with the extremely high consideration of pipers featured in the passage from *Togail Bruidne Dá Derga* considered above.[68] Lower grades of musicians, such as the horn-player (*cornaire*) and, according to *Uraicecht Becc*, the piper (*cuislennach*), are considered to belong to subordinate professions (*fodána*), and they do not have an honour-price in their own right; any offence against such a

---

[66] Whitley Stokes (ed. and tr.), *Togail Bruidne Dá Derga: The Destruction of Dá Derga's Hostel* (Paris: Librarie E. Bouillon, 1902), 114. This passage is transmitted in Dublin, Royal Irish Academy, MS 23 E 25 (c. late 11th – early 12th c.) and London, British Library, MS Egerton 92 (c. 15th c.). It is instead absent from Dublin, Trinity College, MS 1318 (c. late 14th – early 15th c.) and Dublin, Royal Irish Academy, MS D iv 2 (c. 15th c.).
[67] Kelly, *A Guide to Early Irish Law*, 64. Sét, a valuable item, 114-115.
[68] Kelly, *A Guide to Early Irish Law*, 64.

person is paid for as a proportion of the honour-price of his employer or master.[69]

Lastly, it seems that music was a vital part of various strands of late-medieval Irish society, as it was employed in both religious and secular events. As a result, there is a solid understanding of the figures of musicians, who "might pursue their hobby for its own sake, gain casual employment or become renowned professionals . . . [and they] were often employed in the retinues of great lords and were valued members of their household."[70] Particular prominence appears to have been given to harpists, who were among the most prestigious of Irish musicians.[71] This was perhaps connected to what Gerald of Wales observed, namely, the fact that the harp (*citharia*), together with the lyre (*tympanum*), was one of the main instruments of the Irish, in which they were "more skilled than any nation."[72]

When all of this is considered, the presence of musical references in *Beathadh Sir Gui o Bharbhuic* could result from an intervention on behalf of the redactor, who was trying to Gaelicise his source text by giving space to an element intrinsically characterising the Irish literary, legal, and social context. Positive evidence, however, prevents us from extending this conclusion to *Bethadh Bibuis o Hamtuir*; the fragmentary and incomplete copy of the text does not contain significant references to musical instruments or musicians. Indeed, the text only mentions bells, which are rung to signal the passing of hosts on the bridge leading to the city of Damascus in one occurrence and to honour Bevis' memory in a procession in the city of Coilin in another.[73]

Final Considerations

This descriptive comparison between *Beathadh Sir Gui o Bharbhuic* and *Bethadh Bibuis o Hamtuir*, along with their sources, has evidenced how the adaptations underwent a substantial Gaelicisation. This result was accomplished by emphasising three elements distinctively connected to late-medieval Irish society, jurisprudence, history, and literature:

---

[69] Kelly, *A Guide to Early Irish Law*, 64.
[70] Downham, *Medieval Ireland*, 327.
[71] Downham, *Medieval Ireland*, 326.
[72] Downham, *Medieval Ireland*, 326.
[73] Robinson, "The Irish Lives," 308, 318.

hospitality, clothing, and music. The Gaelicisation of the adaptations played an essential part in contributing to the literary acculturation of the foreign narrative material and, accordingly, to its successful textual migration into a new reception context. This migration ultimately allowed for the phenomenon of *Kulturtransfer* (cultural transfer), whereby foreign cultural products transition into a new cultural context and influence their later development.[74] In particular, the effect of these adaptations on the Irish tradition, first noted by Alan Bruford, might be seen in a specific type of romance-influenced narrative, usually termed *scéalta romansaíochta* (romantic tales); indeed, these tales began to appear in Ireland around the time that these translations were made and grew rapidly in number over the following centuries.[75]

Hopefully, forthcoming scholarly pursuits will examine the process of Gaelicisation in Early Modern Irish literary translations. The examination of this textual corpus through the integration of Descriptive Translation Studies and philology yields several desirable outcomes. Within the field of Irish studies, it offers valuable insights into the contemporary social, legal, and cultural context, as well as the literary tradition, thus making significant contributions to multiple areas of research. In the realm of medieval studies, it can shed light on the intricate methods and techniques employed by medieval translators, which have often been neglected or dismissed *tout court*. Within the scope of Descriptive Translation Studies, it can enrich the theory itself by incorporating new case studies from the corpus of medieval translations, which has been almost ignored in the theoretical elaboration of the descriptive approach.

---

[74] Erich Poppe, "Cultural Transfer and Textual Migration: Sir Bevis comes to Ireland," in *Hiberno-Continental Cultural and Literary Interactions in the Middle Ages*, eds Wolfram Keller and Dagmar Schlüter (Münster: Nodus Publikationen, 2017), 205–220, at 206.

[75] Alan Bruford, *Gaelic Folk-Tales and Mediaeval Romances: A Study of the Early Modern Irish 'Romantic tales' and their Oral Derivatives* (Dublin: Folklore of Ireland Society, 1969), at 11.

Creating a Welsh-Language Historical Map of Swansea

Geraint Evans

In April 2023 the Historic Towns Trust (HTT) published two historical maps of Swansea and the Mumbles, covering their medieval origins and the industrial period up to 1919. The project was led by Professor Helen Fulton, who is a trustee of the HTT, and in the early stages of the project it became clear that the maps would need to contain so much information that a bilingual map was not practical. The decision was therefore taken to produce two maps, one in English and one in Welsh. A large team of contributors collected the historical information while different editorial teams were responsible for compiling and editing the narrative content of the two maps. The cartographical work on both maps was carried out by Giles Darkes, the cartographic editor for the HTT. When it was published *Mapiau Hanesyddol o Abertawe a'r Mwmbwls* (Historical Maps of Swansea and the Mumbles) became the first Welsh-language map to be produced by the Historic Towns Trust. It is also significant because it is the first substantial Welsh-language map of any town in Wales which has ever been published. This paper will describe some of the linguistic challenges which were faced in mapping a Welsh town which has previously only ever been mapped in English.[1]

The Historic Towns Trust is a charitable, not-for profit organisation which grew out of The British Atlas of Historic Towns Project (HTT). This project was established in 1963 as part of a pan-European initiative to produce atlases and maps of consistent scale and content for the easy comparison of the growth and development of European cities. The Historic Towns Trust covers England, Wales and Scotland while the Irish Historic Towns Atlas, which is funded by the Royal Irish Academy, covers the whole of Ireland. The HTT produces large historical atlases containing a series of maps relating to individual cities as well as historical maps

---

[1] *Mapiau Hanesyddol o Abertawe a'r Mwmbwls*, ed. Geraint Evans, Helen Fulton and Giles Darkes (London: Historic Towns Trust, 2023); *Historical Maps of Swansea and Mumbles*, ed. Helen Fulton and Giles Darkes (London: Historic Towns Trust, 2023).

consisting of maps with text. The historical maps are printed as a folded sheet in a card cover, similar in format to the Ordnance Survey series. Each map includes an introduction and a brief history of the town or city together with a gazetteer of the main features shown on the map. In the case of Swansea, the gazetteer covers the major buildings and streets and some of the main topographical features of the medieval town and its docks. The maps also include some illustrations and topic boxes which explore or illustrate some of the major points of interest. In recent years the HTT's series of historical maps has included *York: from Medieval Times to 1850* (2018), *Medieval London–The City, Westminster and Southwark, 1270 to 1300* (2019), and *Bristol in 1480: a Medieval Merchant City* (2020). The Swansea maps—numbers 13 and 14 in the current series—cover the medieval origins and the industrial town up to 1919. These are the first HTT maps to cover a town in Wales but further projects covering towns in Wales and the March are already being explored. The base map for the Swansea map is the Ordnance Survey of 1923 and like all the other maps in the series the maps are printed at a scale of 1:25000, which is about 25 inches to the mile. An explanatory legend explains how the historical layers have been mapped, with the surviving medieval streets and buildings colour coded against the different strata of historical data which has been included.

Placenames, street names and the politics of Welsh identity

The politics of placenames is an important element in the history of Wales, as it is in Ireland and Scotland and in many other countries whose modern history has been inflected by the legacy of colonialism. It is no coincidence that Cymdeithas yr Iaith [the Welsh Language Society], perhaps the most radical of the nationalist groups in twentieth-century Wales, placed Welsh-language road signs at the forefront of their original campaign strategy in the 1960s and 1970s.[2] Road signs are visible, they name the landscape through which we travel, and the semiotic power of establishing Welsh-language placenames on road signs in Wales was seen as an essential first step in reclaiming Wales as a country whose Brythonic identity is proclaimed by the Welsh language. In the early days of

---

[2] See P. Merriman and R. Jones, "'Symbols of Justice': the Welsh Language Society's Campaign for Bilingual Road Signs in Wales, 1967-1980" in *Journal of Historical Geography*, 35, no. 2 (2009): 350-75.

MAP OF SWANSEA

Cymdeithas yr Iaith, a society which was founded in the wake of Saunders Lewis's 1962 radio talk *Tynged yr Iaith* "The Fate of the Language," there was also much engagement with the significance of priority.[3] Cymdeithas yr Iaith argued that not only should road signs in Wales include the Welsh form of a placename, but they argued that the Welsh form should always come first. This again relates to semiotics. When a small town in north Wales is signed as "Dinbych | Denbigh" the semiotic meaning of the sign is unconsciously read as: "this town is called Dinbych and in English it is known as Denbigh". Not the other way round. At the time, that one small conceptual leap towards the foregrounding of Welsh placenames in Welsh road signs was widely regarded as outrageous by conservative politicians for whom the colonial context was invisible. Only later, as the practice became normalised through repetition, did the priority of Welsh begin to achieve hegemonic acceptance.[4]

At the same time, the academic field of placename studies was busy exploring the origins of place, field, town and street names across Britain and Ireland and the picture that emerged in Wales was a landscape which inevitably carried the linguistic markers of multilingual settlement. Placenames of Wales carry historical markers in Welsh, Latin, Irish, Norse and English, and one thing which becomes clear through placename studies is that language ignores political boundaries. There are English placenames in Wales just as there are Welsh placenames in England and often the same place carries names in different languages at different times in its history. The origin of placenames has always been an important part of Celtic Studies, but in the late twentieth century there was a more popular growth of interest in the origins of Welsh placenames which led to popular segments on BBC Radio Cymru with Professor Bedwyr Lewis Jones devoted to the history of Welsh placenames and a series of small paperbacks published in a series called *Llyfrau Llafar Gwlad* (Country Lore Books)

---

[3] Saunders Lewis, *Tynged yr Iaith* (Caerdydd: BBC, 1962); for a discussion of the impact of *Tynged yr Iaith* and of the language movement in the later twentieth century see Geraint Jenkins, *'Let's Do Our Best for the Ancient Tongue': The Welsh Language in the Twentieth Century* (Aberystwyth: Canolfan Uwchefrydiau Cymreig a Cheltaidd Prifysgol Cymru, 2000).

[4] For a discussion of the politics of road signs in Wales see R. Jones and P. Merriman, "Hot, banal and everyday nationalism: bilingual road signs in Wales" in *Political Geography,* 28, no. 3 (2009): 164-73.

with titles such as *Enwau* (Names), *Enwau Tafarnau Cymru* (Welsh Tavern Names) and *Enwau Lleoedd Bro Dyfrdwy ac Alun* (Placenames of the Dee valley".[5] This popular interest in traditional names and their origins seemed to signal a wider acceptance of the idea that how the Welsh landscape was named was an expression of how Wales saw itself and following the establishment of a Welsh government in Cardiff popular support for bilingual signage in Wales was finally supported by the legislative will of government.

Road signs also have institutional status. They proclaim the name of a place or a street with the authority of the state which erects and maintains them, and it is partly by reflecting the visibility of signage in the built environment that map makers can reinforce the role of language in national identity. A renewed sense of the importance of the language of public signs, in Wales as elsewhere, is perhaps reflected in the drift in academic placename studies away from purely historical and linguistic concerns. This international trend has been explored by scholars such as Reuben Rose-Redwood, whose disciplinary background and interest lies more with political geography than etymology and linguistic taxonomy. Working with ideas from governmentality studies and political semiotics Rose-Redwood has explored some of the wider implications for the future of "critical place-name studies" in which the political economy of toponymic practice might be given a more prominent role.[6] In a wider context Rhys Jones and Huw Lewis have also used the insights of political geography to broaden the discussion about linguistic mapping while examining different ways of mapping the contemporary use of Welsh. Their use of geographical theory has also brought fresh insight into the ways in which institutions such as governments and councils interact or engage with language and languages.[7]

In the field of cartography, the team which created the Swansea map was aware of participating in a long history of mapping the Welsh

---

[5] Bedwyr Lewis Jones, *Enwau* (Llanrwst: Carreg Gwalch, 1991); Myrddin ap Dafydd, *Enwau Tafarnau Cymru* (Llanrwst: Carreg Gwalch, 1988); Hywel Wyn Owen, *Enwau Lleoedd Bro Dyfrdwy ac Alun* (Llanrwst: Carreg Gwalch, 1991).
[6] See R. Rose-Redwood, D. Alderman and M. Azaryahu, "Geographies of toponymic inscription: new Directions in Critical Place-name Studies" in Progress in Human Geography, 34. No. 4 (2010): 453-70.
[7] See R. Jones and H. Lewis, *New Geographies of Language. Language, Culture and Politics in Wales* (London: Palgrave Macmillan, 2019).

MAP OF SWANSEA

landscape, a process which has recently been invigorated by the Welsh government's Mapio Cymru (Mapping Wales) online project. In linguistic terms, however, the challenge for online maps and printed maps is the same. The landscape, towns and streets of Wales have largely been named and signed in English by an English administration and this in turn has helped to shape the use of Welsh in Wales, particularly spoken Welsh, through borrowings and code-switching practices which reflect the institutional status of English. So, while remaining mindful of recent scholarly and political initiatives mapping teams are drawn inevitably into a search for their own language policy, one which aims to balance historical usage, current institutional practice and current linguistic usage with the aspirations of cultural nationalism.

Swansea, Mumbles and Gower

Located on the southeastern coastline of the Gower peninsula, Swansea and the Mumbles are part of an ancient landscape which is historically rich and linguistically diverse.[8] While the medieval town was established around a Norman castle, the modern town of Swansea, which now has a population of about 250,000, grew from the late eighteenth century onwards because of industrialisation. Copper was particularly significant and for a time in the nineteenth century Swansea was the largest copper producer in the world.[9] Industrialisation also led to the construction of new docks and an expansion of the port around the mouth of the river Tawe, features which came to dominate the later industrial town to the south and east of the castle. The docks were heavily bombed in February 1941 in what became known as the 'three nights' blitz' and most of what had survived from the medieval town was destroyed.[10] The post-war reconstruction therefore involved the creation of new streets and the

---

[8] For a comprehensive survey of the history of Swansea in the period covered by the maps see Gerald Gabb, *Swansea and its History II: the Riverside Town* (Swansea: Gerald Gabb, 2019).
[9] For an overview of industrial Swansea see Louise Miskell, *Intelligent Town: An Urban History of Swansea 1760-1855* (Cardiff: University of Wales Press, 2012).
[10] See J.R. Alban *'The 'Three Nights' Blitz': Select Contemporary Reports Relating to Swansea's Air Raids of February 1941* (Swansea: Swansea City Council, 1994).

rebuilding or renaming of some of the old streets so that a historical map up to 1919 recalls a streetscape which is only partly visible in Swansea today.

Placenames around Swansea and on the Gower peninsula are predominantly Welsh but English, Latin, Norman French and Scandinavian influences are also visible.[11] There are some early Celtic Church names and placenames on the Gower peninsula, which was the site of the some of the earliest Christian churches in Wales. One example is Llangynydd/Llangennith, a church which was probably established in the sixth century. The name derives from *llan* plus the personal name Cynydd for the "church of Cynydd" and it is attested as "Iann Cinith" in 1160 and "Langenith" in 1284. Also, in the southern part of Gower is Rhosili from *rhos* plus the personal name 'Sulien' for "Sulien's moorland promontory". This is attested as "Rossili" in 1230 and "Ros ssili" c. 1566. This preserves the memory of an early British saint whose name is related to the name Julian and the placename is interesting linguistically because the unstressed final *-en* of Sulien has been elided over time to produce a place name which carries a regular Welsh stress on the penultimate. The best-known Welsh place name which has survived in the region in modern usage is "Abertawe" itself, a name which is composed of *aber* plus the river name "Tawe" for "mouth of the river Tawe". This is attested as "Abertawe", c. 1191 and as "Aber Tawy" c. 1300. Linked to this as a modern English equivalent is the Scandinavian place name "Swansea" which is derived from the personal name Sveinn plus Old Norse *ey* (island). This survives as "Swensi" on coins of c. 1140, as "Swense" in 1235 and later as Swannesey in 1505 but the likelihood is that in earlier times Swansea and Abertawe referred to separate places. While modern Swansea is associated with the mouth of the river Tawe and the area around the Norman castle, the original "Swensi" or Sfen's island was an older trading post closer to the modern-day Mumbles.[12] The name Mumbles originally referred to the two small islands and adjoining rocks off Mumbles Head, the peninsula to the west of Swansea

---

[11] See H.W. Owen and R. Morgan, *Dictionary of the Place-Names of Wales* (Llandysul: Gomer, 2007); for a discussion of Welsh and English placenames on the Gower peninsula see
Melville Richards, *Enwau Tir a Gwlad* (Caernarfon: Gwasg Gwynedd, 1998), 53-4.

[12] On the early history and locations of Swansea and the Mumbles see vol.1 of Gerald Gabb, *Swansea and its History*.

MAP OF SWANSEA

Bay. This is an obscure name with a much-contested etymology but the editors of the Swansea map supported the view that is likely to be Middle English in origin, deriving from Middle English *momele* "to mumble" and that this perhaps referred to the mumbling sound of the waves in the rocks around the promontory. The name is recorded as "Mommulls" in 1549 and "Mombles" in 1580 and as "y Mwmlws" in a Welsh source of 1609. On the other hand, Blackpill, which lies on Swansea Bay close to the Mumbles, is a more solidly derived English placename. This is Old English or early Middle English *blaec* plus *pyll* for "the black pool". It survives as "Blakepulle" in 1153-84 but has become 'Black Pill' by 1729.

However, there are some obvious differences between the history of placenames in Wales and the history of Welsh street names. The most obvious is that the Welsh language is predominantly visible in the placenames and topographical names of the Welsh countryside, in villages and towns, in farms and field names and in the names of rivers and mountains. But the street names of most of the towns in Wales, including Swansea and Mumbles, are predominantly English, a phenomenon which will be explored in the discussion below.

The history of Welsh-language maps

In discussing the history of Welsh maps there is a distinction to be made between maps of Wales in general and maps of Wales where the placenames and the language of other text on the map is predominantly Welsh. There are many maps of Wales dating from the late Middle Ages and early modern period, but all the early ones which have survived have text in Latin or English. As the Swansea map project developed it became clear that there were very few early Welsh-language maps, and this was confirmed by a search of the material in the map collection in the National Library of Wales. Huw Thomas, the current Curator of Maps, reported that "... there are relatively few maps in Welsh at all. Of some 73,000 catalogue records for maps in our collection just over 800 have any Welsh at all, and [most] of these are bi-lingual." As we might expect, there are a number of early printed Welsh Bibles which include maps but for economic reasons most of these use pre-existing English-language maps. And when it comes to Welsh-language maps of towns and cities the first which has been identified is Jerusalem rather than any of the towns in Wales. Huw Thomas further noted that "Thomas Gee produced two maps of Jerusalem in his

GERAINT EVANS

Encyclopaedia Cambrensis in 1868, one of biblical times and the other of modern Jerusalem. These are the earliest town plans in Welsh that I can find, but obviously [they are not] of a Welsh town."[13] We would expect that in more recent times this might have changed. The Welsh Language Act (1993) established the principle that the Welsh and English languages should be treated equally in the conduct of public business in Wales. Following devolution in 1999 there was a further Welsh Language Act in 2012 and again in 2015 when the Well-being of Future Generations (Wales) Act established that the Welsh government had a statutory duty to work towards achieving a number of well-being goals which included "a Wales of vibrant culture and thriving Welsh language". It was these successive pieces of legislation which led to the appearance of bilingual signage in Wales, following years of grass-roots protest calling for such a move. Legislative change also led to government and local councils beginning to produce standardised lists of bilingual placenames and street names. But it has not yet led to the production of many Welsh-language maps of Welsh towns and the few which have appeared—mostly produced by local councils—are generally bilingual rather than in Welsh, because it is cheaper to produce a single bilingual map than to produce two. The earliest of these which we could identify is a small bilingual street plan of parts of Cardiff which was produced by Cardiff Council in 1997. So, when *Mapiau Hanesyddol o Abertawe a'r Mwmbwls* appeared in April 2023 it was the first substantial Welsh-language map of any town in Wales which had ever been published.

Street names and placenames

The study of placenames has always been an important part of Celtic Studies and discussions about linguistic history continue to rely on primary research in placename studies. By comparison, relatively less work has been done on street names, perhaps because they often become a significant feature only in modern times and relatively few vernacular records survive relating to the names of streets in the Middle Ages.[14] Nevertheless a few guiding principles do emerge from existing work on street names in

---

[13] Huw Thomas, personal correspondence, April 2023.
[14] For a survey of the surviving evidence and an account of the different uses of 'street', 'lane' and 'road' see the Introduction to Eilert Ekwall, *Street-Names of the City of London* (Oxford: Clarendon, 1954).

MAP OF SWANSEA

England, particularly in the work which has been done on medieval London, and these proved to be valuable as the naming of streets in the Welsh map became the most challenging part of the project.

In medieval London almost every street name ended either in 'street' or 'lane' with 'street' used for wider thoroughfares and 'lane' for the smaller connections between them or between the streets and the Thames. This is also the case in medieval Swansea where the earliest names which have survived are mostly in 'street' with one example in 'lane' and nothing in 'alley' or 'hill'. Medieval Swansea's only 'lane' was the perhaps ironically named Welcome Lane which was narrow and steep and therefore easily defensible, and which led from the navigable bank of the river to an eastern gate in the castle wall. Another useful distinction in early street names can be made between 'street' and 'road'. In general, the word 'street' designates a roadway within a town or settlement while 'road' designates a roadway between two towns or districts. The use of names in 'road' within a town or settlement is a modern development. In Swansea there were three main routes out of the town: west towards the Gower, or north, and then northwest or northeast, towards the two nearest abbeys and castles at Carmarthen and Neath. In developing the list of Welsh street names for Swansea we observed this primary distinction between 'stryd' or 'heol' within the town and 'ffordd' as a main route towards another town. We also retained the local usage of 'stryd' where it had become established, as in Stryd y Berllan for Orchard Street, but inclined towards 'heol' in general, recognising the local usage of 'heol' or 'hewl' where northern usage might tend towards 'ffordd'.[15]

In modern spoken English this distinction between 'street' and 'road' can still be heard in different stress patterns.[16] We say Oxford Street, stressing the first element, but Oxford Road, stressing both elements. Oxford Road is a noun phrase with an implied article, 'road' as the head noun and Oxford as the premodifier: it's the road to Oxford or the Oxford Road. But in Oxford Street, 'street' is the unstressed second element of a compound, so Oxford is stressed but street is unstressed, and we can still

---

[15] See the entries for 'heol' and 'ffordd' in *Geiriadur Prifysgol Cymru: a Dictionary of the Welsh Language* (Aberystwyth: University of Wales, 1997-).
[16] See "Street or Road?" in Adrian Room, *The Street Names of England* (London: Stamford, 1992).

hear this distinction in the unconscious stress patterns of native speakers of English.

Street names in Swansea

The Norman borough town of Swansea was established in the twelfth and thirteenth centuries along with a large number of other Norman towns in Wales and all the early street names which have survived are English in origin and appear to be 'born English' names. This is also true, of course, of every Norman town of Wales, as they were established by and for English or Anglo-Norman traders to the exclusion of the Welsh. Interestingly, Ekwall finds a similar phenomenon in the early street names of London, where nearly all the surviving names are Middle English with French being almost invisible and "no London street name now in use [being] recorded in Old English sources."[17]

Henry de Beaumont was granted the lordship of Gower in 1106. The first castle was built quickly of timber and Swansea was established as the *caput* of the lordship of Gower by 1107. The 'New Castle' was built of stone between 1221 and 1284, and it is the remains of this castle which survive today. St. Mary's Church was built about a century later, under the bishopric of Henry de Gower, who was Bishop of St. David's 1328 to 1347. The streetscape of early Swansea was slow to grow beyond the limits of the medieval town and it wasn't until industrialisation that the layout of the modern town began to appear.[18] Most of the earliest street names which have survived in Swansea from before about 1400 are listed below. These are mostly from around the castle and within the walls and defensive ditch of the borough town:

> Castle Street, Castle Bailey Street, Caer Street, Cross Street, Fisher Street, Frog Street, Goat Street, Greenfield Street, Orchard Street, St. Mary's Street, Strand, Wassail Street, Welcome Lane, Wind Street, York Street

These early names are all 'born English' and it is not until the expansion of the town began in the early nineteenth century that new street names began to be adopted which contained any Welsh elements.

---

[17] Ekwall, *Street-Names of the City of London*, 35.
[18] See the discussion of the "Plan of Swansea (1823)" in Gabb, *Swansea and its History*, 1-5.

MAP OF SWANSEA

One key discovery about modern Welsh street names in Swansea was made by Dr. Ben Curtis, the historical researcher who was employed on the project. This is that there was very little evidence of the use of Welsh-language street names in Swansea before the late twentieth century. This was surprising because Swansea was a strongly Welsh speaking town in the eighteenth and nineteenth centuries and was often described as the capital of Welsh non-conformist religion in the late nineteenth and early twentieth centuries; that is, it was the capital of the chapel tradition which was conducted almost entirely in the Welsh language. But what evidence we have suggests that Welsh speakers treated English street names like English placenames and borrowed them into spoken Welsh rather than translating them. In newspapers and other documents of the nineteenth and early twentieth centuries we find streets such as 'High Street' and 'York Street' borrowed as English phrases into Welsh sentences, but often alongside 'Abertawe' rather than 'Swansea'. The practice seems to have been that Welsh speakers in industrial Swansea prior to 1919 regularly translated placenames such as Swansea, Neath and Carmarthen into spoken and written Welsh but that English street names were treated as code-switch borrowings. This does not seem to have been the case in all parts of Wales, but it conforms with the socio-linguistic environment before the late twentieth century where road signs and street signs in Wales, and all public signage in general, were part of an English linguistic domain. The tendency of Welsh speakers was therefore to borrow English street names into Welsh sentences because they were code-switching into an English linguistic domain. This began to change with the language movement of the 1960s, which campaigned for the legal status of the Welsh language and the use of bilingual road signs in Wales, but the practice persists today and can still be widely heard in spoken Welsh. More recently, as mentioned above, the legal status of Welsh did begin to change, especially after devolution, at which point Welsh or bilingual signage began to appear, but this was far from being the case in 1919. Another factor which we discovered is that the responsibility for street names in Wales is devolved to local councils, so the implementation of language policy has not been uniform. Some Welsh councils, and many Welsh speakers, began reclaiming street names by adopting the Welsh version of an English name or by creating Welsh names for new streets. But this was a problem for a Welsh historical map which ends in 1919 because while there is now a tradition of using Welsh street names for some streets in Swansea there is very little recoverable tradition of Welsh speakers using Welsh street names before 1919.

Adding to the complexity Swansea Council developed a policy in 1996 that as Swansea expanded all new street names would be either in Welsh or in English, with a more or less even number approved in both languages. Individual local councils therefore develop policy in response to legislation and statutory guidance, they have the authority to approve new street names and they are also required to pass this information to the National Street Gazetteer, which is the repository for official street names.[19] So there are no new bilingual street names being approved in Swansea and in general Swansea council does not use bilingual street signs although these are common in some other Welsh towns. Some of the older English street names in Swansea, such as High Street and Orchard Street, have developed modern Welsh equivalents which are used by Welsh speakers—Y Stryd Fawr and Stryd y Berllan—and these are signed bilingually, but very few bilingual street names are visible in Swansea today. For example, Swansea's new Arena Theatre, which opened in 2022, can be reached by a new pedestrian bridge which spans Oystermouth Road, linking the harbourside theatre with the streets around St. Mary's church. The council signage on the approach to the bridge refers in English to the "New Oystermouth Road Bridge" and in Welsh to "Pont Newydd Oystermouth Road", retaining the English street name in the Welsh phrase.

What kind of language policy could therefore be employed for a historical map of Swansea which is also the first substantial Welsh-language map of any town in Wales? After much discussion the editorial team decided against using English names for most Swansea streets before 1919 and decided instead to use Welsh names for all the streets which still survived and for which a Welsh form was now in use. For older streets which no longer existed we retained the English name, and for surviving streets which had not developed a contemporary Welsh form we also retained the English original, noting this decision at the head of the Gazetteer:

> *Ychydig iawn o dystiolaeth sydd wedi goroesi am y defnydd o enwau strydoedd Cymraeg yn Abertawe erbyn 1919. Ond*

---

[19] Correspondence with the Office responsible for Street Naming and Numbering (SNN) in Swansea, December 2022.

MAP OF SWANSEA

gan mai dyma'r map Cymraeg cyntaf o Abertawe a'r Mwmbwls penderfynnwyd mabwysiadu rhai enwau strydoedd Cymraeg ar gyfer y map gan nodi yma nad yw hyn yn adlewyrchu'r arfer hanesyddol ym mhob achos.

Very little evidence has survived about the use of Welsh street names in Swansea prior to 1919. But as this is the first Welsh-language map of Swansea and the Mumbles it was decided to adopt some Welsh street names for the map while noting here that this does not necessarily reflect historical usage in every case.

Most British street names have a two-part form: an individual name such as 'High' or 'York', which is sometimes known as the specific, and an indicator name such as 'street' or 'lane', which is sometimes known as the generic. A few street names, especially topographical street names, have only one element and Swansea examples include The Burrows and The Strand. 'High Street' is probably the most widespread street name in England and Wales and in early towns many of the thoroughfares which lead out of town from the High Street will be suffixed as 'road'.[20] In the case of Swansea the street called High Street simply becomes Carmarthen Road as it heads north out of the town.

In linguistic terms there are four kinds of street name that appear in the two historical maps of Swansea. There are English names with English individual elements, English names with Welsh individual elements, Welsh names with English individual elements and Welsh names with Welsh individual elements. Here are some examples: English names with English elements include High Street, Frog Street, Oystermouth Road and Nelson Terrace. English names with Welsh elements include St. Illtyd's Crescent, Dyvatty Street, Hafod Street and Waun-Wen Road. Welsh street names with English elements which appear on the Welsh map include Stryd Adelaide, Heol Foxhole, Heol Victoria and Parêd y Cei while Welsh names with Welsh elements include Stryd y Berllan, Cilgant Illtud Sant, Heol Ystumllwynarth and Lôn y Castell. The English element can sometimes take on a Welsh form when it's included in a Welsh street name as in Parêd

---

[20] See John **Field,** "Street Names" in *The Local Historian,* 16, no. 4 (November 1984): 195-203.

y Cei, where the English elements 'parade' and 'quay' are borrowed into Welsh using Welsh orthography. More commonly, a Welsh individual element is borrowed into English where it is either translated or adopted as a borrowing with English orthography. Examples included Carmarthen Road, Dinevor Place and St. Illtyd's Crescent.

In the Welsh street names, there are also patterns of usage similar to the English street names so that 'heol' or 'ffordd'—like the uses of 'street' or 'road'—can indicate the difference between a street in the town and the beginnings of a road to another town. Modern urban development can, of course, render this early distinction invisible in the modern town but in the medieval and early modern town there are usually very few roads in and out of the town. Swansea is approached from the south and east by water and the position of the castle and town walls make it particularly difficult to approach from the east, so there are essentially only two routes out of the town on foot. High Street runs north from the castle's North Gate and soon forks northwest into the Carmarthen Road, and northeast into Neath Road. As the names suggest, these are the main roads to Carmarthen, which was the largest town in Wales prior to the industrial revolution; and to Neath, another Norman town, with a Cistercian monastery, once the largest abbey in Wales; and a Norman castle which is still visible as a ruin and still visible in the Welsh place name: Castell-nedd. There were two early streets leading west, which probably merged into the modern St. Helen's Road. These are the aptly named Greenfield Street, which emerged from the Wassail Gate in the southwest; and Gower Street, which emerged from the West Gate. As that latter name indicates, this was the main route from Swansea to Gower.

Some early Swansea street names

Looking at the medieval street names which are listed above there is no Welsh visible in the individual elements. At first sight 'Caer Street' looks promising as this is a street which is adjacent to the castle, but it turns out not to be a Welsh name. The form 'Caer' first appears in the 1800s adopted, it seems, by Welsh speakers who thought they recognised in the English name an echo of the Welsh word 'caer' which means castle. The earlier form—which is well attested—was 'Carr Street' a name which probably comes from Middle English 'cart' reflecting the location of the original market which was located at the top of Wind Street under the walls of the castle.

MAP OF SWANSEA

Wind Street is also a fascinating name and, in its layout, the most visibly medieval street to have survived in Swansea. Wind Street and the parallel development of Fisher Street represent the two oldest trading streets in Swansea, and the width of Wind Street as it survives today seems to indicate that as it was laid out it adhered to the precept from the time of Henry I whereby a street "or *heaghstraet, strata regia, cyninges straet* or the like . . . was to be sufficiently broad for two loaded carts to meet [and pass]".[21] The two oldest identifiable pubs in Swansea still stand on these two streets—the Cross Keys in Fisher Street and the No Sign, as it's now known, in Wind Street. This street name is recorded as 'Wyne Street' in 1567 and 'Winstrett' in 1579 and the street is still pronounced locally as 'Wind Street'—rhyming with 'find' or 'kind'—a name which is popularly understood to refer to windyness. This popular understanding is based partly on the Elizabethan pronunciation of 'wind' as in the song from *As You Like It* (Act II, Scene VII), where the rhyme suggests the pronunciation:

> Blow, blow, thou winter wind,
> Thou art not so unkind
> As man's ingratitude.[22]

But the evidence suggests that the name probably relates to the sale of wine or, more likely still, to the Middle English word 'wind' as in a narrow or winding street or lane. The really interesting thing is that this folk etymology from 'windy' has informed the recent Welsh coinage of 'Stryd y Gwynt' ("the street of the wind") which in the last twenty years has been widely used locally and is now recognised by Swansea council. So, we have used 'Stryd y Gwynt' as the street name on the Welsh map while explaining in the Gazetteer that this is a modern coinage based on a folk etymology. It is also interesting to note that there are a number of other examples of streets called 'Wind Street' in Wales and where they occur in local authorities which do use bilingual street names these have also become 'Stryd y Gwynt'. There are examples in Castell Nedd/Neath, Llandysul and Conwy, all of which were Norman market towns, while in the modern town of

---

[21] Ekwall, *Street-Names of the City of London*, 1-2.
[22] William Shakespeare, *As You Like It*, ed. Agnes Latham (London: Methuen, 1975), 58.

GERAINT EVANS

Rhydaman/Ammanford the Welsh form of 'Wind Street' is 'Ffordd y Gwynt'.

Another interesting early name is Frog Street, which runs along the southern side of St. Mary's church, which was a Norman foundation. Frog Street runs east into Fisher Street which in turn becomes York Street. Because of the apparent similarity between the two elements 'Frog' and 'Efrog' we wondered whether it was possible that the name 'Fisher Street' had intruded into what was once a continuously named street, known by the individual element 'York' to English speakers and as 'Efrog' to Welsh speakers. The idea was tantalising, but no evidence could be found and Fisher Street—together with Wind Street—has a strong claim to being the oldest commercial street in Swansea. In addition to the early attestation of 'Fisher Street' in its present location the pattern of different parts of what is now a single street being known by different names is also seen elsewhere at a time when the modern use of street numbers had not yet been adopted. Ekwall lists a number of examples for medieval London. There are also other examples of 'Frog Street' running along the south side of a medieval church. One is at the mostly fifteenth-century church of St. Mary in Tenby, in southwest Wales and another is the originally ninth-century church of St. Edmund in Exeter. There was also a Frog Row in medieval Nantwich and all of these streets are adjacent to water, as was Frog Street in Swansea, so 'frog' seems here to be a descriptive English element which is unrelated to Welsh 'Efrog' and refers, as elsewhere, to the amphibious creatures who thrived in land which was marshy or close to running water. In medieval Swansea Frog Street intersected Cross Street, which ran along the eastern edge of the medieval church, suggesting that the name was originally Christian rather than topographical. Sadly, the visibility of medieval Swansea was further diminished in the 1950s when Cross Street was renamed Princess Way as part of the post-war re-development.

Much of medieval Swansea was damaged or destroyed in the Second World War by the bombing raids which targeted the docks and most of the medieval buildings have therefore been lost, together with some of the oldest streets. Frog Street had already been demolished during slum clearances in the late nineteenth century when Fisher Street and Cross Street were demolished and renamed in the late 1950s. But part of York Street does survive under its original name as does Wind Street, which still winds

MAP OF SWANSEA

down from the ruins of the medieval castle and still supports a thriving trade in cheap wine as it is now the focus of student nightlife in Swansea.

Conclusion

Street names are an important element of urban history, but this project has highlighted some of the problems involved in researching aspects of linguistic history for which few written records have survived. Future projects will doubtless build on the lessons learned in the Swansea project but in many cases, they may also wish to adopt our policy of assimilating contemporary Welsh street name forms into a reconstructed historical map of lost oral practice. In the wake of recent changes to governance in Wales and to changes in the legal status of the language, our decision to adopt contemporary Welsh forms into an historical map can be seen as a contribution to a wider project of nation building as the newly acquired legal status of the Welsh language in Wales is integrated into popular culture and scholarly practice.

The Historic Towns Trust is already developing plans for future maps of Welsh towns and their medieval origins. The HTT has now adopted as policy a commitment that all future historical maps of towns in Wales will result in two maps, one in Welsh and one in English. This decision can be seen as a direct consequence of the legal recognition of Welsh as an official language and the subsequent increased visibility of Welsh in the built environment of contemporary Wales. The success of the Swansea map has also shown that Welsh-language maps of Welsh towns can make an original and important contributions to the study of urban history and linguistic development in Britain.

The Irish Progressive: Investigating Early Hiberno-English Texts

Dolores Fors

One prominent feature of Hiberno-English is called the 'Irish English progressive.' This is a linguistic feature which is typically recognized as *do* + *be* + V-*ing*,[1] meaning a structure that includes *do* and *be* paired with a verb finalized by the *ing*-suffix, as seen in one of the 'tokens' (findings in a corpus search) from this study, "Don't be talking to me, you sneaking, skulking villain." [2] It is a feature which is hypothesized to have been introduced through the influence of the Irish language. Most studies of the Irish English progressive so far have focused on the twentieth and twenty-first centuries. In this study I focus on an earlier time period, namely from the beginning of the seventeenth to the end of the nineteenth century. I do this in order to trace the historical development of the Irish English progressive and to track the impact that this has had on the standard English progressive.

Through the use of 'corpora' (large sets of language data) and 'corpus linguistics' (the use of corpora to carry out quantitative studies) I aim to showcase the frequency and distribution of this feature, as well as to give some contextual insight on its usage. The order in which I will do this is, first, to give an overview on the research questions, and then to discuss the Irish English progressive as a feature. After this comes a discussion about the habitual aspect, followed by a discussion of Celtic Englishes. I will subsequently assess data, and then delineate the theoretical framework and methodology which will be applied to that assessment. Lastly, I will briefly discuss limitations of the research before finally presenting the results of the study and readdressing the research questions.

---

[1] Raymond Hickey, *Irish English: History and Present-Day Forms* (Cambridge: Cambridge University Press, 2007), 216.
[2] Corpus of Electronic Texts (CELT), accessed January 9, 2022, https://celt.ucc.ie/published/E850000-007.html.

IRISH PROGRESSIVE

Research questions

My research set out with the goal of answering several research questions. These questions were refined as a single, primary question, namely:

> What is the distribution of the Irish English progressive in Hiberno-English from the beginning of the seventeenth to the end of the nineteenth century?

Followed by two subsidiary questions, namely:

- What is the frequency of the *be + verb* ending in *-ing* structure, or the standard progressive, regardless of the habitual aspect?

- How can the distribution of the Irish English progressive be categorized into different sentence types based on previous studies of the topic

The Irish English progressive

The Irish English progressive replicates the form of the progressive aspect in standard English, but represents another aspect. Aspect of a verb says something about when the action of a verb is taking place: if it is ongoing, if it has passed and so forth. In standard English, the progressive aspect is formed by the BE-copula followed by a verb ending in *-ing*.[3] One example of this would be 'I am presenting.' The Irish English progressive, on the other hand, is used to express another aspect, namely the habitual aspect.[4] The habitual aspect will be discussed later. The Irish English progressive is thus recognized as an occurrence of the progressive aspect form, which, however, communicates habitual aspect in its sense. Aoife Ní Mhurchú describes it as follows:

> Though similar in syntax to the Standard English present progressive, save for the *do*-auxiliary, this structure does

---

[3] Jan Svartvik, Randolph Quirk, and David Crystal, *A Comprehensive Grammar of the English Language* (Harlow: Longman, 1985), 211.
[4] Hickey, *Irish English,* 217.

not express progressivity, but rather highlights the habitual nature of the main verb.[5]

The habitual aspect in the Irish English progressive construction thus emphasizes when something happens repeatedly or habitually, even though the form mostly mimics that of the progressive aspect in standard English.

The Irish English progressive is a multifaceted feature which varies in construction and form. As mentioned, it is often associated with the cemented construction *do + be + verb* ending in *-ing*. However, despite the *do* often being referred to as a set part of the Irish English progressive, the construction can also function without the *do*.[6] Several other varieties of structures exist in Irish English which convey the habitual aspect by centering on the *be*-copula. One example is 'bees' as in 'I bees reading,'[7] while other constructions utilize adjectives instead of progressive participial verbal formations in *-ing*: an example of this is, 'I do be hungry.'[8] The Irish English progressive may additionally be found in African American Vernacular English.[9] This may reflect Irish influence in areas simultaneously inhabited by African and Irish immigrants.

The habitual aspect

It is established, then, that the Irish English progressive is an expression of the habitual aspect. In the Irish language, the habitual aspect is conveyed in part as a conjugated aspectual form, and this is often paired with a verb conjugated in the progressive aspect or an adjective.[10] In this study, however, I focus on structures where the predicate is a verb, not an adjective. One typical habitual construction in Irish involves the habitual conjugation of the verb *bí* paired with the particle *ag* and a verbal noun,[11]

---

[5] Aoife Ní Mhurchú, "What's Left to Say About Irish English Progressives? 'I'm Not Going Having Any Conversation with You,'" *Corpus pragmatics: international journal of corpus linguistics and pragmatics* 2, no. 3 (2018): 292.
[6] Ní Mhurchú, "What's Left to Say About Irish English Progressives?," 292.
[7] Hickey, *Irish English*, 236-237.
[8] Ní Mhurchú, "What's Left to Say About Irish English Progressives?," 292.
[9] John R. Rickford, "Social Contact and Linguistic Diffusion: Hiberno-English and New World Black English," *Language (Baltimore)* 62, no. 2 (1986): 282.
[10] Nancy Stenson, *Modern Irish: A Comprehensive Grammar* (Milton: Routledge, 2019), 59.
[11] Hickey, *Irish English*, 213.

such as in '*Bíonn mé ag scríobh*' or '*Bím ag scríobh*,' ('I am often writing'). The latter example showcases how the habitual aspectual form of *bí* also has person conjugations. It might, then, be translated as "I do be writing," using the Irish English progressive. This is the grammatical setup that is said to be mimicked in English by Irish English speakers through the feature that this study focuses on.

Celtic Englishes

Since, as previously mentioned, the Irish English progressive is a multifaceted feature that alters a sentence from several linguistic perspectives, it is interesting to research. Its unique structure allows for significant discussion of many points pertinent to the study of Hiberno-English as well as of Celtic Englishes. The scope of this study covers both older texts and relatively recent texts, with the aim of facilitating further understanding not only of the substrate effect Irish might have had on English, but also of the L1 and L2 processes that exist in this linguistic domain. L1 and L2 are terms commonly used when dealing with language acquisition and linguistic dynamics, where L1 stands for 'first language,' and L2 for 'second language.' The studied feature of this paper is a product of these dynamics.

The term "Celtic Englishes" was introduced by Marku Fillpula. Fillpula explains that Celtic Englishes can be recognised as varieties of English that have come into being within Celtic language- speaking areas where English has existed simultaneously.[12] The traces of the Celtic language in question can show themselves in many different ways. These include phonetic influences that deviate from a standard dialect. Or certain constructions or grammatical features may be borrowed into English, or vice versa. Or lastly, the features may be lexical, in the form of code-switching, or the use of certain specific words or terminology from Celtic languages.

Overall, the influence of the Celtic language group on English is a matter of debate. The full picture of what impact these languages might have had on the core makeup and more recent features of English is still not clear. The study of the Irish English progressive is one step toward learning

---

[12] Markku Filppula, "More on the English progressive and the Celtic connection," *The Celtic Englishes* 3, (2003): 150-168.

more about exactly that. When dealing with the influence of Celtic on English, the three most common areas of research are Scotland, Wales, and Ireland. All three of these areas at present have speakers both of Celtic languages and of English. Celtic languages, however, were the dominant languages in many regions of the Isles prior to the spread of English.[13] It has been proposed that when English was introduced in many of these regions, the respective Celtic languages began to exert a substratal influence on English.[14] The aforementioned dialects of Hiberno-English, Welsh English, and Hebridean English, which resulted from this process are therefore often grouped as Celtic Englishes.[15]

My research focuses, then, on one of the aforementioned dialects, namely Hiberno-English. Hiberno-English applies to varieties of English from all of Ireland, but possesses two recognized sub-varieties, in the northern and southern part of the island of Ireland, called simply *Northern Hiberno-English* and *Southern Hiberno-English*.[16] Ireland still has a relatively large number of Irish speakers, and, due to its isolated geography, Hiberno-English has developed and been maintained with stability. The dialect is recognized and popularized by many features such as different vowel sounds, periphrastic *do*, and the habitual aspect in verbs.[17] Irish as a language differs from English on many levels, which makes its influence upon English all the more noticeable.

The history of Ireland subsumes several periods during which Irish and English could have coalesced into Hiberno-English. While the invasion and occupation of Britain by the Anglo-Saxons during the early fifth century are believed to have initiated not only the English language, but indeed the Celtic Englishes that exist today, it was not until the twelfth century that English was properly introduced in Ireland, where its spread was periodically uneven.[18] The dominance of the Irish language was first

---

[13] Markku Filppula, Juhani Klemola, and Heli Pitkänen, ed., *The Celtic roots of English* (Joensuu: University of Joensuu, Faculty of Humanities, 2002): 2-4.
[14] Markku Filppula, "Inversion in embedded questions in some regional varieties of English," in *Generative Theory and Corpus Studies: a Dialogue from 10 ICEHL, Mouton de Gruyter* (2000): 440.
[15] Filppula, "More on the English progressive," 150-168.
[16] Filppula, "Inversion in embedded questions," 440.
[17] Hickey, *Irish English*, 218; 213.
[18] Hickey, *Irish English*, 31.

challenged in year 1366, when decrees were promulgated to prohibit the Irish language and culture in favor of cultivating an Anglo-Norman identity in Ireland.[19] The time that ensued was turbulent, with increasing influence exerted by the neighbouring country, England, and by the English monarchy, which was extended to Ireland in 1541.[20] The power of the monarchy was reimposed, and again, the English language, along with English law.[21] During the eighteenth century Irish identity, and along with it the Irish language, experienced some revitalization.[22] Despite this, however, the Irish language was recognized in Ireland as being endangered by the mid-nineteenth century.[23]

Data

The data selected for this study has been taken from CELT, or the Corpus of Electronic Texts.[24] This corpus is web-based, and consists of a vast selection of source texts from several languages, including Hiberno-English, French, and Latin. However, the main portion of the corpus consists of texts in the Irish language. Since this study, texts in Hiberno-English from this period were selected and extracted from the web-corpus. The data was then reviewed, and non-relevant sections were removed. Once the individual texts were prepared, they were added to several directories, which in turn were organized and processed through the corpus software AntConc. See Table 1 for more information on the makeup of the corpus.

---

[19] Hickey, *Irish English*, 419.
[20] Hickey, *Irish English*, 419.
[21] Reg Hindley, *The Death of the Irish Language: A Qualified Obituary* (London: Routledge, 1990), 5.
[22] Hickey, *Irish English*, 420-421.
[23] Hindley, *The Death of the Irish Language*, 8.
[24] CELT, accessed January 9, 2022, https://celt.ucc.ie/engpage.html.

Time period	Genre	Word count	Number of texts
17th century	Mixed	285,824	69
18th century	Mixed	557,929	44
19th century	Mixed	527,152	299
Total		1,370,905	412

Table 1: total word count per century

A broad variety of genres and texts is available for the Hiberno-English portion of *CELT*. These include books, poems, lyrics, news, letters, dialogue, and miscellaneous. Some notable authors such as William Shakespeare and Oscar Wilde can be found in the corpus. The *CELT* corpus has not been annotated, and one thus depends heavily on the capabilities of the corpus tool, in this case AntConc, in order to find 'collocates'(words that co-occur frequently) and to perform the correct searches.

Methodology

This is a quantitative study which utilizes some qualitative methods to expand the results. The results of the corpus searches have been manually validated to ascertain that each token encountered is a plausible instance of the Irish English progressive. The results are presented both in comparison to the overall word count and through a normalization process. The normalization process indicates how often the construction appears per one million words. The search string used for finding the tokens consisted of searching for words ending in *-ing* preceded by the verb in its *be*-form, as well as some cases which included different personal pronouns before the verb. The words which had an *ing*-suffix but which were not verbs were sorted out.

As mentioned, the auxiliary *do* is not obligatory in the Irish English progressive construction. In this study, the most common form of the Irish English progressive consisted of cases where the *do* did co-occur. It is important to consider the collocates in searching for *be* + *verbs* ending in *-ing*, as collocates and context are vital when distinguishing between the standard English progressive and the Irish English progressive. The formula for this requires that the search does not include any 'lemmas' (including all inflections of a word) of the verb *be,* and that requirement excludes many instances of the standard English progressive. For instance, in a search, 'I am running' would be written 'I be running,' disregarding the subject-verb agreement. Another important component in the formula is that the structure must be capable of being understood to communicate a habitual sense, even if it is complemented by an adverb.

Limitations

Several limitations have been placed upon this study. First, the data is not organized according to genre, and no division has been made between originally spoken data, such as transcriptions, and written data. This impedes refinement of the results in terms of frequency distribution between genres. Second, the Irish English progressive occurs frequently in speech, but is evident less frequently in its written forms, and the present research does not address that question. Third, several texts from the dataset might be analyzed through other linguistic approaches, such as discourse analysis, in order to provide a deeper understanding of the Hiberno-English profile and of the possible manner in and extent to which the Irish English progressive occurs within it. Finally, many of the genres included, such as poems, fiction, and lyrics are often subjected to different exaggerations of dialectal varieties. This can be explained as being due to nationalism, nostalgia, character distinctions, comedic effect, other stylistic domains, or "stage Irish." Thus, many of the sources may not represent authentic examples of the targeted construction. Authenticity is another reason to consider a more qualitative approach to many of these texts.

Results

The three centuries showed different results and frequencies. Although neither the seventeenth nor the eighteenth century showed any occurrence of the Irish English progressive, they nonetheless differed from one another in other ways. The seventeenth century manifested some examples of structures analogous to the Irish English progressive, but the eighteenth century did not. See Table 2 for more an overview of the frequency results.

Century	Word count	*Be* + V-*ing*	Irish English progressive
17th	285,824	26	0
18th	557,929	13	0
19th	527,152	207	31
Total	1,370,905	246	31
Normalized frequency	N/A	179.44	22.6

Table 2: summary of the progressive *be* + V-*ing*

As can be seen in the table, the Irish English progressive and the *be* + *verbs* ending in -*ing*, or standard progressive, seem to have increased significantly and simultaneously during the nineteenth century.

Readdressing research questions

The first question:

> What is the distribution of the Irish English progressive in Hiberno-English from the beginning of the seventeenth to the end of the nineteenth century?

The distribution of the Irish English progressive increased chronologically, and with considerable contrast, considering that the seventeenth and eighteenth centuries showed no instances of this phenomenon. Based on this pattern, it might be argued that the Irish English progressive developed as a feature of Hiberno-English at a stage later than the eighteenth century, at least broadly considered. It is possible that a rise in Irish nationalism coinciding with the nineteenth century enhanced the use of certain dialectal features, owing to a desire on the part of speakers to express their culture or their membership within that culture or community. As mentioned, during the seventeenth and eighteenth centuries many Irish speakers had to supress both their language and their culture due to oppression from England and its monarchy.

IRISH PROGRESSIVE

The second research question:

What is the distribution of the **be** + **Verb** ending in **-ing** structure, or the standard progressive, regardless of the habitual aspect?

The distribution shows that the standard English progressive seems to have increased in frequency, at least in the form of *be* + *verb* ending in *-ing*, where the *be* search excludes lemmas. It is not clear whether increasing use of the progressive as a grammatical feature in Standard English set the scene for the Irish English progressive to emerge, or whether the habitual aspect transferred from Irish might have laid the foundation for this increase in the use progressive verbs.

The third research question:

How can the distribution of the Irish English progressive be categorized into different sentence types based on previous studies of the topic?

The study categorized the findings into the sentence types imperative and interrogative, as these were the ones identified. See table 3 below for sentence type distribution.

Sentence types	Occurrences	Normalized frequency
Imperative	15	28.45
Interrogative	2	3.8
Other	14	26.5
Total	31	58.8

Table 3: sentence type distribution

Since only the nineteenth century produced results which could be categorized according to the parameters of the question, that century alone offered a table covering the sought-after distribution and categorization into sentence types. The results show that the imperative sentence type was most frequent.

Conclusions

To sum up, utilizing corpus linguistic techniques to examine a discrete set of historical texts I have been able to offer new findings on the Irish English progressive and on the habitual aspect in Irish English. In particular, I suggest that while the seventeenth and eighteenth centuries offer us no written occurrences of the Irish English progressive, the nineteenth century appears to mark the real beginning of this feature, where imperative sentence structures seem to be dominant. I argue that overall use of the English progressive increased significantly during the same time the Irish English progressive came into being.

Acknowledgements

Lastly, I would like to give some acknowledgements. I would like first to thank both my supervisors, Gregory Darwin and Dan McIntyre, for sharing their vast knowledge and for the great support they have given me in my work as a PhD student so far. In addition, I would like to thank associate professor Christer Geisler for his immense help in writing this paper. I would also like give thanks to Uppsala university and the English department there, for letting me grow as a scholar and for offering such a thriving environment in which to do so.

The Early Medieval Topography and Toponymy of Armagh City: Trían Saxan and Connections with Anglo-Saxon England

Mícheál B. Ó Mainnín

Seissedhach do gran chorca
no trian d'airnibh dubcorcra
no do dercnaibh darach duinn
no do chnoibh falach finncuill–
fo ·gabhar cen tacha tinn
(i nArd) Macha ar oen (pinginn.)

A sixth-measure of oaten grain, /or a third-measure of dark purple sloes, / or of acorns of the brown oak, / or of nuts of a fair hazel cluster—/ all are to be had in full abundance / at Ard Macha for one penny.[1]

---

[1] Séan Mac Airt and Gearóid Mac Niocaill ed. and trans., *The Annals of Ulster (to A.D. 1131) (AU²)* (Dublin: Dublin Institute for Advanced Studies, 1983), s.a. 1032. The readings in the last line are confirmed by the copy of the text preserved in the *Annals of the Four Masters*: John O'Donovan, ed. and trans., *Annála Ríoghachta Éireann: Annals of the Kingdom of Ireland by the Four Masters, from the Earliest Period to the Year 1616 (AFM)*, 7 vols. (Dublin: Hodges, Smith and Co., 1848-51; reprint Dublin: de Búrca 1990), s.a. 1031. This set of annals also provides a preface to the verse: *Flaithbhertach Ua Néill do thoidheacht ó Róimh. As fri reimhes Flaithbhertaigh fo gaibhthi an connradh dimhór in Ard Macha amail as follus isin rand* . . . (Flaithbheartach Ua Neill returned from Rome. It was during the reign of Flaithbheartach that the very great bargain used to be got at Ard-Macha, as is evident in this quatrain . . .). There is no mention of Flaithbhertach, high-king of Ailech, in the corresponding entry in *AU* where the verse follows on the notice concerned with the death of Máel Tuile, bishop of Armagh, and his replacement by Áed ua Forréid. Flaithbhertach, who died in 1036, is given the epithet *in trosdáin* ("[Flaithbhertach] of the [pilgrim's] staff") in his obit in the Annals of Loch Cé, W.M. Hennessy, ed. and trans., *Annals of Loch Cé, A Chronicle of Irish Affairs from A.D. 1014 to A.D. 1590 (ALC)*, 2 vols. (London: Longmans & Co, 1871), s.a. 1036. The Annals of Loch Cé do not preserve the verse on Armagh, however.

MÍCHEÁL Ó MAINNÍN

Medieval Armagh and the 'Monastic Town'

Armagh city, ecclesiastical capital of Ireland, has more textual references to it than any other ecclesiastical settlement in early medieval Ireland.[2] The above verse, recorded in hand H[1] in the margin of the Trinity College Dublin copy of the Annals of Ulster, manuscript 1282 (H.1.8), under the year 1032, points to a thriving market economy in Armagh at a time when its affairs were of particular concern to the compilers and were probably being recorded locally.[3] In addition, one lexical item in the verse stands out in the present context, the word *trían* 'a third' which we encounter in the topography of the settlement in three distinct names: *Trían Mór*, *Trían Masáin* and *Trían Saxan*.[4] This essay is concerned with the origin and application of one of these names, Trían Saxan, and the potential light which it casts on connections between the church of Armagh and Anglo-Saxon England in the early medieval period in particular.

The annals abound with references to Armagh (in particular to its churches and other elements of its ecclesiastical topography) and build on the glimpses of the medieval settlement that are afforded to us by earlier sources which are concerned with the life of Saint Patrick. In the seventh-century Liber Angeli, for example, which has been described as constituting the 'foundation charter' of the city,[5] the core of the ecclesiastical settlement is described as an *urbs* (and also a *civitas*), in contradistinction to its

---

[2] Nicholas B. Aitchison, *Armagh and the Royal Centres in Early Medieval Ireland. Monuments, Cosmology and the Past* (Woodbridge: Boydell & Brewer), 225; Thomas Charles-Edwards, *Early Christian Ireland* (Cambridge: Cambridge University Press, 2000), 161.

[3] *AU*[2], Foreword, xii; Aitchison, *Armagh and the Royal Centres*, 226.

[4] On the basic meaning of *trían* (Modern Irish *trian*), "third part", see *Electronic Dictionary of the Irish Language* (*eDIL*), s.v. "1 trían," accessed 21 February 2024, http://www.dil.ie/41887. The Dictionary also notes that the word has the meaning "district, quarter" when applied to towns, and there is no doubting the ample evidence for this meaning in later place-names (see further below). However, it is my belief that trían is best understood in its primary sense as "third part/one of three parts" in the topography of medieval Armagh.

[5] Edel Bhreathnach, *Ireland in the Medieval World, AD 400-1000. Landscape, Kingship and Religion* (Dublin: Four Courts Press, 2014), 29, 194.

suburbana, the territory immediately surrounding it.[6] The extent to which this is an indication of some degree of urbanisation in Armagh (embryonic or otherwise) has been contested by scholars, with John Bradley and Charles Doherty in particular arguing the case for the existence in Ireland of pre-Viking 'monastic towns,' but with others taking a more skeptical view (for example, Howard Clarke, Colmán Etchingham, Cathy Swift, and Mary Valante).[7] Having said that, Anngret Simms and Howard Clarke

---

[6] Ludwig Bieler, *The Patrician Texts in the Book of Armagh*, Scriptores Latini Hiberniae 10 (Dublin: Dublin Institute for Advanced Studies, 1979), 184, ll. 5, 23, 25; 186, l. 18.

[7] The following list of sources is not exhaustive: R.A. Butlin, "Urban and Proto-Urban Settlements in Pre-Norman Ireland," in *The Development of the Irish Town*, ed. R.A. Butlin (London: Croom Helm, 1977); Helmut Jäger, "Entwicklungsphasen irischer Städte im Mittelalter," in *Civitatum Communitas: Studien zum Europäischen Städtewesen. Festschrift Heinz Stoob zum 65. Geburtstag*, ed. Franz Petri, Heinz Quirin and Helmut Jäger, 2 vols. (Cologne: Böhlau, 1984), 71-95; Charles Doherty, "The Monastic Town in Early Medieval Ireland," in *The Comparative History of Urban Origins in non-Roman Europe: Ireland, Wales, Denmark, Germany, Poland and Russia from the Ninth to the Thirteenth Century*, ed. H.B. Clarke and Anngret Simms (Oxford: British Archaeological Reports, 1985), 45-75; Leo Swan, "Monastic Proto-towns in Early Medieval Ireland: The Evidence of Aerial Photography, Plan Analysis and Survey," in *The Comparative History of Urban Origins in non-Roman Europe* [. . .]., ed. H.B. Clarke and Anngret Simms (Oxford: British Archaeological Reports, 1985), 77-102; Brian Graham, "Urban Genesis in Early Medieval Ireland," *Journal of Historical Geography* 13 (1987): 3-16; John Bradley, "The Monastic Town of Clonmacnoise," in *Clonmacnoise Studies Volume 1: Seminar Papers 1994*, ed. Heather A. King (Dublin: Dúchas, the Heritage Service, 1998); Mary Valante, "Reassessing the Irish 'Monastic Town'," *Irish Historical Studies* 31.121 (1998): 1-18; John Bradley, "Towards a Definition of the Irish Monastic Town," in *Aedificia Nova: Studies in Honour of Rosemary Cramp*, ed. C.E. Karkov and Helen Damico (Kalamazoo: Medieval Academy of America, 2008), 325-60; Colmán Etchingham, *The Irish Monastic Town: Is this a Valid Concept?* Kathleen Hughes Memorial Lectures 8 (Cambridge: University of Cambridge, Department of Anglo-Saxon, Norse and Celtic, 2010); H.B. Clarke, "Quo Vadis? Mapping the Irish 'Monastic Town'," in *Princes, Prelates and Poets in Medieval Ireland: Essays in Honour of Katharine Simms*, ed. Sean Duffy (Dublin: Four Courts Press, 2013), 261-78; Brian Graham, "Beyond the Fascicles: Spatial Form

recently have made a distinction between "three early medieval groups of proto-towns: Gaelic monastic towns, Viking seaports and Gaelic market towns," arguing that "Gaelic monastic towns are a distinctly Irish species resulting from the important role played by Early Christian monasteries as central places." Furthermore,

> [i]n canonical writings the precincts of monastic towns are described as consisting of three zones: *sanctus, sanctior and sanctissimus,* with the most holy at the core.[8] Each of these functional zones had their own enclosures and . . . these enclosures are reflected in the present-day composite town-plans of towns with their origin in monastic life. This is particularly obvious on the 1:2500 plans of Kells, Armagh and Tuam. The proto-urban functions of these early monastic places can be summarised as centre of education (schooling), patron of the arts (high crosses), keeper of treasures (in round towers), a provider of sanctuary and the location of a market.[9]

---

and Social Process," in *Maps & Texts. Exploring the Irish Historic Towns Atlas*, ed. H.B. Clarke and Sarah Gearty (Dublin: Royal Irish Academy, 2013), 257-65; Aidan O'Sullivan, Finbar McCormick, Thomas Kerr and Lorcan Harney, *Early Medieval Ireland AD 400-1100: The Evidence from Archaeological Excavations* (Dublin: Royal Irish Academy, 2014); Rebecca Wall Forrestal, "Studying Early Medieval Irish Urbanization: Problems and Possibilities," in *Space and Settlement in Medieval Ireland*, ed. Vicky McAlister and Terry Barry (Dublin: Four Courts Press, 2015); Catherine Swift, "Religion," in *More Maps & Texts. Sources and the Irish Historic Towns Atlas*, ed. H.B. Clarke and Sarah Gearty (Dublin: Royal Irish Academy, 2018), 67-86; Cóilín Ó Drisceoil, "From Gaelic Church Settlements to Anglo-Norman Towns: Problems and Possibilities," in H.B. Clarke and Sarah Gearty, eds., *More Maps & Texts. Sources and the Irish Historic Towns Atlas* (Dublin: Royal Irish Academy, 2018), 115-33.

[8] The reference here is to *Collectio Canonum Hibernensis*; see David Jenkins, *'Holy, Holier, Holiest': The Sacred Topography of the Early Medieval Irish Church* (Turnhout: Brepols, 2010).

[9] "Anngret Simms on the 'Monastic Town'," Royal Irish Academy February 2017; updated April 2020, accessed January 30, 2024, https://www.ria.ie/anngret-simms-monastic-town

MEDIEVAL ARMAGH

As can be seen from two interpretive plans of early medieval Armagh, one produced for the *Irish Historic Towns Atlas* (*IHTA*) in 2007 and the other by Tomás Ó Carragáin in 2010,[10] the inner enclosure of Armagh would come to encompass (in the fullness of time) not only the principal church but also subsidiary churches and the round tower. The second enclosure contained the abbot's house and the priory of the Céili Dé.[11] The area covered within these two enclosures is referred to collectively as *Ráith Arda Macha* 'the close of Ard Macha' (sometimes abbreviated as the Ráith).[12] A third enclosure is not marked on the *IHTA* map, but is thought to be discernible in the contemporary street plan (as noted by Simms above and illustrated by Ó Carragáin).[13]

Triads and Trians

The existence at monastic sites of three enclosures distinguished from each other in terms of relative sanctity is paralleled in Armagh by the

---

[10] Catherine McCullough and W.H. Crawford, *Irish Historic Towns Atlas No. 18. Armagh* (Dublin: Royal Irish Academy, 2007), 1; Tomás Ó Carragáin, *Churches in Early Medieval Ireland. Architecture, Ritual and Memory* (New Haven: Yale University Press, 2010), 62, fig. 64.

[11] The plans produced for the *IHTA* and by Ó Carragáin do not agree entirely; the latter locates the Abbey of Saints Peter and Paul outside the second enclosure whereas the former is not clear on where the boundary runs at this point. Also, Trían Mór is west of the medieval church according to Ó Carragáin (and Aitchison, *Armagh and the Royal Centres*, 247, fig. 61) but is placed to the south on the *IHTA* plan.

[12] For discussion of this name and its application, see Mícheál B. Ó Mainnín, "Narrative Construction and Toponymic Exploitation: *Ard Macha* and Related Names in Medieval Irish Texts," *Aiste. Studies in Gaelic Literature* 3 (2010): 1-19.

[13] Ó Carragáin, *Churches in Early Medieval Ireland*, 62, fig. 64. See also Aitchison, *Armagh and the Royal Centres*, 221, fig. 56, and 238, fig. 59; Kathleen Hughes and Ann Hamlin, *The Modern Traveller to the Early Irish Church* (Dublin: Four Courts, 1997; first edition 1977), 55-6. However, for a cautionary note on the interpretation of street patterns and their identification with earlier enclosures, see Ó Drisceoil, "From Gaelic Church Settlements to Anglo-Norman Towns," 128.

existence of other 'triads'.[14] One is the dedication of churches to all three national saints—Patrick, Brigit and Columba—and the location of these churches is of great interest: the church of St Patrick, as patron of Armagh, is at the centre; and beyond the most sacred core are St. Columba's Church to the north and St. Bridget's Church to the south, reflecting the location of their main churches elsewhere in Iona and Kildare.[15] Another triad is the division of the settlement beyond the Ráith into three *trena*,[16] the plural form of the word trían which we encountered in our item of verse at the

---

[14] It has been noted that "nowhere ... does one get triads with such profusion as in the Celtic languages," although "the case for a special Celtic cult of threeness is unproven." See Fergus Kelly, "Thinking in Threes: The Triad in Early Irish Literature", Sir John Rhŷs Memorial Lecture, *Proceedings of the British Academy* 125 (2004): 1-18, at 1-3. However, it is of interest in the present context that the text entitled *Trecheng Breth Féne (The Triads of Ireland)* begins with a list of the characteristics of thirty-one churches, the first of which is Armagh, and that the compiler is thought to have been a cleric; idem, 3, 6. It is also interesting to note that *Bethu Phátraic*, the Irish Life of the patron saint of Armagh, is divided into three books, hence its English title, the *Tripartite Life of Patrick*. Charles-Edwards, *Early Christian Ireland*, 191 and 346, notes that this structure is not particularly common in hagiographical texts more generally (although it is also found in *Vita Columbae*). The number three is of special significance in the Christian tradition because of the core doctrine of the holy trinity and it is possible that this is also relevant here.
[15] Aitchison, *Armagh and the Royal Centres*, 250-1.
[16] The thirds are referred to collectively in the annals in 1020: *Ard Macha do loscadh a tertkalaind Mái cona durthigib uile cenmotha in teach screbtra nama. ⁊ roloisced illtighi isna Trenaib ⁊ in damhliag mor, ⁊ in cloiccthech cona clogaib, ⁊ Damlíag na Togha ⁊ Damliag in Stabuill ⁊ in cathair proicepta ⁊ imadh oír ⁊ argait, ⁊ sét archena* (Armagh was burnt on the 3d of the Kalends of May, with all its prayer-houses, except only the library; and many houses were burnt in the Thirds, and the great stone-house, and the belfry with its bells, and the stone-house of the Togha(?), and the Stone-house of the Barn, and the pulpit, and abundance of gold and silver, and treasures besides.) Whitley Stokes ed. and trans., "The Annals of Tigernach," *Revue Celtique* 16 (1895): 374–419; 17 (1896): 6–33, 116–263, 337–420; 18 (1897): 9–59, 150–303, s.a. 1020. Reprinted in 2 vols. (Felinfach: Llanerch Publishers, 1993). The Trena are not mentioned in the version of this annal in AU, and the word has been mis-transcribed in AFM, s.a. 1020 (. . .ro loisccthi iol taighe is na treabhaibh . . .).

MEDIEVAL ARMAGH

outset:[17] *Trían Mór* 'great third', *Trían Masáin* 'Masán's third',[18] and *Trían Saxan* 'third of the Saxons/English'. All three names are encountered in the annals: Trían Mór is possibly implied in the reference to Trían Arda Macha

---

[17] On the declension of *trían* (Modern Irish *trian*), see *eDIL*, s.v. "1 trían," accessed 21 February 2024, http://www.dil.ie/41887 The nominative plural form as noted here is *trena* and this is also attested in the Early Modern Irish grammatical tracts which permit either *treana* or *trín* in the plural. That the *-e-* in *treana* is short in quantity is supported by the dative plural form in an accompanying line of verse from a poem by Gofraidh Fionn Ó Dálaigh (where the short vowel is confirmed by the deibhidhe rhyme): "rí nimhe 'n-a thrí **trean**aibh / go dtí im chridhe a chr**eideamh**ain." (The bold font illustrates the rhyming segments.) See Osborn Bergin, "Irish Grammatical Tracts [II, §§12-87]", supplement to *Ériu* 9 (1921-3), 61-124, at 121, §76, and Lambert McKenna ed. and trans, *Aithdioghluim Dána*, 2 vols. (Dublin: Irish Texts Society, 1939-40), I, §69, p. 263, v. 9cd.

[18] For discussion of this name, see Mícheál B. Ó Mainnín, "The Pan-Gaelic Onomasticon: The Case of *Gleann Masáin* and *Trian Masáin*," in *Onomastications: A Festschrift for Simon Taylor*, ed. Thomas Clancy (Glasgow, at press).

in the year 987,[19] and is recorded for certain in 1009,[20] 1092,[21] 1112,[22] 1150,[23] 1170[24] and 1173;[25] Trían Masáin is on record in 1112[26] and 1121;[27]

---

[19] *Laidhgnén, mac Cearbhaill, tighearna Fernmhaighe, do mharbhadh for lár Trín Arda Macha, lá Fearghal, mac Conaing, tighearna Oiligh,* ⁊ *la Cenél Eóghain* "Laidhgnen, son of Cearbhall, lord of Fearnmhagh, was slain in the middle of Trian-Arda-Macha, by Fearghal, son of Conaing, lord of Oileach, and the Cinel-Eoghain" (AFM, s.a. 987). Note, also, the use of singular trían in the phrase 'eter ráith ⁊ trían' (AU², s.a. 1074, 1189) discussed below; it could be argued that, rather than being used collectively with reference to all of the trena, the employment of trían in the phrase is primarily with the largest of the three 'thirds' in mind: Trían Mór. For the suggestion that trían is to be equated with suburbana in Liber Angeli, see note 35 below.

[20] *Maelan, .i. in Gai Moir, rí H. Dorthaind, do marbad do Cheniul Eogain i nArd Macha for lar Trin Moir tria comerghi na da sluagh* "Maelán i.e. of the large spear, king of Uí Dorthainn, was killed by the Cenél Eógain in the middle of the Trian Mór in Ard Macha as a result of a commotion of the two armies" (AU², s.a. 1009).

[21] *Raith Ard Macha cona tempull do loscadh i .iiii. Kł. September* ⁊ *sreth do triun mor* ⁊ *sreth do triun Saxan* (The *Ráith* of Ard Macha with its church was burned on the fourth of the Kalends of September [29 Aug.], and a stretch of the *Trian Mór* and a stretch of *Trian Saxan*) (AU², s.a. 1092). Cf. also AFM and ALC, s.a. 1092.

[22] *Raith Arda Macha cona tempull do loscadh in .x. Kł. Aprilis* ⁊ *da sreith Trin Masan* ⁊ *in tres sreith do Triun Mor* "The ráith of Ard Macha with its church was burned on the tenth of the Kalends of April [23 March], and two stretches of the Trian Masan and a third stretch of Trian Mór" (*AU²*, s.a. 1112; cf. AFM, s.a. 1112).

[23] *An leth tuaiscertach do Triun mhór Arda Macha do losccadh aidhche fhéile Cianáin* "The northern half of the Trian-mor of Ard-Macha was burned on the night of the festival of Cianan" (AFM, s.a. 1150).

[24] *Concobhar, mac Muircertaigh hUi Lochlainn, ri Ceneoil-Eogain,* ⁊ *ridomna Erenn uile, do marbadh do Aedh Bic Mac Canae* ⁊ *do Uib-Caraca[i]n, Dia-Sathairn Casc, ar lar Trin moir i n-Ard-Macha* "Concobhar, son of Muirchertach Ua Lochlainn, king of Cenel-Eogain, royal heir of all Ireland, was killed by Aedh Mac Cana the Little and by the Ui Caraca[i]n, Easter [Holy] Saturday [April 4], in the centre of the Great Third in Ard-Macha." William M. Hennessy and Bartholomew Mac Carthy, ed. and trans. *Annála Uladh: Annals of Ulster otherwise Annala Senait, Annals of Senat: A Chronicle of Irish Affairs from A.D.*

and Trían Saxan in 1092 and 1127.[28] By contrast, none of these names is recorded in Patrician material although there is a solitary reference to *Trían Conchobair* 'Conchobar's third' in *Bethu Phátraic*, the Irish Life of

---

431 to A.D. 1540 (AU[1]), 4 vols. (Dublin: A. Thom and Co. for Her Majesty's Stationery Office, 1887-1901; reprint, de Búrca 1998), s.a. 1170. Cf. also AFM, s.a. 1170.

[25] *Crech mor la Aedh Mac Oengusa ⁊ la Clainn-Aedha, co roaircset Trian mor (i n-Ard Macha). Ocus romarbadh in fer sin i cind tri mis, iar n-arcain Aird-Macha do* "Great foray by Aedh Mac Oenghusa and by the Clann-Aedha, so that they pillaged the Great Third (in Ard-Macha). And that man was killed before three months, after the pillaging of Ard Macha by him" (AU[1], s.a 1173).

[26] Cf. note 22 above.

[27] *Da sreith Trin Mhasan o dhorus Ratha co crois mBrigte do loscadh* "Two stretches of Trian Masan from the gate of the *ráith* to the cross of Brigit were burned" (AU[2], s.a. 1121). Cf also AFM, s.a. 1121. This event is not recorded in ALC.

[28] These references are discussed individually below.

MÍCHEÁL Ó MAINNÍN

Patrick.[29] This appears to be located in the vicinity of Armagh and may be an alias for the greatest of the three trena: Trían Mór.[30]

The word trian (earlier trían) is reasonably well-attested in Irish toponymy (although, in contrast, strikingly rare as a place-name element in Gaelic Scotland). It is also present historically in the Isle of Man where it became established as the term for the basic unit in the island's historical

---

[29] Kathleen Mulchrone, ed. and trans., *Bethu Phátraic. The Tripartite Life of Patrick. Volume I. Text and Sources* (Dublin: Royal Irish Academy, 1939), 140, l. 2789; Whitley Stokes, ed. and trans., *The Tripartite Life of Patrick with Other Documents Relating to That Saint*, 2 vols., Rerum Britannicarum Medii Aevi Scriptores 89 (London: Eyre and Spottiswoode, 1887), 1:236. See also *Trianconcavair ager iuxta Ardmacham*, John Colgan, *Trias Thaumaturga* with an Introduction by Pádraig Ó Riain (Dublin: Edmund Burke, 1997), 718 (index). Originally published as *Triadis Thaumaturgae seu Divorum Patricii, Columbae, et Brigidae, Trium Veteris et Maioris Scotiae, seu Hiberniae, Sanctorum Insulae* (Louvain: The Irish College 1647). The reference cited to the text is 'pa. 133, c, 77' but I have been unable to locate it on that page. There is a later reference in 1367 to a Trientulcha (probably representing the Irish *Trian Tulcha* "third of the hill(ock) or mound") in the Register of Archbishop Sweteman where it is said to be located in the Archbishop's "tenement of Armagh." Brendan Smith ed. and trans., *The Register of Milo Sweteman, Archbishop of Armagh, 1361-1380* (Dublin: Irish Manuscripts Commission, 1996), 132, §134. It is not clear what relationship there may be (if any) between this trían and the three trena of the annals. On the declension and translation of tulach, see *eDIL*, s.v. "tulach," accessed 31 January 2024, http://www.dil.ie/42443

[30] On the comparable use of the aliases *Ard Saileach*, *Druim Sailech* and *Ráith Sailech* for *Ard Macha* as a whole, see Ó Mainnín, "Narrative Construction and Toponymic Exploitation", 5-10. There is a reference to what must be a distinct Trían Conchobair in *Mesca Ulad* where the province of Ulster is divided into three portions assigned to Conchobor, Fintan mac Néill Níamglonnaig and Cú Chulainn. Conchobar's portion is said to extend from Tráig Bali to Tráig Tola (*á Thráig Bali co Tráig Tola i nUltaib*); J. Carmichael Watson ed., *Mesca Ulad* (Dublin: Dublin Institute for Advanced Studies, 1941), 2, ll. 26-7. Aitchison has suggested that Armagh's trena are "not thirds, but quarters" and cites the occurrence of Trían Conchobair in *Bethu Phátraic* as evidence for this. However, he suggests elsewhere that Trían Conchobair may have been an earlier name for Trían Saxan, which seems to support the view that the Ráith of Ard Macha was surrounded by three 'thirds' rather than four 'quarters'; see Aitchison, *Armagh and the Royal Centres*, 229, 251.

administrative system, in descending order: sheadings, parishes, treens, quarterlands and intacks.[31] It is now obsolete, however, as an administrative unit. To return to Ireland, the Placenames Database of Ireland (logainm.ie) lists 67 contemporary placenames which contain the word trian (and its diminutive triainín) as a generic or specific element (including two instances which parallel our Trían Mór, one in Sligo and one in Leitrim). There are possibly a further 8 examples of trian in the Northern Ireland counties, giving a provisional total of 75 for the whole island of Ireland. The element has a marked western concentration and there are many examples also in the south; there are no examples at all, however, from County Armagh.[32] With regards to the medieval period, the revised version of *Onomasticon Goedelicum* notes 18 place-names with trían as a generic (excluding our names in Armagh city).[33] While the great majority of these do not appear to have any ecclesiastical connection, the annals allude to two other monasteries in a manner which provides striking parallels with Armagh. In the year 1111, lightning struck Downpatrick and set fire to its monastery, *eter ráith ⁊ trian* 'both fort/close and third'.[34] The phraseology of the coupling of ráith and trían here is exactly the same as elsewhere in

---

[31] George Broderick, *Placenames of the Isle of Man*, 7 vols. (Tübingen: Niemeyer, 1994–2005), 1:xiv-xvii.

[32] See https://www.placenamesni.org for names containing the anglicised versions 'trean', 'treen', 'trin' and 'trien', accessed January 31, 2024. The one example marked in Armagh in the distribution map for trian on logainm.ie, Tuath Threana (Tiranny), is not derived from the place-name element *trian* but from a personal name Trian. Accessed January 31, 2024, Logainm. The Placenames Database of Ireland, https://www.logainm.ie/ga /gluais/206-trian. Logainm prefers the form placename.

[33] Donnchadh Ó Corráin, A Digital Edition of Edmund Hogan's *Onomasticon Goedelicum* (Dublin 1910). Revised and Corrected by Donnchadh Ó Corráin, accessed 31 January 2024, https://www.dias.ie/2017/04/01/onomasticon-goedelicum/

[34] *Teine di ait do loscadh Duin da Lethglas eter raith ⁊ trian* "Lightning burned Dún da Lethglas, both *ráith* and *trian*" (AU², s.a. 1111). See, also, AFM, s.a. 1111 and *ALC* s.a. 1111. It is possible that the division of ecclesiastical sites into trena (at Armagh and perhaps elsewhere) was employed as a form of fire break, see Doherty, "The Monastic Town", 66, and Ciarán J. Devlin, *The Making of Medieval Derry* (Dublin: Four Courts Press, 2018; first edition 2013), 133.

the annals with reference to Armagh;[35] in 1074,[36] and again in 1189,[37] we are told that Armagh was burned "eter ráith ⁊ trían." Our second example relates to the death of one Aillill mac Eughain in 908 who is described as *princeps Triuin Corcaighi* (superior or abbot of the Trían of Cork) in his obit in the Annals of Ulster (AU², s.a. 908).[38] It has also been suggested by Nick Aitchison that Clonmacnoise may have had a similar coupling of ráith and trían, but this is less certain.[39]

Location of Trían Saxan

A striking feature of the contemporary streetscape of Armagh city is the presence in its nomenclature of a further triad: Irish Street, Scotch Street and English Street. Intriguingly, in the light of the parallels noted a moment ago, the urban centre of Downpatrick is also divided into Irish Street, Scotch

---

[35] Note Aitchison, *Armagh and the Royal Centres*, 227, on the singular use of *trían* here where the phrase "appears to mean all Armagh" and may correspond with the distinction noted above {p. 2} which is made in the Liber Angeli between the *urbs* and *suburbana* of the settlement. However, see also note 19 above.

[36] *Ard Macha do loscadh Dia Mairt iar mBelltaine cona uilibh templaibh ⁊ cloccaibh eter raith ⁊ trian* (Ard Macha was burned on the Tuesday after Mayday [6 May] with all its churches and bells, both the Ráith and the Third) (AU², s.a. 1074; cf. AFM and ALC, s.a. 1074).

[37] *Ard Macha do loscadh o crosa[ibh] Brighti co reicles Brighti, eter Raith ⁊ Trian ⁊ tempul* (Ard-Macha was burned from the crosses of Brigit to the Regular church of Brigit, both Close and Third and church) (AU¹, s.a. 1189; cf. also AFM and ALC, s.a. 1189).

[38] Trían Corcaighi may parallel the reference to Trían Arda Macha (see note 19 above), i.e. the largest trían being associated most closely with the whole settlement.

[39] Aitchison, *Armagh and the Royal Centres*, 228. Two entries in the annals record the burning of a *tertia parte* of Clonmacnoise in the years 818 and 835; however, in 816 and 834, the conflagration afflicted the *maiore parte* (AU¹, s.a. 816, 818, 834, 835). The sense may be quantitative rather than topographical or toponymic (unless we take the latter to be a latinisation of Trían Mór). Note, also, the burning of a *tertia parte* elsewhere, at Swords in 1020: *Cluain Iraird ⁊ Cluain M Nois ⁊ Sord Coluim Cille tertia parte cremate sunt* (Cluain Iraird and Cluain Moccu Nóis and a third of Sord Coluim Cille were [also] burned) (*AU²*, s.a. 1020; see *ALC*, s.a. 1020).

MEDIEVAL ARMAGH

Street and English Street,[40] and the presence of a tripartite division such as this in the urban toponymy of two Ulster towns may not seem surprising in the light of the ethnically distinct landscapes which emerged in this part of Ireland in the aftermath of the Plantation of Ulster.[41] Nonetheless, there is more to the situation than that in Armagh as there is a clear semantic connection between English Street (first on record in Rocque's map of the city in 1760) and one of the three trena, Trían Saxan.[42] Furthermore, evidence for a direct topographical connection between the two names is ascertainable from a comparison of the detail contained in inquisitions and patents which relate to the property of the Abbey of St. Peter and St. Paul in the early seventeenth century and the modern streetscape. These sources allude to a street called Bore(ne)triensassanagh et var.,[43] an anglicised

---

[40] R.H. Buchanan and Anthony Wilson, *Irish Historic Towns Atlas. No. 8 Downpatrick* (Dublin: Royal Irish Academy, 1997), 4-5, 9. Note the 1708 rental which records an Irish Quarter and a Scotch Quarter.

[41] Carrickfergus, for example, had its Irish and Scotch Quarters outside the walls of the town in the seventeenth century and this reflects real ethnic divisions there (Gilbert Camblin, *The Town in Ulster. An Account of the Origin and Building of the Towns of the Province and the Development of Their Rural Setting* [. . .]. (Belfast: Wm. Mullan & Son, 1951), 52); Philip Robinson, *Irish Historic Towns Atlas. No. 2 Carrickfergus* (Dublin: Royal Irish Academy, 1986), 5. In Armagh, however, there does not appear to be any evidence for separate Irish, Scottish, and English settlements within the city.

[42] John Rocque, *A Topographical Map of the County Armagh to which is Anex'd the Plans of Newry and Armagh* (London: J. Rocque, 1760). Paterson states that the name English Street (together with Irish Street) first makes its appearance in the rentals in 1671, ten years later than the first occurrence of "Scottish Street" in a rental dating to *c*.1661 (T.G.F Paterson, "Armagh City Streets," in *Harvest Home. The Last Sheaf. A Selection from the Writings of T.G.F. Paterson Relating to County Armagh*, edited with an Introduction by E. Estyn Evans (Dundalk: Dundalgan Press for the Armagh County Museum, 1975; first published as "Armagh Street-names" in the *Bulletin of the Ulster Place-Name Society* 1 (1952-3): 18-24), 46-55, at 49). However, this is not noted in *IHTA Armagh*, 10-2 (for the sources, see 27 (s.v. Rentals)).

[43] The spelling with the article is more frequent (although not all of the sources concerned are independent witnesses). *Inquisitionum in Officio Rotulorum Cancellariae Hiberniae Asservatorum Repertorium* vol. ii (Ulster), ed. James

spelling which may represent the Irish *Bóthar Triain/Trín Sasanach* 'Trian Sasanach road' or *Bóthar an Triain/Trín Sasanaigh* 'road of the *Trian Sasanach*' (in the latter, Sasanach functions as a qualifying adjective while, in the former, it is a substantive). It is clear from the context that this street is to be identified with modern Abbey Street which joins Upper English Street north of the medieval cathedral.[44] This is extremely valuable evidence in determining the location of one of our three trena as William Reeves has noted: Trían Saxan was the trían or third which covered an area now "embraced by Upper English and Abbey Streets, and from it English Street probably derived its name".[45]

Trían Saxan in the Annals and Later Sources

There are two references in the annals to Trían Saxan, as we have seen, and these date to the end of the eleventh and early twelfth centuries. However, there is evidence to suggest that it (and the other trena) continued to be preserved as part of the topography of the city until the later Middle Ages and into the seventeenth century. Both Trían Saxan (Ternsaxan *recte* Trensaxan) and Trían Mór (trenmor) are recorded in the Register of Archbishop Sweteman in a rental which, if contemporary with the tenure of the archbishop, dates to the period 1361x80,[46] and Trían Saxan appears in a

---

Hardiman (Dublin: George and John Grierson and Martin Keene, 1829), 4 Jacobus I (1614); *Irish Patent Rolls of James I: Facsimile of the Irish Record Commissioner's Calendar Prepared Prior to 1830*. Foreword by Margaret C. Griffith (Dublin: Stationery Office for the Irish Manuscripts Commission, 1966), 391b (1618), 534a (1620).

[44] See *IHTA Armagh*, 10, which does not identify Borenetriensassenagh and its variants directly with English Street but there seems no reason to doubt the connection between the two names.

[45] William Reeves, *The Ancient Churches of Armagh* (Lusk: printed for the author, 1860; reprinted in the *Ulster Journal of Archaeology* 2 (1896): 194-204; 3 (1897): 193-5; 4 (1898): 205-28; 5 (1899): 220-7; 6 (1900): 24-33, at 212. See also Paterson, "Armagh City Streets," 47.

[46] The title and earlier part of the document is lost; we have nothing to date it precisely, therefore. Smith, *The Register of Milo Sweteman*, 153, §155.

later rental dating to 1660 in the form *Trensasina*.⁴⁷ This suggests that the name now had taken on the modern form of the word in Irish for 'English (people)' and was known in Irish as Trian Sasanach (and this is also clear from the form used in the road name noted above).

To return to the annals, the earliest of our two references, dating to 1092, records the burning of 'a stretch' of Trían Saxan and also of Trían Mór (presumably with reference to a row of houses) in a fire which seems to have decimated the Ráith.⁴⁸ The annal entry of 1127 makes more gruesome reading; it records the beheading of one Raghnall, grandson of Riabach, by the Airthir who had found him (taking refuge, possibly) in a house in Trían Saxan:

> *Airthir do ghabail taighi Flainn m Sinaigh i triun Saxan for Raghnall m m Riabaigh, aidhci Luain Inite ⁊ a dichennadh leó.*

> The Airthir stormed a house belonging to Flann son of Sínach in the Trian Saxan against Raghnall grandson of Riabach on the eve of Shrove Monday [14 Feb.] and he was beheaded by them (AU², s.a. 1127)⁴⁹

Flann was clearly a member of Clann Sínaich, the family which held the abbacy of Armagh in continuous succession from the time of Dub dá Leithe (d. 998), brother of the illustrious poet Eochaid ua Flainn/Flannucáin (d. 1004), until the death of Muirchertach in 1134.⁵⁰ There is no mention of a 'Flann son of Sínach' in the surviving genealogies, as far as I am aware.⁵¹

---

[47] Glancy appends the title "St." to his transcription of the name from this source but this is absent from the copy of the original document in the Public Record Office of Northern Ireland, T/729/1B, 163-4. Michael Glancy, "The Incidence of the Plantation on the City of Armagh," *Seanchas Ard Mhacha* 1.2 (1955): 115-60, at 133.
[48] See note 21 above.
[49] Cf. *ALC*, s.a. 1127 which also records this event.
[50] Mícheál B. Ó Mainnín, "Eochaid ua Flainn is Eochaid ua Flannucáin: Súil Úr ar an bhFianaise," Léann. Iris Chumann Léann na Litríochta 2 (2009): 75-104, at 79-80.
[51] For the genealogies relating to Clann Sínaich, see Nollaig Ó Muraíle ed. and trans., *Leabhar Mór na nGenealach: The Great Book of Irish Genealogies*,

However, eight years later in 1135 the Annals of the Four Masters record the death of one Fland Ua Sionaigh, 'keeper of the Crozier of Jesus (*Bachall Íosa*)',[52] which was the chief relic of the church of Armagh and reputed to have belonged to Saint Patrick.[53] Fland Ua Sionaigh is identifiable with Flann son of Colmán son of Sínach in the genealogies;[54] it is possible, therefore, that the form of his name in the annal of 1135 is to be taken literally as Fland ua Sionaigh 'Fland grandson of Sínach' rather than as evidence of an otherwise unattested surname Ua Sionaigh.[55] If so, the

---

Compiled (1645-66) by Dubhaltach Mac Fhirbhisigh (Dublin: de Búrca, 2003), 5 vols., §309.1-4; J.B. Arthurs, "Early Septs and Territories of Co. Armagh," *Bulletin of the Ulster Place-names Society* 2 (1954): 45-55, at 51; M.A. O'Brien, *Corpus Genealogiarum Hibernian*, vol. 1 (Dublin: Dublin Institute for Advanced Studies, 1962), 146 e 12 (cf. also 334 ab 45); Kuno Meyer, "The Laud Genealogies and Tribal Histories," *Zeitschrift für celtische Philologie* 8 (1912): 291-338, at 323.

[52] *Fland Ua Sionaigh, maor bachla Iosa, décc iar naithrighe tocchaidhe* "Flann Ua Sinaigh, keeper of the Bachall-Isa, died after good penance" (AFM s.a. 1135).

[53] For discussion and references to *Bachall Íosa*, see Sarah Christine Erskine, "Is the *Cloc in Édachta* St. Patrick's Oldest and Most Important Medieval Bell-relic?" *Journal of the Royal Society of Antiquaries of Ireland* 142–143 (2012–2013): 74–85; idem, "St. Patrick's Bachall Isu: its Origins, Traditions, and Rise to Prominence as Armagh's Premier Relic," *Eolas* 6 (2013): 41–67. Aitchison, *Armagh and the Royal Centres*, 258-9, 273; Charles-Edwards, *Early Christian Ireland*, 278-9; A.T. Lucas, "The Social Role of Relics and Reliquaries in Ancient Ireland," *Journal of the Royal Society of Antiquaries of Ireland* 116 (1986): 5-37.

[54] Ó Muraíle, *Leabhar Mór na nGenealach*, §309.1; Arthurs, "Early Septs and Territories of Co. Armagh," 51.

[55] There is no evidence for a surname Ua Síonaigh in Armagh. However, there is little evidence for a surname Mac/Mac Meic Síonaigh either; see further Ó Mainnín, "Eochaid ua Flainn," 89-90. If there had been such a surname in the past, it is possible that there might have been variation between the *Ua* and *Mac Meic* prefixes (as in Ua/Mac Meic Lachlainn). The latter formation was contracted to *Mac* (as in Mac Lachlainn) from the twelfth century and new surnames in *Mac*, which skipped out the "*mac meic* phase" altogether, developed from about 1200; Matthew Hammond, "The Development of *Mac* Surnames in the Gaelic World," in *Personal Names and Naming Practices in Medieval Scotland* (Woodbridge: Boydell & Brewer, 2019), 100–143, at 103, 129. See also Diarmuid Ó Murchadha, "The Formation of Gaelic Surnames in Ireland:

'Flann m[ac] Sínaigh' alluded to in the annal of 1127 might possibly have been a brother of Colmán. A further possibility is that the annal has omitted a second *m* (compare *Raghnall m[ac] m[eic] Riabaigh* in the same entry) in which case the Flann in both the annals of 1127 and 1135 may refer to the same person: *Flann m[ac] m[eic] Sínaigh* alias *Fland ua Sionaigh*. Reeves also notes that the keeper of the Book of Armagh (*Canóin Pátraicc*) had a tenement near the foot of Abbey Street; and suggests that the keeper of St. Patrick's Bell also dwelt hereabouts "in all probability".[56] It is clear, therefore, that Trían Saxan had some very important residents, some of whom also held extensive lands in the rural hinterland by virtue of their office as in the case of the parish of *Baile an Mhaoir*/Ballymoyer 'the farmstead of the maor/steward' in south Armagh, which derives its name from its possession by the hereditary keeper of the Book of Armagh, and *Lurga Uí Mhealláin*/Lurgyvallen, which preserves the memory of the hereditary keepers of St. Patrick's Bell.

Irish Connections with Anglo-Saxon England

What of the Saxain from whom Trían Saxan derived its name? Have we a context in which their presence in medieval Armagh may be explained? It would be impossible to cover adequately all the possibilities here; Fiona Edmonds has considered an extensive sweep of time in the relationship between Ireland and England (from the seventh to the eleventh centuries) and shown that the links between the Gaelic world and Northumbria in particular were enduring, varied and dynamic. Indeed, she has argued that the eleventh century was "a high-point of Gaelic linguistic influence on the former Northumbrian kingdom", albeit this influence was not just transmitted from Ireland but also from the Isle of Man and Scotland.[57] There is more than one potential horizon for contact between Armagh and England, therefore; we should note, for example, the presence

---

Choosing the Eponyms," *Nomina. Journal of the Society for Name Studies in Britain and Ireland* 22 (1999): 25-43; Kay Muhr and Liam Ó hAisibéil, *The Oxford Dictionary of Family Names of Ireland (ODFNI)* (Oxford: Oxford University Press, 2021), xxv-xxvi, 506-7, 592.

[56] Reeves, *The Ancient Churches of Armagh*, 212.

[57] Fiona Edmonds, *Gaelic Influence in the Northumbrian Kingdom: the Golden Age and the Viking Age* (Woodbridge: Boydell, 2019), 172; see also 15, 18, 219-22.

of Irish scholars at the courts of King Alfred the Great and King Æthelstan in the late ninth and early tenth centuries, and the particular link provided by the Gospels of Macdurnan—named for their scribe Máel Brígte mac Tornáin (d. 927), abbot of Armagh—which Æthelstan presented to Christ Church Canterbury.[58]

I have chosen to focus on the early medieval period, the Golden Age of ecclesiastical connection between Ireland and England, because of Armagh's prominence in the history of the Irish church.[59] Connections between Ireland and England in this domain have been the subject of considerable interest, and the impact of the establishment of an Irish monastery on the island of Lindisfarne in Northumbria by Saint Aidan in or around 635 AD is well known. The invitation to Aidan was extended by Oswald son of Æthelfrith who, as a Northumbrian prince, had spent a period of exile in Iona (founded in 563 AD) and Scottish Dál Riada from 616 (during the reign of King Edwin of Northumbria), but who had returned with his brother Oswiu to Northumbria upon Edwin's death in 633.[60] Oswald was to succeed his own brother, Eanfrith, as king in *c.* 634 and he, in turn, was succeeded by Oswiu in *c.*642. Indeed, Oswiu's son, Aldfrith (d. 705),[61] is known as Fland Fína mac Ossu in Irish tradition and is credited

---

[58] See Hughes, "Evidence for Contacts between the Churches of the Irish and the English," 65-6; Dáibhí Ó Cróinín, *Early Medieval Ireland 400-1200* (London and New York: Longman, 1995), 229.

[59] I acknowledge the temporal distance between this period and the earliest reference in the sources to Trían Saxan (in 1092). However, there can be considerable gaps in the record and the name is likely to be much earlier in date (see further below). Note the striking example of the name Slieve Carna on William Bald's map of County Mayo (1816) which appears as *Mons Cairnn* in the eight-century Additamenta in the Book of Armagh. No record of the name survives in the intervening period of over 1000 years; Nollaig Ó Muraíle, "Some Thoughts on Matters Onomastic," *Journal of the Galway Archaeological and Historical Society* 53 (2001): 23-46, at 30.

[60] For more detail on this and on what follows, see Colin A. Ireland, *The Gaelic Background of Old English Poetry before Bede* (Berlin and New York: De Gruyter, 2022).

[61] His mother was Irish, and he is said to have been a grandson on the maternal side of Colmán Rímid (d. 604), joint high-king of Ireland. Colin A. Ireland, "Aldfrith of Northumbria and the Irish Genealogies," *Celtica* 22 (1991): 64-78, at 68.

with works in Irish, particularly *Bríathra/Roscada Flainn Fína maic Ossu*.[62] We are also aware of Irish connections with other English churches including York, Glastonbury, and Canterbury (in the latter case involving the attendance of Irish students at the 'Canterbury School' founded by the archbishop, Theodore of Tarsus, and his companion, Hadrian, sometime after his appointment in AD 669).[63]

In terms of traffic in the other direction, the Synod of Whitby, called in 664 to settle the question of the calculation of the date of Easter, resulted in Colmán (then bishop at Lindisfarne) withdrawing at first to Iona for four years and then permanently to Ireland in protest at the decision to abandon the 'northern' Irish custom. Having first settled in Inishbofin off the coast of Galway in 668, he and his community (which included English monks) established the monastery known as *Mag nÉo na Sacsan* 'Mayo of the Saxons' (now Mayo Abbey in Co. Mayo) sometime around the year 673 which continued to maintain a strong connection with England until the end of the eighth century.[64] Indeed, the three bishops of Mayo in our period of

---

[62] Colin A. Ireland, ed. and trans., *Old Irish Wisdom Attributed to Aldfrith of Northumbria: An Edition of Bríathra Flainn Fhína maic Ossu*, MRTS, 205 (Tempe, Arizona: Arizona Center for Medieval and Renaissance Studies, 1999). For the possibility that Bangor was the place where Aldfrith was educated, see Ireland, *The Gaelic Background of Old English Poetry*, 75, 180, 194, 333. See also, Colin A. Ireland, "Where Was King Aldfrith of Northumbria Educated? An Exploration of Seventh-Century Insular Learning," *Traditio* 70 (2015): 29-73.

[63] On connections with various parts of England, see Ireland, *The Gaelic Background of Old English Poetry*, 4, 220-1, 226-7, 260, 294, 299; Charles-Edwards, *Early Christian Ireland*, 8-9, 309-11, 437; Michael W. Herren, "Scholarly Contacts between the Irish and the Southern English in the Seventh Century," *Peritia. Journal of the Medieval Academy of Ireland* 12 (1998): 24-53; Clare Stancliffe, "The Irish Tradition in Northumbria after the Synod of Whitby," in *The Lindisfarne Gospels: New Perspectives*, ed. Richard Gameson (Leiden: Brill, 2017), 19-42.

[64] For the possible date of the foundation of Mag nÉo na Sacsan and some general discussion of the endurance of its connections with England, see Ireland, *The Gaelic Background of Old English Poetry*, 225-6, 326-9, 350. On continuing connections between Ireland and Northumbria in the aftermath of the Synod of Whitby, see Kathleen Hughes, "Evidence for Contacts between the Churches of the Irish and the English from the Synod of Whitby to the Viking Age," in

whom the records speak with certainty were all English: Eadwine (d. 773) from 768,[65] Leodfrith from 773, and Ealdwulf from 786.[66] Garallt, whose obit is recorded in the annals in 732,[67] was also English although his status as a bishop is less certain.[68] In any case, there is evidence that Mag nÉo was at the centre of a larger "cluster of pilgrim houses" in south Connacht, including *Tech Saxan* "house of the Saxons" (Tisaxon in Monivea in Galway),[69] which has been described as a 'daughter-house' of Mayo.[70] There is a second Tech Saxan/Tisaxon in Cork (a parish name and the name of two related townlands within that parish, Tisaxon Beg and Tisaxon

---

England before the Conquest: Studies in Primary Sources Presented to Dorothy Whitelock, ed. Peter Clemoes and Kathleen Hughes (Cambridge: Cambridge University Press, 1971), 49-67.

[65] See *AU²*, s.a. 773 for his death notice where his name is Gaelicised as Aedán. His name is now thought to be preserved in the place-name Islandeady in Mayo. Fiachra Mac Gabhann, "The Place-Names of Mayo," in *Mayo. History and Society*, ed. Gerard Moran and Nollaig Ó Muraíle (Dublin: Geography Publications, 2014), 101-32, at 107, 123 n. 1; 127 n. 70. Mac Gabhann cites Nollaig Ó Muraíle as his source for this suggestion; the latter had previously held a different view. Nollaig Ó Muraíle, *Mayo Places: Their Names and Origins* (Dublin: FNT, 1985), 49-50.

[66] Vera Orschel, "The Early History of Mayo of the Saxons," in *Mayo History and Society*, ed. Gerard Moran and Nollaig Ó Muraíle (Dublin: Geography Publications, 2014), 77-99, at 85-6, 88-9. Máire Ní Mhaonaigh, "Of Saxons, a Viking and Normans: Colmán, Gerald and the Monastery of Mayo," in *Proceedings of the British Academy* 157: *Anglo-Saxon/Irish Relations before the Vikings*, ed. James Graham-Campbell and Michael Ryan (Oxford: Oxford University Press for the British Academy, 2009), 411-26, at 417.

[67] *Pontifex Maighe Heu Saxonum, Garaalt, obiit* "The pontiff of Mag Eó na Saxan, Gerald, died" (AU², s.a. 732).

[68] Orschel, "The Early History of Mayo of the Saxons," 81, 84, 85; see also Ní Mhaonaigh, "Of Saxons, a Viking and Normans," 417-9.

[69] Logainm. The Placenames Database of Ireland, https://www.logainm.ie/ga/20264, accessed 31 January 2024.

[70] Joseph Mannion, "Tech Saxan: An Anglo-Saxon Monastic Settlement in Early Medieval East Galway," *Journal of the Galway Archaeological and Historical Society* 60 (2008): 9-21, at 16. Note also *Cnoc Sacsan* (now Knocksaxon in Templemore in Mayo) and possibly Inis an Ghaill Chrábhaidh and Teampall an Oilithrigh elsewhere in Connacht which possibly may be connected with Anglo-Saxon clerics; Orschel, "The Early History of Mayo of the Saxons," 82-3.

More),[71] and further evidence for connections with England elsewhere in that county in the case of *Tulach Léis* (Tullylease) which has been recorded in the form Tulach Léis na Saxan et var. in *Félire Óengusso* "The Martyrology of Oengus."[72] A richly decorated slab "with close Anglo-Saxon parallels" commemorating an Anglo-Saxon saint "Berechtuine" survives in Tullylease;[73] this saint is to be distinguished from another Anglo-Saxon saint, Berrihert, whose cult is celebrated elsewhere in Munster.[74] The latter is commemorated in the townland name Cill Bheircheirt (Kilberrihert/Kilberehert), of which there are two examples in Cork (one in the parish of Aghabulloge,[75] and the other in Knocktemple),[76] and one in Kerry.[77] There is also a Saint Beirrihert's Kyle (derived from the Irish *Cill Bheircheirt*) in the Glen of Aherlow in Tipperary.[78] This suggests

---

[71] Logainm. The Placenames Database of Ireland, https://www.logainm.ie/ga/767 See also https://www.logainm.ie/ga/11109 and https://www.logainm.ie/ga/11110, accessed 31 January 2024.

[72] Whitley Stokes, ed. and trans., *Félire Óengusso Céli Dé. The Martyrology of Oengus the Culdee*, Henry Bradshaw Society 29 (London: Harrison and Sons, 1905), 256, 258n8.

[73] Its inscription reads *quicumquae hunc titulum legerit orat pro berechtuine* and it has been noted that the Greek cross on the slab is reminiscent of the cross on folio 26v of the Lindisfarne Gospels; see Isabel Henderson and Elisabeth Okasha, "The Early Christian Inscribed and Carved Stones of Tullylease, Co. Cork," *Cambridge Medieval Celtic Studies* 24 (1992): 1-36, at 15-7, 22-4, 34. See also Hughes and Hamlin, *The Modern Traveller to the Early Irish Church*, 91.

[74] Fiona Edmonds, "The Practicalities of Communication between Northumbrian and Irish Churches, *c*.635-735," in *Proceedings of the British Academy* 157: *Anglo-Saxon/Irish Relations before the Vikings*, ed. James Graham-Campbell and Michael Ryan (Oxford: Oxford University Press for the British Academy, 2009), 129-47, at 143-4.

[75] Logainm. The Placenames Database of Ireland, https://www.logainm.ie/ga/11437, accessed 31 January 2024.

[76] Logainm. The Placenames Database of Ireland, https://www.logainm.ie/ga/10700, accessed 31 January 2024.

[77] Logainm. The Placenames Database of Ireland, https://www.logainm.ie/ga/24628, accessed 31 January 2024.

[78] Logainm. The Placenames Database of Ireland, https://www.logainm.ie/ga/1416113, accessed 31 January 2024. There is another

the existence of a related cluster of names in these three counties. There are also dedications to Saint Cuthbert of Lindisfarne in Ireland: *Cill Mochuidbhricht*/Kilmahuddrick, a townland and parish in Dublin,[79] and possibly Mulhuddart, another parish in Dublin (whose current Irish name has been confirmed as Mullach Eadrad which may suggest another possibility, a connection with St. Eadbert of Lindisfarne).[80] There is one further monastery which (as in the case of Mayo) received special mention in the Venerable Bede's *Historia Ecclesiastica Gentis Anglorum* although there is no evidence for any formal nexus which connected them.[81] This is the monastery of Rath Melsigi which was located in the townland and parish of Clonmelsh in County Carlow,[82] and which had Anglo-Saxons among its community from 651,[83] seventeen years prior to the arrival of their

---

ecclesiastical site nearby at Toureen Peacaun (https://www.logainm.ie/ga/1416133) which has been shown to have an Anglo-Saxon connection. The inscription on its east cross includes an English female name, "Osgyth"; see Gifford Charles-Edwards, "The East Cross Inscription from Toureen Peacaun: Some Concrete Evidence," *Journal of the Royal Society of Antiquaries in Ireland* 132 (2002): 114-26.

[79] Logainm. The Placenames Database of Ireland, https://www.logainm.ie/ga/859 and https://www.logainm.ie/ga/17351, accessed 31 January 2024. See further Edmonds, *Gaelic Influence in the Northumbrian Kingdom*, 143-4.

[80] Logainm. The Placenames Database of Ireland, https://www.logainm.ie/ga/17103; see also https://www.logainm.ie/ga/867, https://www.logainm.ie/ga/867, accessed 31 January 2024. Mulhuddart has a related (but now obsolete) name, Cloghranhiddert, which alludes to the same personage; see Colm Ó Lochlainn, "The Placename Eadar," *The Irish Book Lover* 31 (1949): 56-7; Myles V. Ronan, "Mulhuddard and Cloghran-Hiddert," *Journal of the Royal Society of Antiquaries of Ireland* 70.10 (1940): 182-93.

[81] Bertram Colgrave and R.A.B. Mynors, ed. and trans., *Bede's Ecclesiastical History of the English People* (Oxford: Oxford University, 1969), III.27, 312-3.

[82] Clonmelsh clearly retains in anglicised form the second element of the name Rath Melsigi. The ecclesiastical site extended also into what is now the contiguous townland of Garryhundon; see Thomas Fanning, "Appendix: Some Field Monuments in the Townlands of Clonmelsh and Garryhundon, Co. Carlow," *Peritia: Journal of the Medieval Academy of Ireland* 3 (1984): 43-9.

[83] See Dáibhí Ó Cróinín, "Rath Melsigi, Willibrord, and the Earliest Echternach Manuscripts," *Peritia. Journal of the Medieval Academy of Ireland* 3 (1984): 17-

countrymen in Mayo. Bede mentions some of them by name,[84] including Ecgberht who has been described as "the leading English churchman resident in Ireland" in his time, not least because of his role in establishing missions on the continent and in helping to establish the Roman Easter in Iona and among the Picts.[85] While there is no evidence of any direct connection between Rath Melsigi and Mayo, it has been suggested that the Carlow foundation was a daughter-house of the monastery of Bangor in County Down.[86]

Despite the evidence for the presence of prominent English churchmen and Anglo-Saxon communities in Ireland in our period, we have no direct evidence for the presence of significant numbers of Englishmen among the ecclesiastical community at Armagh (other than in the name Trían Saxan).

49; Idem, "*Pater* Ecgberct of Rath Melsigi: The Hero of Bede's *Historia Ecclesiastica*?" O'Reilly Memorial Lecture at University College Cork, April 27, 2023, accessed 23 February 2024, https://www.youtube.com/watch?v=eVnwTocMzXk

[84] Bede names a "dozen or so" in his *Historia* "and the names of others of what must have been a fairly sizeable group of exiles can be gleaned from other sources" (Ó Cróinín, "Rath Melsigi, Willibrord, and the Earliest Echternach Manuscripts," 22. Some were to achieve great prominence such as Chad, later bishop of York and Lichfield (see Charles-Edwards, *Early Christian Ireland*, 8n2; 9, 314, 320; Ireland, *The Gaelic Background of Old English Poetry*, 230-2, et passim). On Bede and the Irish, see Alan Thacker, "Bede and the Irish," in *Beda Venerabilis: Historian, Monk and Northumbrian*, ed. L.A.J.R. Houwen and A.A. MacDonald, Mediaevalia Groningana 19 (Groningen: E. Forsten: 1996), 31-59, and Sarah McCann, "*Plures de Scottorum Regione*: Bede, Ireland and the Irish," *Eolas* 8 (2015): 20-38. The latter notes that the Irish, who permeate Bede's text, are from various parts of Ireland (and Scottish Dál Riata, presumably), and are found all over Britain. Furthermore, "of the forty-two individuals in the text who can arguably be identified as Irish, only seven are unnamed" (26-8). Further evidence of Bede's favourable view of the Irish is his criticism of the Northumbrian attack on Brega in Ireland at the behest of King Ecgfrith in AD 684 whose army "wretchedly devastated a harmless race that had always been most friendly to the English" (*uastauit misere gentem innoxiam et nationi Anglorum semper amicissimam*), Colgrave and Mynors, *Bede's Ecclesiastical History*, IV.26 (24), 426-7

[85] Charles-Edwards, *Early Christian Ireland*, 435; see also 336-7 and 436-7.

[86] Ireland, *The Gaelic Background of Old English Poetry*, 75, 180, 194, 333.

However, there is the possibility that Trían Saxan in Armagh derived its name from the presence of English students in the city rather than clerics. Aldhelm, abbot of Malmesbury and, subsequently, bishop of Sherborne, wrote in *c*.680 of "thronging students by the fleetload" going to Ireland to study,[87] and Bede (d. 735) in his *Historia* distinguishes between those who went to study and those who went to train in the monastic life.[88] Armagh is frequently mentioned as a centre of education in the annals,[89] and Seathrún

---

[87] *Cur, inquam, Hibernia, quo catervatim istinc lectitantes classibus advecti confluunt, ineffabili quodam privilegio efferatur* . . . (Why, I ask, is Ireland, whither assemble the thronging students by the fleetload, exalted with a sort of ineffable privilege . . .) Rudolf Ehwald, ed., "Epistolae," in Monumenta Germaniae Historica. Auctores Antiquissimi 15. Aldhelmi Opera (Berlin: Weidmann, 1919), 475-503, at 492, ll. 9-10; Michael Lapidge and Michael Herren, trans., *Aldhelm. The Prose Works* (Ipswich: D.S. Brewer; Totowa, New Jersey: Rowman and Littlefield, 1979), 163. See Ireland, *The Gaelic Background of Old English Poetry*, 225, on the possible date of Aldhelm's letter.

[88] *Erant ibidem eo tempore multi nobilium simul et mediocrium de gente Anglorum, qui tempore Finani et Colmani episcoporum, relicta insula patria, uel diuinae lectionis uel continentioris uitae gratia illo secesserant. Et quidam quidem mox se monasticae conuersationi fideliter mancipauerunt; aliii magis circueundo per cellas magistrorum lectioni operam dare gaudebant. Quos omnes Scotti libentissime suscipientes, uictum eis cotidianum sine pretio, libros quoque ad legendum et magisterium gratuitum praebere curabant* (At this time there were many in England, both nobles and commons, who, in the days of Bishops Finan and Colman, had left their own country and retired to Ireland either for the sake of religious studies or to live a more ascetic life. In course of time some of these devoted themselves faithfully to the monastic life, while others preferred to travel round to the cells of various teachers and apply themselves to study. The Irish welcomed them all gladly, gave them their daily food, and also provided them with books to read and with instruction, without asking for any payment.) Colgrave and Mynors, *Bede's Ecclesiastical History*, III.27, 312-3.

[89] For reference to the death of students through illness in Armagh, and to the destruction by fire there of the "houses of the students", see *AFM*, s.a. 1011 and 1020. Note also "the killing of the lector and master of the students" in Armagh (AU^2, s.a. 1042). Much later, the clergy of Ireland at the Synod of Clane in 1162 "determined that no one should be a lector in any church in Ireland who was not an alumnus of Ard-Macha before" (*ro chinnset clérigh Éreann na badh ferleighinn i ccill i nErinn an fer na badh dalta Arda Macha cédus*) (AFM, s.a.

MEDIEVAL ARMAGH

Céitinn (Geoffrey Keating) made what seems an extravagant claim that the school at Armagh, one of four chief schools in Ireland, catered for 7,000 students.[90] We have additional evidence from the seventeenth century: John Colgan expressed the view that the name Trían Saxan was "most likely" derived from the residence of Anglo-Saxon students there.[91] Further evidence may be provided in the middle of the century by Toirdhealbhach Ó Mealláin, chaplain to Féilim Ó Néill, in his diary of the Irish uprising in 1641-2, *Cín Lae Uí Mhealláin*:

> *Do loisgeadh Ard Macha, in tempoll mór gona chlogás, gona chloguibh, gona organuibh, gona fhuineoguibh gloine, agus in chathair uile gona tighibh fionnaolta mailli re a roibh do leabhraibh i stuidigh na Sasanach, diachta, loighice agus fallsa.*

Armagh was burned, the great church with its bell-tower and bells, its organs, its glass windows, and the whole city with its white-limed houses together with all the books of

---

1162). Seven years later, the king of Ireland undertook to provide for the instruction in Armagh of students from Ireland and Scotland: *Isin bliadhain cétna dorat Ruaidhri hUa Conchobair . . . deich m-bú cecha bliadhna uadh féin ₇ ó cach righ i n-a dhegaidh co brath do ferleiginn Aird-Macha, i n-onóir Patraic, ar leighinn do dhenamh do macaibh leighinn Erenn ₇ Alban* (In the same year, Ruaidhri Ua Concobair . . . gave ten cows every year from himself and from every king after him to doom to the lector of Ard-Macha, in honour of [St.] Patrick, to give lectures to students of Ireland and Scotland.) (AU¹, s.a. 1169; cf. AFM, *s.a.* 1169).

[90] *Do bhádar iomorro gus an am-so cheithre príomhscola i nÉirinn, .i. scol i nArd Macha mar a rabhadar seacht míle mac léighinn do réir shearnolla fríoth i nOxford . . .* (Now up to this time there were four chief schools in Ireland, to wit, a school at Ard Macha in which there were seven thousand students according to an old scroll which was found in Oxford . . .). David Comyn and P.S. Dinneen ed. and trans., *Foras Feasa ar Éirinn le Seathrún Céitinn D.D.: the History of Ireland by Geoffrey* Keating D.D., 4 vols. (London, Irish Texts Society, 1902–14), 3:162-5, ll. 2574-7.

[91] *Quarta, Trian-Saxon; id est, tertia portio Saxonum, appellata: quod nomen videtur adepta ex eo, quod vle [r. vel] mercatores (quod verosimiliùs est) studiosi Anglosaxones illi inhabitauerint* (Colgan, *Trias Thaumaturga*, 300).

theology, logic and philosophy, in the Study of the English.[92]

Although this is a late reference, there seems no strong reason to doubt the veracity of its testimony regarding the memory of the presence of English students in Armagh in the past and the potential link to Trían Saxan.[93]

Conclusion

It has been shown that of 75 entries relating to Anglo-Saxon England in the Irish annals up to 1000 AD, 66% of these belong to the period *c.* 580-

---

[92] Tadhg Ó Donnchadha ed., "Cín Lae Ó Mealláin," *Analecta Hibernica* 3 (1931): 1-61, at 11 (May 1642), ll. 10-4. The translation is my own. See also the unpublished doctoral thesis on this text: Máire Nic Cathmhaoil, "The Seventeenth Century Text 'Cín Lae Uí Mhealláin' with Introduction, Translation and Notes," Ulster University, 2006.

[93] The word *stuidigh* is clearly a borrowing of English 'study'; *DIL* cites only one other example (*eDIL* s.v. stuidig) and that is from the *The Flight of the Earls* dating to the beginning of the seventeenth century: *Éirghid go teaghdhas stuidéir an iarla. Orgáin iongantacha adhmaid . . . go n-iliomad leabhar cantaireachta agus starthach 'sa stuite sin* (They then went to the earl's study. In that study there were wonderful wooden organs . . . as well as numerous books on singing and history). Nollaig Ó Muraíle ed. and trans., *Turas na dTaoiseach nUltach as Éirinn. From Ráth Maoláin to Rome. Tadhg Ó Cianáin's Contemporary Narrative of the Journey into Exile of the Ulster Chieftains and Their Followers, 1607-8 [. . .]*. (Rome: Pontifical Irish College, 2007), 170-1. Paterson, has taken this reference to allude potentially to the destruction by O'Neill's forces of the Royal School, first built in the course of the Plantation of Ulster on the site of *Reiclés Coluim Chille* "the church of St Columba" *c.*1614-15. See T.G.F. Paterson, "Proposals for a University at Armagh," in *Harvest Home. The Last Sheaf. A Selection from the Writings of T.G.F. Paterson Relating to County Armagh*, edited with an Introduction by E. Estyn Evans (Dundalk: Dundalgan Press for the Armagh County Museum, 1975), 56-72, at 58; and idem, "The Royal School of Armagh," in *Harvest Home* [. . .]. 12-24, at 13-5. However, there is no evidence that stuidigh might be applied to a school in the conventional sense and *stuidigh na Sasanach* is translated elsewhere as "the studies of the English quarter". See Charles Dillon trans., *"Cín Lae Uí Mhealláin*: Friar O Mellan Journal," *Dúiche Néill* 10 (1995-6): 130-207, at 146.

c. 750, and are largely preoccupied with Northumbria.[94] The seventh and eighth centuries have been described by Kathleen Hughes as the "time of greatest mutual influence" between the Irish and English churches when "clergy seemed to have moved freely between the two countries and settled permanently and happily in each other's lands . . .".[95] Dáibhí Ó Cróinín also stresses this freedom of movement, and adds that there "was nothing surprising to find Irish, English, British, and Pictish royalty and their ecclesiastical relations—with the occasional Frank added for good measure —living together in places like Iona and Lindisfarne, Mayo and Rath Melsigi, and several other monasteries."[96] What is surprising, perhaps, is that the major church settlement of Armagh, which had been promoting the cult of Saint Patrick in pressing its claims for primacy over all of Ireland from the seventh century, and had an indisputable reputation for teaching and scholarship, is conspicuous by its absence from records which shed light on Irish-English contact, other than the preservation in the annals of the toponym Trían Saxan which implies an English presence there.[97] Bede only gives an account of three monasteries in Ireland in his *Historia*: Inishbofin, Mayo and Rath Melsigi.[98] However, he does state that, while some of the English devoted themselves to monastic life, "others preferred to travel round to the cells of various teachers and apply themselves to study" and it is hard to imagine that Armagh would not be on the list of

---

[94] Hermann Moisl, "The Bernician Royal Dynasty and the Irish in the Seventh Century," *Peritia. Journal of the Medieval Academy of Ireland* 2 (1983): 103-26, at 106-7.

[95] Hughes, "Evidence for Contacts between the Churches of the Irish and the English," 67.

[96] Dáibhí Ó Cróinín, "The Earliest Echternach Liturgical Manuscript Fragments: Irish or Anglo-Saxon?" in Rachel Moss, Felicity O'Mahony, Jane Maxwell (eds), *An Insular Odyssey. Manuscript Culture in Early Christian Ireland and Beyond* (Dublin: Four Courts Press, 2017), 55–75, at 74.

[97] Hughes "Evidence for Contacts between the Churches of the Irish and the English," 53, alludes to Trían Saxan in venturing the opinion that "round 800, there were various groups of Englishmen in Ireland who were afterwards forgotten." See also the unidentified churches at Rigair and Cluain Mucceda which are associated with English clergy in the *Litany of Irish Saints*. Charles Plummer, ed. and trans., *Irish Litanies, Text and Translation* (London: Henry Bradshaw Society, 1925), 129, 133.

[98] He also alludes to Colum Cille's connection with Durrow (*HE* III.4).

desirable Irish destinations.[99] Furthermore, the *Martyrology of Óengus*, which is thought to be of Armagh provenance,[100] includes Northumbrian kings and clerics in its calendar of feast days and illustrates that scholars working in Armagh were conscious of the English connection to the Irish church. Interestingly, Anglo-Saxon coins dating to the late eighth century have been recovered in Armagh and provide concrete evidence of Armagh's involvement in the Irish-English trading nexus.[101]

The establishment of the precise period in which Anglo-Saxon clerics and/or students may have been resident in Armagh is hampered by the paucity of evidence. Our earliest reference to Trían Saxan dates to 1092, but the evidence of the existence of trena more generally at Armagh by 987 suggests the latter date as a potential terminus ante quem (and there is also the comparative evidence of trena elsewhere, particularly Cork in 908 and, possibly, earlier at Clonmacnoise). However, it is likely that the ecclesiastical topography of Armagh is much older; indeed, Nick Aitchison has suggested that the contrast between Ráith and Trían (in the phrase eter ráith ₇ trian) is reflected in the distinction in the seventh-century Liber Angeli between *urbs* and *suburbana*.[102]

The middle of the seventh century was the highpoint of traffic from Northumbria to Ireland according to Bede; he specified the period of the bishoprics of Fínán and Colmán in that regard (*HE* III.27), i.e. the years 651-64, which coincide with the middle of King Oswiu's reign (642-70).

---

[99] Armagh also had the attraction of the relics it claimed to have of Peter, Paul, Stephen and Laurence. See Bieler, *The Patrician Texts in the Book of Armagh*, 186 (*Liber Angeli*, ch. 19), and Charles-Edwards, *Early Christian Ireland*, 427.
[100] Pádraig Ó Riain, "The Martyrology of Óengus: The Transmission of the Text," *Studia Hibernica* 31 (2000-1): 221-42. Note the names Oswald, Aldfrith, Wihtberht, Benedict and Cuthbert.
[101] Raghnall Ó Floinn, "The Anglo-Saxon Connection: Irish Metalwork, AD 400-800," in *Proceedings of the British Academy* 157: *Anglo-Saxon/Irish Relations before the Vikings*, ed. James Graham-Campbell and Michael Ryan (Oxford: Oxford University Press for the British Academy, 2009), 231-51, at 235.
[102] Aitchison, *Armagh and the Royal Centres*, 226-7. As far as the archaeological record is concerned, it may be added that the area of the city in which *Trían Saxan* was located (Abbey Street and Upper English Street) has not yet yielded any evidence prior to the eighth century. Gail Roberta Matthews, "The Early History and Archaeology of Armagh City," PhD dissertation, Queen's University Belfast 2000, 3 vols., 180.

Bede also noted that Oswiu, being "well-versed" in the Irish language, "considered that nothing was better than what they [the Irish] had taught" (*HE* III.25), and Colin Ireland has argued that the increase in traffic of students across the Irish Sea during Oswiu's time must reflect a "deliberate educational policy" on the king's part.[103] Oswiu is said to have had a liaison with a woman of Cenél nÉogain stock in Ireland (possibly named Fín), and their son Aldfrith alias Flann Fína is described as "the enduring heir of Bangor" (*comarbae búan Bennchoir*) in the *Martyrology of Óengus*; together with other circumstantial evidence, this has been taken to suggest that Aldfrith was probably educated in Bangor sometime in the 660s.[104] It is not clear whether this was before or after the dispute over the Easter question at the Synod of Whitby in 664; Wilfrid, the chief proponent of Roman orthodoxy at Whitby (and subsequently Bishop of York) is said in his Life by Stephen of Ripon to have credited himself with rooting out the "poisonous weeds" planted by the Irish and converting the "Northumbrian race to the true Easter".[105] It would appear from the letters of Aldhelm that some of Wilfrid's supporters sought to dissuade English students from studying in Ireland in the aftermath of the Synod of Whitby;[106] traffic to Ireland continued "by the fleet load", however, as Aldhelm himself acknowledged, and this persisted into the eighth century as evidenced in the correspondence of Alcuin of York.[107] Aldhelm had also noted the flow in the other direction and described Archbishop Theodore as being "hemmed

---

[103] Ireland, The Gaelic Background of Old English Poetry, 271; see also 179.

[104] Stokes, *Félire Óengusso*, 251; Ireland, "Where was King Aldfrith of Northumbria Educated?," 64-5; Ireland, *The Gaelic Background of Old English Poetry*, 194, 221-2, 258, 266. For evidence that Aldfrith was in Iona c.684, a year before succeeding to the kingship of Northumbria, see idem, *The Gaelic Background of Old English Poetry*, 282-4, 350. There is no evidence that the purpose of his trip there was to pursue his education; Ireland suggests rather that "it should be interpreted in political terms," ibid., 284.

[105] Bertram Colgrave ed. and trans, *The Life of Bishop Wilfrid by Eddius Stephanus* (Cambridge: Cambridge University Press, 1927); Ireland, *The Gaelic Background of Old English Poetry*, 240, 259.

[106] Ehwald, "Epistolae," 5; Lapidge and Herren, *Aldhelm: The Prose Works*, 163; Charles-Edwards, *Early Christian Ireland*, 337.

[107] See Hughes, "Evidence for Contacts between the Churches of the Irish and the English," 56; Ireland, *The Gaelic Background of Old English Poetry*, 89-90, 328, 372.

in by a mass of Irish students" at the Canterbury School which Aldhelm wished to promote as an alternative to study in Ireland.[108] The broader context of this promotion of Canterbury is the extension of the power of the kings of Northumbria and the push by the church for the consolidation of orthodoxy in the period after the synod of 664. King Oswiu and King Ecgberht of Kent had collaborated in sending a delegation to Rome seeking the appointment of a new archbishop of Canterbury later that year (*HE* III.29, IV.1), thereby initiating a chain of events which culminated in the foundation of the school at Canterbury in 669 and the appointment of Wilfrid as bishop of York in the same year (Wilfrid first having been consecrated to York in 664-5).[109] At a papal synod in Rome in 680, Wilfrid is said to have taken it upon himself to confess "the true and catholic faith for all the northern part of Britain and Ireland . . .", and the attack on *Brega* in Ireland, which was initiated by King Ecgfrith (Oswiu's son) in 684, doubtless would have added to Irish concerns regarding the coalescence of English political and ecclesiastical interests, and attempts to assert metropolitan power.[110] It is scarcely coincidental that the church community of Armagh conformed to the Roman Easter soon thereafter (*c*.686); there is no direct evidence for the precise date but it must have been before the *Idacht or Testimony of Bishop Áed* (dated 685 x 688) in which Áed submitted his diocese of Sleaty to the authority of Armagh (as this is most unlikely to have been possible while Armagh remained attached to the unorthodox Irish Easter).[111] Sleaty is located in Leinster, in the valley of the River Barrow in which Rath Melsigi and other establishments (which had long been orthodox) were located, and this provides another avenue by

---

[108] Ireland, The Gaelic Background of Old English Poetry, 226-7.
[109] Charles-Edwards, *Early Christian Ireland*, 429-30; Ireland, *The Gaelic Background of Old English Poetry*, 214.
[110] Charles-Edwards, *Early Christian Ireland*, 416, 433.
[111] Charles-Edwards, *Early Christian Ireland*, 428-9, 433-6, and 439-40. Bishop Áed, who died in 700, was responsible for commissioning Muirchú to write his Vita Patricii. Both of them appear as guarantors in Cáin Adomnáin, promulgated in Birr in 697, in which Armagh is given pride of place by coming first in the list of guarantors (closely followed by the abbot of Bangor, Rath Melsigi's mother-house possibly, which appears in third position. See Máirín Ní Dhonnchadha, "The Guarantor List of Cáin Adomnáin", *Peritia* 1 (1982): 198-215, §1, 3.

which Armagh would have come into contact with English ecclesiastics in Ireland, perhaps.[112]

As regards the presence of English clerics and/or students in Armagh itself, it is of great interest that Rome, on which Armagh modelled itself as a sacred city, also had an English district, Borgo Saxonum, "named after the *Schola Saxonum* that was founded there, apparently by King Ine of Wessex, in 727."[113] It may be, then, that the origin of Trían Saxan may lie in Armagh's attempts to assert itself (and outmanoeuvre Canterbury and York) in the period post *c*.686 by proclaiming its credentials in terms of orthodoxy and primacy over Ireland in a variety of ways.[114] The presence within its bounds of churches dedicated to Brigit and Columba (whenever they were constructed) can be seen as a statement of authority over Kildare and Iona (and the monasteries of the Columban federation within Ireland); Kildare's challenge to the primacy of Armagh had faltered by the end of the seventh century, and Iona's influence declined with the downturn in Columban fortunes in the early ninth century (and the contraction of communication between Iona and Ireland in the Viking Age).[115] In the case of Trían Saxan, the name may be a very direct expression of *romanitas* (not least in the light of the parallel with Rome), and confirmation of the facts on the ground: Armagh's ability to attract students from England despite

---

[112] On the Barrow Valley as forming "an active corridor in the ecclesiastical and intellectual activities of the seventh century", see Ireland, *The Gaelic Background of Old English Poetry*, 347.

[113] Ó Carragáin, *Churches in Early Medieval Ireland*, 221. Intriguingly, King Ine's sister, Cuthburh, was married to Aldfrith of Northumbria who had died earlier in 705; Ireland, *The Gaelic Background of Old English Poetry*, 290-1.

[114] For a detailed discussion of "the significance of contact with Rome in the development of Armagh's claims to greatness' as evidenced in the *Liber Angeli*, see Richard Sharpe, "Armagh and Rome in the Seventh Century," in *Irland und Europa: die Kirche im Frühmittelalter / Ireland and Europe: the Early Church*, ed. Próinséas Ní Chatháin and Michael Richter (Stuttgart: Klett-Cotta, 1984), 58–72, at 59. Sharpe also notes, however, that despite invoking Rome, Armagh did not have the power to impose its authority at this particular time (72).

[115] Máire Herbert, *Iona, Kells and Derry. The History and Hagiography of the Monastic Familia of Columba* (Oxford: Clarendon Press, 1988; reprint 1996), 71; Charles-Edwards, *Early Christian Ireland*, 428-9. For the suggestion that these churches in Armagh were actually staffed from Kildare and Iona, see Ó Carragáin, *Churches in Early Medieval Ireland*, 220.

the existence there of Canterbury and other prestigious schools and the desire of some to stem the flow to Ireland and to assert metropolitan authority over both islands. Bede, on the other hand, approved of Englishmen pursuing an education in Ireland;[116] one wonders, therefore, if any significance can be attached to the absence of any mention of Armagh and its 'Saxon' district in his *Historia*? If this is significant, it may imply that Trían Saxan in Armagh postdates the foundation of the *Schola Saxonum* in Rome in 727 and the completion of Bede's *Historia* in 731. Another way of considering the issue is in the light of the impact of Viking attacks, including the first raid on a monastery, none other than Lindisfarne, in 793. On the Irish side, Rechru was the first to be attacked, two years later in 795,[117] and the annals record Armagh being plundered three times in 832. It would seem likely that whatever draw the city may have had on the pool of students in England in the past, this may have been ruptured by these developments and that Trían Saxan may commemorate the presence of English students in Armagh at a period earlier than the year *c*. 800.

---

[116] See Charles-Edwards, *Early Christian Ireland*, 343. On Bede's sense of debt to the Irish for transmission of the faith to Northumbria, and his view of Ecgbert's persuasion of Iona to adopt the orthodox dating system of Easter in 716 as repayment of that debt, see *HE* (V.22).

[117] *Loscadh Rechrainne o geinntib ⁊ Sci do [cho]scradh ⁊ do lomadh* (The burning of Rechru by the heathens, and Scí was overwhelmed and laid waste) (AU², s.a. 795). While the wider geographical context here may suggest the identification of Rechru with Rathlin Island in County Antrim, there was a second Rechru further south off the coast of Dublin (now Lambay Island) and it was the location of a monastery founded by Ségéne, abbot of Iona, in 635 AD. See Charles-Edwards, *Early Christian Ireland*, 250.

Old Irish in the PaVeDa:
Issues, Perspectives, and Two Case Studies

Elisa Roma and Chiara Zanchi

1. Introduction[1]

In this paper we present the first steps toward including Old Irish data in the Pavia Verbs Database (PaVeDa), a new database which is intended to allow for the crosslinguistic study of valency classes and valency alternations, also in a diachronic fashion. We will touch upon the issues related to such an undertaking, as well as upon the promising perspectives such an addition to the PaVeDa brings about, through the lenses of two case studies.

The paper unfolds as follows: Section 2 familiarizes the reader with the PaVeDa and with its predecessor, the Valency Pattern Leipzig (ValPaL) database; Section 3 outlines the methodology along with the main issues regarding data extraction and data selection for Old Irish; Sections 4 and 5 dwell on a couple of case studies based on the data that have been collected so far: basic valency orientation in Old Irish[2] and valency patterns of

---

[1] Research for the PaVeDa and this paper is supported by European Union funding – NextGenerationEU – Missione 4 Istruzione e ricerca – componente 2, investimento 1.1 "Fondo per il Programma Nazionale della Ricerca (PNR) e Progetti di Ricerca di Rilevante Interesse Nazionale (PRIN)" progetto 20223XH5XM "Verbs' constructional patterns across languages: a multi-dimensional investigation" CUP F53D23004570006. This paper is the result of sustained collaboration between the two authors. For the Italian academic purposes, Elisa Roma is responsible for Sections 3, 4, 5, 6, while Chiara Zanchi is responsible for Sections 1 and 2.

[2] Johanna Nichols, David A. Peterson, and Jonathan Barnes, "Transitivizing and Detransitivizing Languages", *Linguistic Typology* 8, no. 2 (7 July 2004): 149–211, https://doi.org/10.1515/lity.2004.005.

ditransitive verbs,[3] respectively; Section 6 briefly draws some general conclusions.

2. What is the PaVeDa?

The PaVeDa is an open-source relational database aimed at investigating verb argument structure across languages,[4] which is currently under construction at the University of Pavia and the University of Naples "Federico II".[5] Built in the framework of the Valency Patterns Leipzig project,[6] the PaVeDa is devised to expand and enhance the ValPaL database.[7] In particular, the PaVeDa contains additional features and languages as compared to the ValPaL database. Specifically, the PaVeDa features (or will feature) languages from families currently not represented, or underrepresented in the ValPaL database, as well as ancient and medieval

---

[3] Andrej Malchukov, Martin Haspelmath, and Bernard Comrie, "Ditransitive Constructions: A Typological Overview", in *Studies in Ditransitive Constructions. A Comparative Handbook*, eds. Malchukov Andrej, Martin Haspelmath, and Bernard Comrie (Berlin: De Gruyter Mouton, 2010), 1–64, https://doi.org/10.1515/9783110220377.1.

[4] See Chiara Zanchi, Silvia Luraghi, and Claudia Roberta Combei, "PaVeDa - Pavia Verbs Database: Challenges and Perspectives", in *Proceedings of the 4th Workshop on Research in Computational Linguistic Typology and Multilingual NLP*, ed. Ekaterina Vylomova, Edoardo Ponti, and Ryan Cotterell (SIGTYP 2022, Seattle, Washington: Association for Computational Linguistics, 2022), 99–102, https://doi.org/10.18653/v1/2022.sigtyp-1.14. See also Silvia Luraghi, Alessio Palmero Aprosio, Chiara Zanchi, and Martina Giuliani, "Introducing PaVeDa–Pavia Verbs Database: Valency Patterns and Pattern Comparison in Ancient Indo-European Languages", in *Proceedings of the Second Workshop on Language Technologies for Historical and Ancient Languages*, ed. Rachele Sprugnoli and Marco Passarotti (LT4HALA 2024, Turin, Italy: ELRA and ICCL, 2024), 79–88, https://aclanthology.org/2024.lt4hala-1.10.pdf. [accessed 11-22-2024].

[5] The current version of the database can be accessed at the following website: https://paveda.unipv.it. [accessed 11-22-2024].

[6] Andrej Malchukov and Bernard Comrie, eds., *Valency Classes in the World's Languages*, Comparative Handbooks of Linguistics (Berlin: De Gruyter Mouton, 2015).

[7] Iren Hartmann, Martin Haspelmath, and Bradley Taylor, eds., *The Valency Patterns Leipzig Online Database* (Leipzig: Max Planck Institute for Evolutionary Anthropology, 2013), https://valpal.info/. [accessed 11-22-2024].

varieties. The aim of these additions is to provide a database to compare valency patterns and alternations[8] of cognate languages. Furthermore, the inclusion of different stages of a language will allow for diachronic generalizations.

The ValPaL database has been a groundbreaking tool to support and systematize research on verb classes. The core of the database includes 80 distinct verb meanings (e.g. ASK FOR, FILL, TEACH, etc.) and their translational equivalents in 36 languages. Only for some languages, additional verb meanings and proxies have been included, up to a total of 162 verb meanings. For each verb meaning, its typical context, role frame, and microroles (that is, verb-specific semantic roles) are specified:

(1) a. Verb meaning: FILL
b. Typical context: The girl filled the glass with water.
c. Role frame: A fills P (with X)
d. Microroles: filler, filled container, filling material, fill causer, fill beneficiary

Then, for each translational equivalent of the meaning, the coding set associated with each microrole is stored in the database, together with the verb's basic valency pattern. This is in the form of a sentence frame with examples, and alternations, occasionally also with examples. Using the verb meaning in (1) FILL, corresponding to the Italian verb *riempire*, the following pieces of information are given in the ValPaL database:

---

[8] Within the ValPaL framework, an alternation is defined "as a set of two different coding frames that are productively (or at least regularly) associated with both members of a set of verb pairs sharing the same verb stem. Alternations may be coded (marked by an affix on the verb, or by an auxiliary, [. . .]) or uncoded [. . .]."

(2) a. Microrole table:

#	Microrole	Coding set	Argument type
1	filler	V.subj	A
2	filled container	Ø	P
3	filling material	*con*+NP	I

b. Basic coding frame: 1 > V.subj[1] > 2 (*con*+3)

c. Regular alternations: passive, reflexive passive, anticausative, indirect/dative reflexive, oblique subject, impersonal of reflexives, impersonal passive, indirect reciprocal reflexive

d. Marginal alternations: object omission

In (2a), the microroles are matched with their encodings and argument types, specifically, a subject (Agent-like argument) with no case marking agreeing with the verb, an object (Patient-like argument) with no case marking, and an (Instrument) flagged with the preposition *con* 'with'. The basic coding frame (2b) also indicates word order through angle brackets, agreement through square brackets, and argument optionality through round brackets. Each alternation in (2c-d) receives similarly detailed illustration as the basic coding frame.

The ValPaL data mostly come from contributors' intuitions or existing literature, and only occasionally examples are elicited during fieldwork and/or extracted from corpora. Further open issues in the ValPaL database are some inconsistencies in the data (e.g., in the way microroles are stored, see the discussion in Section 5.3 concerning the verb meaning FILL), limited and unbalanced language sample, and the total absence of historical varieties. Additionally, given that basic valency frames and alternations are stored in the ValPaL database at a language-specific level, the resource does not support comparative visualization of similar basic patterns and alternations across languages, nor of possible cognate lemmas.

Therefore, the expansion planned and partially implemented for the PaVeDa[9] has an ambitious goal, as it not only involves the addition of new data, but it also affects the very structure of the relational database aiming at cross-linguistic and diachronic comparison of verb frames. As for data collection, for the time being, the Pavia team has already collected or is collecting data from ancient and medieval Indo-European languages whose modern stages are already in the ValPaL databases (such as Early Latin, Old English, Old High German and Classical Armenian), from languages that do not have direct modern descendants (such as Gothic), or from languages whose modern stages were not or are not yet included in the database (such as Classical and Late Greek and Old Irish). Non-Indo-European languages which have been taken into account in the PaVeDa data collection are Turkish, Finnish, Hungarian, Chuvash, Modern Hebrew and Siwi/Figuig Berber. As for database structure, the Pavia team has already introduced a new analytical layer for alternations, which clusters each language-specific alternation into four categories, namely, "rearranging", "decreasing", "augmenting", and "identifying" alternations.[10] This layer constitutes a first step toward the cross-linguistic comparison of alternations. Furthermore, an option has been implemented to directly compare a verb meaning, its basic frames and alternations in two given languages. Finally, the PaVeDa already allows visualizing all attested alternations of all stored languages for a given meaning (e.g., for FILL there are 183) or to selectively visualize all and only the alternations belonging to one of the four categories of alternations introduced above. A further analytical layer for classifying alternations will be added in the future. It is intended to operate at an intermediate level of granularity between language-specific alternations and the over-generalizing level already added to the database and just briefly discussed.

The addition of ancient languages has brought new challenges to the table. For past varieties of a language, one cannot rely on native speaker's intuitions, but rather must depend on scholars' competence, previous

---

[9] See footnote 4.
[10] For the meanings of the labels see Malchukov and Comrie, *Valency Classes in the World's Languages*.

studies, reference grammars, and obviously on corpora. This corpus-based turn triggered by ancient languages had the consequence that for both ancient and modern languages the PaVeDa contributors need to extract, select, and analyze data from corpora for the sake of database consistency. New practical and theoretical issues have arisen as a result of this undertaking, pertaining to corpus availability and corpus representativeness.[11] Some of these will be tackled in Section 3 by dwelling on data extraction for Old Irish.

3. The search methodology for Old Irish

The search methodology for Old Irish counterparts of verb meanings, both for the ValPaL/PaVeDa meanings and Nichols et al.[12] pairs, includes first a search for the meaning in the advanced search function in eDIL.[13] The verbal lexeme that is most frequent in Corpus PalaeoHibernicum[14] (CorPH) is then selected. If eDIL gives no results, the meaning is searched directly in CorPH filtering the meaning column in the lemma page. Where there are no results in either source, synonyms or proxies are searched for (e.g. BLINK > WINK, AMUSE > ENTERTAIN).

For small corpus languages such as Gothic, all occurrences have been included in the PaVeDa.[15] For ancient languages with larger corpora such as Ancient Greek, all occurrences of the selected verbs have been included if the frequency is lower than one hundred tokens, but a stratified random

---

[11] Sophie Raineri and Camille Debras, "Corpora and Representativeness: Where to Go from Now?", *CogniTextes* 19, no. Volume 19 (17 June 2019), https://doi.org/10.4000/cognitextes.1311. [accessed 11-22-2024].

[12] Nichols, et al., "Transitivizing and Detransitivizing Languages".

[13] eDIL, *An Electronic Dictionary of the Irish Language, Based on the Contributions to a Dictionary of the Irish Language* (Dublin: Royal Irish Academy, 1913-1976) (www.dil.ie 2019), 2019. [accessed 11-22-2024].

[14] David Stifter et al., "Corpus PalaeoHibernicum (CorPH) v1.0", 2021, https://chronhib.maynoothuniversity.ie/chronhibWebsite/home. [accessed 11-22-2024].

[15] See Chiara Zanchi and Matteo Tarsi, "Valency Patterns and Alternations in Gothic", in *Valency over Time*, ed. Silvia Luraghi and Elisa Roma (Berlin: De Gruyter Mouton, 2021), 31–88, https://doi.org/10.1515/9783110755657-003.

sample has been used if its frequency is higher than one hundred.[16] CorPH, as compared to the Gothic and Ancient Greek corpora, is a medium size corpus: it includes 13,123 verb occurrences and 5,340 verbal noun occurrences. However, very few verbs enjoy more than one hundred occurrences: among the ValPaL meanings, in fact, only *do·beir* GIVE and *as·beir* SAY. Therefore, all occurrences are included in the analysis and used to identify the basic argument frame. If an alternation turns out to have only one instance in the corpus, it is included in the alternation list; if there are no instances, it is not included, although one may not expect the alternation to be ruled out with that verb. Occasionally, eDIL and the Würzburg Glosses[17] (Wb) are also used as sources when CorPH appears to have a casual gap: for example, CorPH happens to have no occurrences of the verbal noun *fubthad* of *fo·botha* 'frighten', but the non-finite alternation has been included in the database, referring to an instance given by eDIL.[18] For the verbal noun *foít* of *foídid* 'send', CorPH only offers a single instance with no arguments, so for the non-finite alternation the construction attested in Wb 15a15 has been used. Note that the non-finite alternation has generally not been taken into account for other languages in the PaVeDa (this is not required by the ValPaL and PaVeDa guidelines), but it has been considered a major one for Old Irish.

3.1 The selection process

For a given meaning, the search output in eDIL often includes more than one verb. Frequency in CorPH, as already stated, is a major criterion to select the Old Irish counterpart. However, other criteria also play a role. For example, for EAT, *ithid* has been preferred to *ar·beir biuth* despite its

---

[16] Chiara Zanchi and Guglielmo Inglese, "Ancient Greek Valency Patterns and Alternations". Paper Presented at the 3rd International Colloquium on Ancient Greek Linguistics, Universidad Autónoma de Madrid, Spain, 16-18 June 2022.
[17] The Würzburg glosses were searched using Kavanagh's lexicon (Séamus Kavanagh, *A Lexicon of the Old Irish Glosses in the Würzburg Manuscript of the Epistles of St. Paul*, ed. Dagmar Wodtko, Mitteilungen Der Prähistorischen Kommission 45 (Vienna: Verlag der Österreichischen Akademie der Wissenschaften, 2001). Quotations are from Adrian Doyle's online edition (Adrian Doyle, "Würzburg Irish Glosses", 2018, https://wuerzburg.ie/. [accessed 11-22-2024].)
[18] Trip. 142.17, dil.ie/24739.

lower frequency (6 occurrences as against 65), because of morphological complexity and because ar·beir biuth can also mean 'employ, use, enjoy'. Sometimes a verb with low frequency was preferred because its occurrences grant semantic closeness to the ValPaL given examples:[19] *fo·áitbi* has been preferred to *con·tibi* for LAUGH because its single occurrence in CorPH, Tur. 62 *amal foraitbi intsarra thall intan asrobrad frie conmberad macc* "like that Sarah laughed, when she had been told that she would bear a child", is very close to the example given in the ValPaL database "The little girl laughed". On the other hand, con·tibi (3 occurrences in CorPH) means LAUGH ABOUT, which is listed as a separate meaning in the ValPaL ("The woman laughed about the dog"). *As·indet* has been preferred to *ad·fét* for the meaning TELL because ad·fét employs the verbal noun of *as·indet*. In cases of conflict and uncertainty, both lemmas have been included, for example for NAME both *ainmmnigidir* and *as·beir (do)* have been taken into account.

A second issue is the selection of the basic coding frame as opposed to the alternations. For example, for ASK FOR the ValPaL database gives an example where the askee is optional while the requested thing is not: "The boy asked (his parents) for money". The frame with the requested object for *guidid* has therefore been considered the basic one, while frames with the askee have been listed as alternations.

With ASK FOR the frame suggested by the ValPaL database is also the most frequent one with the Old Irish verb guidid, but in other cases the most frequent frame in CorPH might be with a passive form. For example this happens with *línaid* FILL (6 occurrences for the active, 7 for the passive). In other cases, the most frequent frame might in fact be constrained, being attested only with arguments that are not full nominals. For example with *labraithir* TALK, the most frequent frame has a direct object corresponding to the talked about content, but this direct object only surfaces as a pronominal object or as the head of a relative clause. Thus, since the ValPaL database provides examples with both talkee (addressee) and talked about content as optional, i.e. 'The boy talked (to the girl) (about

---

[19] For a discussion on this semantic criterion see also Martina Giuliani and Chiara Zanchi, "Contributing to a new database on valency classes with Latin data. Challenges and perspectives", in *Proceedings of the International Colloquium on Latin Linguistics 2023*, ed. Lucie Pultrová and Martina Vaníková (Berlin: De Gruyter Mouton, 2024).

her dog)', the pattern without the direct object has been considered the basic one.

The third issue concerning frame selection is a major one, and has to do with the relationship between causatives ('The boy burnt his report card') vs. anticausatives ('The house is burning') or induced vs. plain in Nichols et al.'s terminology, an important alternation that we shall be looking at in Section 4. For meanings such as BURN, the ValPaL database chose the anticausative, or plain, version as basic and added the transitive, causative/induced counterpart separately afterwards as an alternation. On the other hand, the couplet FEAR and FRIGHTEN, which entertain the same relationship, both belong to the initial list of eighty core meanings in the ValPaL database, presumably because they are so lexicalized in English, the working metalanguage. Conversely, for NAME the initial, basic meaning was transitive and BE NAMED was added afterwards. For BREAK and HIDE only the causative meanings are included, and this raises some problems in dealing with basic valency orientation, since intransitive counterparts (anticausatives or plain, see Section 4 below) may appear only as alternations, although they may in fact be basic.

Table 1 in the Appendix shows the list of core verb meanings in the ValPaL database that are going to be included in the PaVeDa and the Old Irish counterparts reckoned to date, that is 72 out of 87.[20]

The meanings FORGIVE and PUNISH are additional; they were included in Roma's 2021 study on non-finite constructions[21] and have been added in the database because of their overall frequency. BE ANGRY on the other hand is included in Nichols et al.'s list[22] of verb meanings devised to determine basic valency orientation.

---

[20] The list of reckoned verb meanings presented at the Colloquium, which included only 40 items, has been updated as of March 2024, but the selection of ditransitives of Section 5 relies on the original sample, which did not include the non-prototypical ditransitives (three-place predicates) BEAT, COVER, POUR, PUSH.

[21] Elisa Roma, "Valency Patterns of Old Irish Verbs: Finite and Non-Finite Syntax", in *Valency over Time*, ed. Silvia Luraghi and Elisa Roma (Berlin: De Gruyter Mouton, 2021), 89–132, https://doi.org/10.1515/9783110755657-004.

[22] Nichols, et al., "Transitivizing and Detransitivizing Languages", 156.

4. Case study I: Old Irish Basic Valency orientation

Basic Valency orientation as defined by Nichols et al. 2004 is a preference that the verbal lexicon of languages exhibits in lexicalizing transitive and intransitive verb meaning pairs. "Transitivizing" languages are languages where intransitive verbs in verb pairs are more basic, that is, morphologically less marked and complex, than transitive ones, which require extra-marking. For example, a transitivizing language is one where FRIGHTEN is derived from FEAR and this derivation pattern applies repeatedly across verb meanings. On the other hand, "detransitivizing" languages are languages where transitive verbs are more basic than intransitive ones, and intransitive counterparts are systematically derived from transitive ones. For example, the meaning FEAR is expressed through a derived form of FRIGHTEN, such as 'be frightened'. Note that the intransitive counterparts, such as for example FEAR, or BURN (as in 'The house is burning'), are termed "plain" by Nichols et al., while the causative counterparts, such as FRIGHTEN, or BURN (as in 'The boy burnt the paper'), are termed "induced".

These two basic valency types with their corresponding morphological processes, as well as the other valency types detected by Nichols et al. 2004 are detailed in what follows and displayed in Table 2. So-called "augmentation" is the morphological process that corresponds to the transitivizing type (Table 2, row a), while "reduction" is the correspondence featured by "detransitivizing" languages (Table 2, row b). Together, these two types of relationship make up the category of "oriented languages". All other types are "non-oriented", as the direction of the derivation cannot be assessed. Non-oriented languages can be of the "neutral" type, if they show overt morphological marking for both plain and induced verbs, as happens with double derivation (Table 2, row c), auxiliary change (Table 2, row d) and ablaut or vowel alternation (Table 2, row e); or they can be indeterminate languages, if they lack overt marking for both members of the pair, as is the case with conjugation class change (Table 2, row f), suppletion (Table 2, row g) and lability or ambivalency (Table 2, row h), that is, when the same lemma performs both duties. Nichols and associates originally compared eighteen plain-induced verb pairs in eighty languages.[23] These were considered representative of the verbal lexicon. In a more recent version of the methodology,[24] plain verbs are further distinguished into continuous, stative predicates and bounded, change of state telic verbs (for example BE AFRAID vs. GET SCARED, BURN vs. CATCH FIRE, BOIL vs. COME TO A BOIL, BE SITTING vs. SIT DOWN, SEE vs. CATCH SIGHT). Six additional meanings are also added to the list, and proxies, that is, semantically similar verbs, are also suggested. The resulting twenty-four verb pairs are further divided into animate and inanimate, according to the animacy of most frequent, likely or possible subjects with the plain verb. In the list below in Table 3, so-called animate verbs are nos. 1-9 and 19-21, while inanimate verbs are nos. 10-18 and 22-24.

---

[23] The list is to be found in the Appendix, Nichols, et al., "Transitivizing and Detransitivizing Languages", 207–9.
[24] Johanna Nichols, "Realization of the Causative Alternation: Revised Wordlist and Examples", 2017, Available at https://www.academia.edu/34318209/Realization_of_the_ causative_alternation_Revised_wordlist_and_examples.

	language	verb pair Plain	induced	correspondence type	basic valency type
a.	Ingush	*wa.d.ozh* 'to fall (down)'	*wa.d.uozha-d.u* 'to drop'	AUGMENTATION	TRANSITIVIZING
b.	Russian	*serdit'sja* 'to be(come) angry'	*serdit* 'to make angey'	REDUCTION	DETRANSITIVIZING
c.	Siberian Yupik	*aghagh-nga-* 'to hang (intr.)'	*aghagh-te* 'to hang (tr.)'	DOUBLE DERIVATION	
d.	Hausa	*yi dariya* 'to laugh'	*ba dariya* 'to make laugh'	AUXILIARY CHANGE	NEUTRAL
e.	Lai	*ʔa-thin phaan* 'to be afraid'	*ʔa-thin phaʔn* 'to frighten'	ABLAUT	
f.	W. Armenian	*var.i-* 'to burn (intr.)'	*var.e-* 'to burn (tr.)'	CONJUGATION CLASS CHANGE	
g.	English	*Die*	*kill*	SUPPLETION	INDETERMINATE
h.	Ingush	*woma-d.u* 'to learn'	*woma-d.u* 'to teach'	LIABILITY	

Table 2. Corresponsdence types (adapted from Nichols et al. 2004)

OLD IRISH VERBS DATABASE

Table 3 reports a list of verb pairs selected through CorPH but supplemented through eDIL, according to the procedure set out for the PaVeDa and detailed above in section 3. To determine basic valency orientation, however, in many cases more than one predicate has been selected for Old Irish in order to capture all attested morphological relationships between pairs. For example, for the meaning BOIL (atelic) the copular predicate *is brothach* and the deponent verb *bruthnaigidir*, both attested in CorPH, are taken into account. For the meaning KILL, although *orgaid* in CorPH is more frequent than *marbaid* (23 occurrences vs. 14), marbaid has also been taken into account due to its relationship with the plain continuous predicate *marb* 'dead'. For BREAK, *boingid*, *brisid* and its more frequent compound *for·brisi* have all been taken into account (brisid only features one occurrence, which however has the core expected meaning, while for·brisi has eight occurrences but more frequently expresses the meaning 'overthrow' in CorPH). For KNOW/LEARN and TEACH, besides the verbs attested in CorPH, *fo·gleinn* and *for·cain*, along with *etar·gnin* and *etargnaigidir*, the verb *múinid*, which is attested in Wb along with for·cain, has also been considered. Note that this multiple-choice strategy is different from the one devised, for example, by Inglese for Latin.[25]

---

[25] Guglielmo Inglese, "Anticausativization and Basic Valency Orientation in Latin", in *Valency over Time*, ed. Silvia Luraghi and Elisa Roma (Berlin: De Gruyter Mouton, 2021), 133–68, https://doi.org/10.1515/9783110755657-005.

Pair	non-causal continuous	plain (bounded)	induced/causal	OI lemma plain atelic	OI lemma plain	OI lemma induced
1	laugh		make laugh, amuse, strike as funny	fo·áitbi, tibid (gen)	con·tibi (fo·áitbi)	ar·peiti
2	dead	die	kill	is marb	at·baill	marbaid (orgaid)
3	sit, be sitting	sit down	seat, have sit, make sit, let sit	saidid	saidid	suidigidir
4	eat	eat (up)	feed, give food	ithid	ithid, ar·beir biuth	ar·biatha (alaid, biathaid)
5	know, be learning	learn, master	teach	etar·gnin	fo·gleinn (múinid reflexive)	for·cain (múinid), etargnaigidir
6	see	catch sight	show	ad·cí	ad·cí (imm·accai)	do·adbat (foillsigidir)
7	be angry	get, become angry	anger, make angry	is fercach, fercaigidir	fercaigidir (londaigidir, fercaigidir passive)	fercaigidir (londaigidir)
8	fear, be afraid	get scared, take fright	frighten, scare	ad·ágathar	fo·botha	fo·botha (úamnaigid)
9	hide, be hiding	go into hiding	hide, conceal, put into hiding	ceilid reflexive	ceilid reflexive	ceilid, con·ceil (do·eim)
10	boil	come to a boil	(bring to) boil	is brothach, bruthnaigidir	berbaid passive (bruthnaigidir)	berbaid
11	burn	catch fire	burn, set afire	loscaid passive (bruthnaigidir)	lasaid	loscaid (lasaid)
12	be broken	break	break	is briste/ forbriste	boingid passive, for·brisi/brisid passive	for·brisi (boingid, brisid)
13	be open	open	open	ar·oslaici /airsailcthe (passive)	ar·oslaici (passive, reflexive)	ar·oslaici (oslaicid)
14	dry	get dry, dry	dry (out)	is tírim	tírmaigid	tírmaigid

Table 3. Old Irish verb pairs in Nichols' (2017) list

15	be straight	straighten (out)	straighten, make straight	is díriuch	dírgid	dírgid
16	hang		hang (up)	ar·rócaib passive	ar·rócaib passive (crochaid passive)	ar·rócaib (crochaid)
17	upside down, capsized	turn over, flip, capsize	turn over, flip, capsize	attá druim tar ais, druim tar druim	imm·soí passive	fo·ceird tar cend imm·soí (imm·cloí)
18	fall	fall	drop, make fall	do·tuit	do·tuit	sligid (ísligidir)
19	awake	wake up	awaken, wake up	(cen cotlud)	do·fiuchra, do·fiuschi	do·díuschi, do·fiuschi
20	asleep	fall asleep	put to sleep	con·tuili, attá ina chotlud	con·tuili	fo·ceird ina chotlud
21	run	(run off)	make run, have run	reithid	reithid, do·reith, teichid	reithid
22	shine	light up	light, turn on	do·aitni, as·tóidi	lasaid	soillsigidir, in·sorchaigedar, for·osna
23	shake	shake, tremble	shake, make tremble		crethaid	fo·crotha, crothaid, bertaigidir
24	roar	roar, rattle, buzz	make roar		beicid, búiridir, géisid	

Table 3 *continued*. Old Irish verb pairs in Nichols' (2017) list

Table 4 reports the attested types of correspondence, i.e. morphological relationship, between pairs.

pair	plain (bounded)	TYPE OF CORRESPONDENCE
1	laugh	SUPPLETION
2	die	SUPPLETION
3	sit down	AUGMENTATION
4	eat (up)	SUPPLETION
5a	learn, master	SUPPLETION
5b	learn, master	REDUCTION
5c	learn, master	AUGMENTATION
6	catch sight	SUPPLETION
7	get, become angry	LABILITY
8a	get scared, take fright	LABILITY
8b	get scared, take fright	SUPPLETION
9	go into hiding	REDUCTION/VOICE
10	come to a boil	REDUCTION/VOICE

11a	catch fire	REDUCTION
11b	catch fire	SUPPLETION
11c	catch fire	LABILITY
12	break	REDUCTION/VOICE
13a	open	LABILITY
13b	open	REDUCTION
14	get dry, dry out	LABILITY
15	straighten (out)	LABILITY
16	hang	REDUCTION/VOICE
17	turn over, flip, capsize	REDUCTION/VOICE
18	fall	SUPPLETION
19a	wake up	SUPPLETION, LABILITY
19b	wake up	AUGMENTATION?
20	fall asleep	SUPPLETION
21	(run off)	LABILITY
22	light up	SUPPLETION
23a	shake, tremble	SUPPLETION
23b	shake, tremble	ABLAUT?
24	roar, rattle, buzz	

Table 4: Types of correspondence between Old Irish verb pairs

Augmentation appears to be very limited in Old Irish (three instances), as the only couplets that instantiate this relationship are *saidid* ~ *suidigidir* 'sit down' vs. 'seat' and *etar·gnin* ~ *etargnaigidir* 'know, be learning' vs. 'make known', possibly also *do·fiuschi* ~ *do·diuschi* 'wake up' vs. 'awake' (though *do·fiuschi* is also labile according to eDIL). On the other hand, suppletion, as in *at·baill* 'die' ~ *marbaid* 'kill', is very common (11 instances of this type of correspondence), as well as reduction, that is passivization or reflexivization of causatives, as for example with *berbaid* 'boil' and *ceilid* 'hide' (nine instances of this correspondence). Lability, as for example with *tírmaigid* 'dry' or *ar·oslaici* 'open' is also well represented (seven couplets).

Lability is quite frequent in fact for the verbs in Nichols' list[26], especially for the relationship between plain telic meanings and causatives/induced, which can be considered the basic one. Lability is attested for the following verbs:

---

[26] "Realization of the Causative Alternation: Revised Wordlist and Examples", 156.

OLD IRISH VERBS DATABASE

fercaigidir and *londaigidir* 'get angry' and 'make angry'
fo·botha 'get scared' and 'frighten'
ar·oslaici 'open' tr. and intr.
lasaid 'catch fire' and 'set afire'
tírmaigid[27] 'get dry' and 'dry out'
dírgid 'straighten' and 'make straight'
do·fiuschi 'wake up' and 'awake'
reithid 'run' and 'make run'

Note that sometimes lability is uncovered in CorPH only by the use of the passive or reflexive alongside the active/deponent with the same meaning (e.g. *ar·oslaici*, *fercaigidir*, examples (3) and (4)), sometimes by the use of the acive/deponent with both meanings and valency patterns, while the passive may not be attested (e.g. *fo·botha*, examples (5) and (6)).[28]

(3) *ate   æm   ní   fercaigedar*
truly indeed NEG be_angry.PRS.3SG
'No, indeed, He is not angry' (Ml 24b18, ID S0006-758[29])

(4) *ar-nach-ad-fercaigther-su   etir*
so_that-NEG-2SG.OBJ-be_angry.PRS.SBJV.2SG-2SG at_all
'that you should not be angry at all' (Mon. Tall. 249, ID S0070-249)

(5) *co-fo<ta>bothad*
<3PL.OBJ>that-frighten.PST.SBJV.3SG
'that he might terrify them' (Ml 33b16, ID S0006-1489)

---

[27] The lemma is given as *tírmaigidir* in CorPH, but deponent inflection is not attested in the corpus, and eDIL only gives active forms (the lemma is *tírmaigid*, *tirmaigid*).

[28] Morphological glosses conform to the Leipzig Glossing rules (https://www.eva.mpg.de/lingua/pdf/Glossing-Rules.pdf; accessed 11-22-2024). The abbreviation DEP is used for "dependent".

[29] Examples (3-14) are taken from CorPH (see footnote 14) and from Doyle's digital edition of the Würzburg Glosses (see footnote 17); for each example the Text Unit ID in CorPH is given after the original locus, as abbreviated in CorPH (Ml = Milan Glosses, Mon. Tall. = Monastery of Tallaght, Sg = St Gall Glosses).

(6) *fobothaim*
(be)frighten(ed).PRS.1SG
'I am frightened' (Sg 146b13, ID S0007-2461)

Lability is registered by eDIL for *lasaid, tírmaigid(ir), dírgid, do·fiuschi*, but in CorPH only the transitive, causative meaning is attested for these verbs, while for *reithid* it is the induced, causative meaning reported in eDIL that is not attested in CorPH. For *ar·oslaici*, eDIL does not clearly distinguish the two constructions but only mentions the fact that in the Old Irish glosses it may correspond to Latin *pandere, aperire* and *reserare* 'open', but also to intransitive *patere* 'be open'.

To sum up, and to compare Old Irish with other Indo-European languages taken into account by Nichols, Old Irish appears to be mostly indeterminate for animate verbs, as the most frequent pattern is suppletion, and detransitivizing for inanimate verbs, as reduction (voice) prevails for these pairs. Homeric Greek in particular has a similar active vs. middle voice alternation for inanimate verbs, e.g. καί-ω *kaí-ō* 'burn (tr.)' vs. middle καί-ομαι *kaí-omai* 'burn (intr.)'[30]. Therefore, the Old Irish distribution would fit into Nichols et al.'s conclusion that western Indo-European languages, such as Greek, Germanic and Slavic languages, tend to be detransitivising while eastern ones such as Hindi, Armenian, Ossetic, tend to be transitivising.

However, this conclusion has been questioned for German by Plank and Lahiri[31], who have noted that what looked like ablaut alternations, and thus correspond to an indeterminate type, in many cases are in fact instances of umlaut, due to derivation of weak verbs from strong ones through suffixation. Additionally, it has been recently argued that the earliest Germanic representative, Gothic, can be chiefly classified as transitivizing[32].

---

[30] See Eleonora Sausa, "Basic Valency Orientation in Homeric Greek", *Folia Linguistica* 50, no. Historica-vol-37 (1 November 2016): 205–38, https://doi.org/10.1515/flih-2016-0007.
[31] Frans Plank and Aditi Lahiri, "Macroscopic and Microscopic Typology: Basic Valence Orientation, More Pertinacious than Meets the Naked Eye", *Linguistic Typology* 19, no. 1 (1 May 2015): 1–54, https://doi.org/10.1515/lingty-2015-0001.
[32] Matteo Tarsi and Chiara Zanchi, "Basic Valency Orientation in Gothic", *Indogermanische Forschungen,* forthcoming.

Similarly, in Old Irish a frequent derivation pattern for induced/causative counterparts is a transitivising pattern that derives weak, frequently deponent verbs, from nouns or verbal nouns of plain counterparts. In Nichols' list we have the following couplets:

> *suidigidir* 'place, make sit' from *suide* (verbal noun of *saidid* 'sit')
> *etargnaigidir* 'make known' from *etargnae* (verbal noun of *etar·gnin* 'know')
> *foillsigidir* 'make clear' from *follus* 'clear'
> *fercaigidir* (labile/ambivalent) 'make angry' from *ferc* 'anger' as well as *londaigidir* (labile/ambivalent) 'make angry' from *lond* 'angry'
> *dírgid* (labile/ambivalent) 'straighten, make straight' from *díriuch* 'straight' and *con·dírgedar*, used to translate compounds of Latin *rego*, e.g. *dirigo*
> *ísligidir* 'bring low' from *ísel* 'low'
> *marbaid* 'kill' from *marb* 'dead'
> *tírmaigid* (labile/ambivalent) 'get dry, dry out' from *tírim* 'dry'

It is important to note that this relationship is concealed if only verbal lemmas are compared synchronically and that, while these formations probably reflect different chronological layers, as the alternation between deponent and non-deponent inflection suggests, they belong to a well-established augmentation derivation pattern in Old Irish.

5. Case study II: Old Irish ditransitives

The second case study we will tackle based on the Old Irish PaVeDa data concerns the verb frames of ditransitives.[33] Ditransitive constructions consist of a ditransitive verb, an agent argument (A), a recipient-like argument (R), and a theme-like argument (T).

Three alignment types are distinguished in the typological literature, which include what are usually termed dative (and locative) alternations:

---

[33] Andrej Malchukov, Martin Haspelmath, and Bernard Comrie (eds.), *Studies in Ditransitive Constructions: A Comparative Handbook* (Berlin: De Gruyter Mouton, 2010).

1.) Indirective alignment, whereby the theme-like argument is the object, and the recipient-like argument receives separate coding, as in *I give the book* (T) *to Mary* (R), *They load boxes* (T) *onto the truck* (R).
2.) Secundative alignment, whereby the recipient-like argument is the object, and the theme-like has separate coding, as in *They load the truck* (R) *with boxes* (T);
3.) Neutral alignment, whereby both the recipient-like and the theme-like argument receive the same coding, as in the Double Accusative Construction, for example *I give her* (R) *the book* (T).

According to the definition given by in Comrie et al.,[34] three-argument constructions in which the two non-agent arguments are not R and T are not ditransitive constructions. However, mental/cognitive transfer verbs such as SHOW and TEACH are readily included among ditransitives and the authors' questionnaire guidelines explicitly suggest including verbs with similar patterns such as English *deny*, *envy*, or German *entziehen* 'withdraw from'.[35] Although physical and mental transfer predicates form, the core of ditransitive predicates from a cross-linguistic perspective,[36] for the present purposes, all three-argument verbs which have a Patient-like or Theme-like argument and a Recipient-like or Goal-like argument have been considered.

A prototypical ditransitive verb in Old Irish is, of course, the physical transfer verb *do·beir* 'give', which consistently adheres to indirective alignment, with theme expressed as object and recipient marked with *do*, as in (7):

---

[34] Malchukov, Haspelmath, and Comrie, "I. Ditransitive Constructions".
[35] Bernard Comrie, Martin Haspelmath, and Andrej Malchukov, "Questionnaire on ditransitive constructions", in Andrej Malchukov, Martin Haspelmath, and Bernard Comrie (eds.), *Studies in Ditransitive Constructions: A Comparative Handbook* (Berlin: De Gruyter Mouton, 2010), 65.
[36] William Croft, *Morphosyntax: Constructions of the World's Languages* (Cambridge, United Kingdom; New York, NY: Cambridge University Press, 2022), para. 7.5.

OLD IRISH VERBS DATABASE

(7) *do<m>berat   ní   do   neuch*
    <DEP>give.PRS.3PL something.ACC to   anyone.DAT
    (ar<da>munethar   feid)
    <3PL.OBJ.REL>honour.PRS.3SG dignity.DAT
    'That they give something to anyone (who worships them)' (Ml 124c16, ID S0006-7491)

The ditransitive verbs reckoned for Old Irish to date are fourteen verbs that correspond to fifteen verb meanings: *do·beir* 'give', *beirid* 'bring' and 'carry', *foídid* 'send', *do·adbat* 'show', *for·cain* 'teach', *as·indet* 'tell', *as·beir* 'say', *guidid* 'ask for', *do·cuirethar* 'put', *fo·ceird* 'throw', *línaid* 'fill', *ainmmnigidir* 'name' (as well as *as·beir* NAME), *do·luigi* 'forgive' and *do·fich* 'punish'. All of these consistently appear in the indirective construction shown above for do·beir, except guidid and for·cain (see 5.1 and 5.2 below), which also admit secundative alignment besides the indirective one (that is to say, they admit the so-called "dative alternation"), *línaid* and *ainmnigidir*, which are only attested in CorPH with the secundative alignment, while the only predicate in the above sample which marginally admits neutral alignment is *as·beir* with the meaning 'name'. We shall take a closer look at the verbs that admit or require secundative alignment here, excluding *ainmnigidir*, which will be dealt with together with as·beir in a separate paper.[37]

5.1 Guidid

When both the askee and the requested thing are overt with guidid, only the indirective pattern is attested in CorPH (six occurrences). The askee therefore appears as direct object in the accusative only when the requested thing is omitted (10 occurrences). Moreover, the askee in that case is either *dia* 'God' (8 instances) or a pronominal infix (2 instances). In Wb, an accusative askee is also most frequently *dia* (4 instances) or a pronominal infix (5 instances), but a different object can also occur (*a macc* 'his son' and *cách* 'everyone'). However, in Wb the secundative alignment is also attested with both roles overtly expressed, the askee and the

---

[37] Elisa Roma, "Differential case marking in Old Irish: nominal and pronominal arguments in valency alternations", to appear in *Noun phrase and pronominal syntax in medieval and early modern Celtic languages*, Special issue of Studia Celtica Posnaniensia, ed. by Elliott Lash.

requested thing, and in that case the requested thing is marked with the preposition *imm* + accusative, which is not found at all in CorPH with guidid, as in (8) and (9).

(8) amal ro<t>gát-sa   im   anad
    as   <2SG.OBJ>PRF.ask.PST.1SG-1SG   about remain.VN.ACC
    in   ephis
    in   Ephesus.DAT
    'as I have asked you to stay in Ephesus' (Wb 27d19)
    (rather than 'about staying', as in Thes., see the Latin text *Sicut rogaui té ut remaneres Ephesi*)

(9) an   nongeiss   cách   imm a   chomalnad
    when DEP.ask.SBJV.2SG everyone.ACC about its fulfil.VN.ACC
    'when you ask everyone for its fulfilment' (Wb 30b4)

Wb also feature an instance of secundative alignment without an overt requested thing (26b8 *guidmini dúib* 'we ask you'). However the gloss appears to be a translation of the Latin *denuntiamus autem uobis*, and the requested thing is represented by the following Latin complement clause introduced by *ut*.

The passive is not very frequent with guidid in CorPH, but there are no occurrences of the passive with secundative alignment, i.e. where the askee would be the subject, either in CorPH or in Würzburg (2 occurrences of passive forms each). The verb guidid is not attested in the St. Gall glosses, and its modern descendant *guigh* apparently only means 'pray' or 'wish'.

In the ancient Indo-European languages already stored in the PaVeDa, the equivalents of ASK FOR (Old Latin *posco*, Ionic-Attic Ancient Greek αἰτέω *aitéō*, Gothic *bidjan*, Old English *axian*) generally feature neutral alignment with the Double Accusative Construction; only Old English *axian* is also attested in the indirective alignment. Data for passivization are available in the PaVeDa for Ionic-Attic Ancient Greek and Old English: in the former, only the askee is passivized, whereas in the latter both the askee and the requested thing can be passivized.

5.2 For·cain

The second verb which allows secundative alignment, *for·cain* 'teach', is attested in CorPH with an overt taught person and taught content only twice. One instance, Ml 54c31, (10) below, has indirective alignment, while the other one, (11) below, again from the Milan glosses, has probably secundative alignment.

(10) [*pro bonís*]   *forcha[na]inn-se*   *doib-som*
     [for good deeds]   REL\teach.IMPF.1SG-1SG   to.3PL-3PL
     'which I used to teach them' (Ml 54c31, ID S0006-3332)

(11) *dond   érchoiliud*   .i.
     to.the.DAT determination.DAT   id est
     for<tan>roichan-ni   *ho*   *fortacht*
     <1PL.OBJ>teach.PRF.2SG-1PL   from   help.DAT
     dund   erchoiliud   *asrochoilsem*
     to.the. DAT determination. DAT   REL\determine.PRF.1PL
     'to the determination, that is, you have instructed us by help to the determination which we have made'[38] (Ml 22c3, ID S0006-592)

In the other five instances of the secundative alignment in CorPH, the taught content is omitted and the sole direct object, taught person, is either a pronominal infix (4 instances) or the head of a relative clause (1 instance). This preference is also reflected in Wb, where among the four instances of secundative alignment, the object is twice a pronominal infix: once the head of a relative clause and once the reciprocal pronoun *alaile* 'each other'.

Differently from guidid, the passive with secundative alignment is attested twice in CorPH, alongside the passive with indirective alignment (3 instances, with no teachee); in Wb, passive with secundative, or rather neutral alignment, only occurs once, with *figura etymologica* (3b23 *a forcital forndobcanar* 'the teaching you are taught'). The verb apparently does not have a modern Irish descendant. Note that a much less frequent verb with the same meaning, *do·inchosaig*, employs neutral alignment once

---

[38] This is a gloss on *decretui* in *nos decretui auxilio commonisti*.

in CorPH (with object infix for teachee and accusative verbal noun for taught content).[39]

As for the verbs representing the meaning TEACH in the other ancient Indo-European languages in the PaVeDa (Old Latin *doceo*, Ionic-Attic Ancient Greek διδάσκω *didáskō,* Gothic *laisjan,* Old English *tǣcan*), they show the same alignment distribution discussed for ASK FOR: generalized Double Accusative Construction with Old English also allowing for the indirective alignment. Passivization is also neutral in Ancient Greek, whereas it is secundative in Old Latin and Gothic, and it follows the indirective alignment in Old English.

5.3 Línaid

The verb *línaid* 'fill' is not a prototypical ditransitive predicate, as defined above, but it is a three-place transfer verb. It only occurs with secundative alignment in CorPH, however all thirteen instances are from a single text, the Milan glosses. The filled container[40] is therefore always the

---

[39] *Poems of Blathmac* 345 *Tos·n-inchoisecht ind óen ré dénom nathrach n-umaide* 'At the same time he taught them the making of brazen serpents'. The only other instance reckoned in CorPH for this verb is *Is maith immurgo lais do neuch do·inchoisc a llessai dóib* 'He thinks it well, however, for anyone, that one should show what is profitable to them' (translation as in CorPH). The syntax and the context rather suggest that *doinchoisc* may be read as a verbal noun, i.e. as *do [th]incoisc*, and consequently *a llessai* as a genitive plural rather than nominative for accusative: 'He thinks it well however for anyone to teach what is profitable to them' (or rather 'to teach them what is profitable to them').

[40] The [filled container] is classified as P in the ValPaL for the meaning FILL, while the container of LOAD, that is the [loading place], is classified as L (locative), and the [loaded thing] as T (theme), rather than X (other), as the [filling material] with FILL. In the database CONCEPTICON (Johann Mattis List et al., eds., *CLLD Concepticon 3.1.0* (Leipzig: Max Planck Institute for Evolutionary Anthropology, 2023), https://concepticon.clld.org/. [accessed on 11-22-2024]), likewise, the action/process FILL is defined as "To make full", while the action/process LOAD as "To put a large quantity of things onto something". There is however no apparent principled reason why filled container and loading place should not be considered as similar semantic roles. The semantic closeness of the recipient-like locative arguments of the two concepts (and of other processes, such as COVER) seems clear given that FILL can be defined as "To

object (or the subject with the seven passive forms, which outnumber active forms by one), but again the third argument, that is, the filling material, only occurs once in CorPH, with the passive, as in (12).

(12) linfider   do   gin[41]   ho
      fill.PASS.DEP.FUT.SG   your   mouth.NOM   from
      rath   in   spiur[ta]   noib
      grace.DAT   the.GEN.SG   spirit.GEN   holy.GEN
      'that your mouth will be filled with the grace of the Holy Spirit'
      (Ml 103a10, ID S0006-6333)

While the filling material in CorPH is flagged by the preposition *ó* + dative, a construction that is not recorded in eDIL, Wb uses the preposition *di* twice (examples 13 and 14), once with the very same word *rath* as in example (12) from the Milan glosses.

(13) ro<n>lín   di   rath
      <1PL.OBJ>PRF.fill.3SG   of   grace.DAT
      in   spirto
      the.GEN.SG   spirit.GEN
      'He has filled us with the grace of the Spirit' (Wb 20d11)

---

put a (large) quantity of things into something so as to make it full" and LOAD as "To make loaded". In the ValPaL, there are languages where the [filled container] is consistently a locative, and the [filling material] is subject (Korean, Jaminjung) and languages where [filling material] and [filled container] are subject and object (Emai); this is the frame at Wb 22b13 *rolín inbith nuile* et caelum *bolad inna idbairtesin* 'the odour of that offering has filled the whole world and the sky'. Korean is said to admit the locative alternation (indirective and secundative alignment) with FILL and COVER, but not with LOAD (only indirective alignment). These patterns emerge more clearly if the microroles are given consistent numbers across languages, which is the coding procedure followed in PaVeDa, see Section 2.

[41] Ms. *gnim*.

(14) [calicem] *líntar   lán   di   fín*
            fill.PASS.REL.PRS.SG full.NOM of   wine.DAT
            for   altóir   demne
            on   altar. DAT demon.GEN.PL
'which is filled full of wine on an altar of demons' (Wb 11b13)

The same preposition *de*, alongside *le*, is used with *líon*, the verb's descendant in Modern Irish. The passive with secundative is quite frequent, as already noted above.

The comparison with the other Indo-European languages in the PaVeDa gives back a consistent picture with FILL verbs: they all (Old Latin *compleo*, Ionic-Attic Ancient Greek πίμπλημι *pímplēmi*, Gothic *fulljan*, Old English *fyllian*) feature the secundative alignment both in the active and in the passive diatheses.

6. Conclusions

The PaVeDa is a new typological database which allows diachronic investigations of valency classes and alternations, in particular of Indo-European languages. The first, time-consuming steps towards adding Old Irish data to the PaVeDa, have been taken. Their inclusion in the database raises issues related to the study of a "corpus language", to data extraction, selection, and analysis, which are on the one hand similar to other languages such as Latin or Ancient Greek but also language- and documentation-specific. A recurrent problem of course is the circumstance that available corpora may not represent certain genres, which attest to certain verb meanings or constructions.

The two case studies presented here, basic valency orientation and alignment alternations with ditransitive verbs, show that despite the initial stage of the project, the PaVeDa promises to be a useful tool to classify Old Irish valency frames and alternations, to point out alternations that are not clearly presented by eDIL as yet, and to compare the frames with semantic equivalents (and verbal cognates) in other languages.

OLD IRISH VERBS DATABASE

Appendix

ASK FOR	guidid	COVER	in·tuigethar	HIDE	ceilid	PLAY 2	imm·beir	SIT DOWN	saidid
BE A HUNTER	is fénnid	CUT	do·fuiben	HIT	ad·cumaing	POUR	do·eissim	STEAL	
BE DRY	is tirim	DIE	at·baill	HUG	*tadaid a di láim imm	PUSH	ad·aig	SMELL	
BE HUNGRY	is goirt	DIG	claidid	JUMP	lingid	PUT	do·cuirethar	TAKE	gaibid
BE SAD	is brónach	DRESS	gaibid (étach) imm	KILL	marbaid	RAIN	snigid (flechud)	TALK	labraithir
BEAT	benaid	DRY	tirmaigid	KNOW	ro·finnadar	ROLL		TEACH	for·cain
BLINK	sméitid	EAT	ithid	LAUGH	fo·daibi	RUN	reithid	TEAR	
BOIL	bruthnaigidir	FEAR	ad·ágathar	LEAVE	fo·ácaib	SAY	as·beir	TELL	as·indet
BOIL TR	berbaid	FEEL COLD	úar do	LIKE	is maith la	SCREAM		THINK	
BREAK	brisid	FEEL PAIN	atá (galar)	LIVE	ad·treba	SEARCH FOR		THROW	fo·ceird
BRING	beirid	FILL	línaid	LOAD	No verbal counterpart	SEE	ad·cí	TIE	
BUILD	con·utaing	FOLLOW	seichithir	LOOK AT	do·éccai	SEND	foídid	TOUCH	
BURN	lasaid	FRIGHTEN	fo·botha	MEET 1	con·ricc	SHAVE	berraid	WASH	
BURN TR	loscaid	GIVE	do·beir	MEET 2	do·ecmaing	SHOUT AT		WIPE	
CARRY	beirid	GO	téit	NAME 1	as·beir do	SHOW	do·adbat	FORGIVE	do·luigi
CLIMB	dringid	GRIND	do·fuaire	NAME 2	ainmmnigidir	SING		BE ANGRY	fercaigidir
COOK	fo·noí	HEAR	ro·cluinethar	PEEL	sceirtid	SINK		PUNISH	do·fich
COUGH	*do·gní cosachtach	HELP	for·tét	PLAY 1	cluichigidir	SIT	saidid	FORGET	

Table 1. Meanings captured and corresponding lemmas for Old Irish in PaVeDa

Abstracts of Presenters at the Forty-second Harvard Celtic Colloquium

Songs from Drowning Women: A Comparative Analysis of "A' Bhean Eudach"/"A Bhean Ud Thall," a Gaelic Variant of "The Twa Sisters" (Child 10)

Lorena Alessandrini

The Scottish Gaelic song-poem "A' Bhean Eudach" ("The Jealous Woman"), also known as "A Bhean Ud Thall" ("O Woman Yonder") or "Bean mhic a' mhaoir" ("The wife of the ground-officer's son"), is the only extant example of a narrative ballad which has transitioned into Gaelic. Despite its unique status, however, the song has been mostly ignored by folklorists and musicologists alike, with the exception of Alan Bruford and Derick Thomson. The story behind the poem, which revolves around the death of a mother who is left to drown by another woman–her sister or her maidservant, depending on the version–who has designs on the mother's husband, is highly reminiscent of the popular international ballad "The Twa Sisters" (Child 10), also known as "The Cruel Sister," which has survived in almost 500 variants (Roud Folksong Index). Versions of "A' Bhean Eudach"/"A Bhean Ud Thall" have been preserved as waulking songs and lullabies throughout the Hebrides and West Highlands, as well as in Ireland and Nova Scotia (Thomson 1992; Shaw 1986).

Both "The Twa Sisters" and "A' Bhean Eudach" center around murder/sororicide, jealousy, and poetic justice; however, the Gaelic versions present significant differences which mark them as a distinct, coherent corpus. Building on the works of Thomson and Bruford, as well as on Paul Brewster's survey of "The Two Sisters" (1953), this study aims at examining a selection of versions of "A' Bhean Eudach" preserved in some of the major collections (e.g., Shaw 1986; Thomson 1992; Tolmie 1997; Gillies 2005), and, through comparative analysis, demonstrating how, in these texts, the narrative framework of the Child ballad has been thematically, geographically, and structurally "Gaelicized." This comparison, I argue, would confirm that "A' Bhean Eudach" is indeed a Gaelic variant of "The Cruel Sister," while suggesting that the whole Gaelic

ABSTRACTS

corpus may be considered as an "ecotype," a term coined by Carl Wilhelm von Sydow to indicate national variants of an international type.

From Eriugena to Duns Scotus: The Development of Medieval Celtic Theology

Dustin A. Ashley

John Scotus Eriugena was a ninth century Irish theologian that was heavily influenced by the Neoplatonic tradition. A significant intellectual of the early monastic period, Eriugena drew upon the works of both the Western and Eastern Church Fathers to produce the *Periphyseon*. Within the text, the reconciles both to produce a theological treatise from a uniquely Irish perspective. However, throughout the text he demonstrates a keen understanding of several Platonic philosophers from a Christian perspective. This includes Plotinus, Porphyry, Proclus, and perhaps Plato.

His influence is present among the theologians from the School of St. Victor, a priory turned school in the twelfth century. Particularly among the Victorine theologians are Hugh and Richard of St. Victor, who systematically explored Eriugena's theological insights on the relationship of science and theology. This is particularly true of Richard, a theologian of Scottish birth, who methodically explored the practice of contemplation as a science and contributed to the understanding of God as infinite. These ideas are later explored by Adam of Dryburgh, whose ideas later impacted the theology of Duns Scotus and served as a unique counterpoint to the divine simplicity of Aquinas' theology.

The theological underpinnings present within Eriugena's work will provide a foundation for understanding these Scottish theologians, and how their combined theological assertions demonstrate a vibrant continuity of Celtic Christian theological development among pre-Reformation theologians.

FORTY-SECOND CELTIC COLLOQUIUM

Columba's Crane: An Exploration in Medieval Irish Ecological History

River Atwood Tabor

The incident of Columba and the Crane–a touching moment within Adomnan's *Vita Columbae*–offers an interpretational cornucopia. This paper will take that moment in literature as a starting point for an examination which focuses not only on the theological implications of Columba's Crane, but by taking this crane as *figura*, we can examine a facet within the ecological history of medieval Ireland. We will begin on the hagiographical level, by looking at how the greeting and brotherhood which St. Columba extends to the windblown crane constitutes a metaphor for the inclusion of animals within the community of Christ. This section will transition to look at how interactions between the Medieval Irish and cranes were recognised in Irish law. Both herons and cranes (Ir. *corr*) were kept as pets and were legally recognised as such, and accorded the appropriate prices and penalties. Indeed, according to Giraldus Cambrensis, there were an abundance of cranes within Medieval Ireland. Now the crane is a visitor almost never seen. The final section of this paper will look at the total reduction of the Irish crane population, with recourse to recordings of crane sightings and available ecological data. In this sense we can see how the crane serves as a 'historical indicator species': its presence and absence is an indication of myriad historical processes.

An Analysis of the *Áes Dána* and their Status in Early Irish Law

Madison S. Bailey

This research aims to analyze and define the *Áes Dána* 'men of art', their status, and their roles within early medieval Irish society through the use of legal tracts and legal analysis. The four main crafts explored include the *cerd* 'smith', *goba* 'ironsmith', *saer* 'wright', and *briugu* 'hospitaller'. This paper also explores women craft-persons including *druinech* 'embroideress', and *ben lamtoruid* 'a woman of profitable handicraft'. The similarities and differences between honour-price and status are defined, as

ABSTRACTS

well as, how these legal ideas affect each craftsperson and the individual craft. The status concepts of *soer* 'free'/ *doer* 'unfree' and *doernemed* 'servile nemed'/ *soernemed* 'free nemed' are defined as a further analysis of status of the Áes dána. Additionally, the social fluidity of the *Áes Dána* as lower status *nemed* and higher status commoners is explored as well as their special advantages and limitations within their society. All these aims are achieved by the use of various legal tracts including *Bretha Crolige* 'Judgements on Sick Maintenance', *Bretha Déin Chécht* 'Judgements of Dían Cécht', *Cáin Lánamna* 'The Regulations of Couples', *Bretha Creidini* 'The Judgements of Creidine', *Uraicecht Becc* 'Small Primer', *Críth Gablach* 'The Branched Purchase', and *Di Astud Chor* 'On The Securing of Contracts'. All of these groups and concepts are examined together to exhibit that early medieval Irish society had a hierarchical fluidity, legal independence, and new definitions of nobility for those who practice craft.

The Fragments of Bignan, an example of the Gwenedeg dialect in Classical Middle Breton?

Myrzinn Boucher-Durand

The two fragments of Bignan are a set of two Middle Breton (twelfth century to 1659) fragments found in the archives of Saint-Brieuc and possibly emanating from the parish of Bignan, near Locminé in the Gwened area. The fragments dated to 1480, have been studied for their language in the nineteenth and twentieth centuries. Though some noted Gwenedeg dialectal traits in the texts, others refuted that possibility : Can a Middle Breton text from the fifteenth century contain traces of the Gwenedeg dialect? This statement presupposes that dialectal variation did not exist in Middle Breton, or at least did not before the late Middle Breton period, which began in 1600. I believe, however, that reexamining the arguments that claim there were no dialectal traces in Middle Breton is now necessary. Indeed, Jorgensen, in his dialectal study of *An Buhez Sant Gwenole,* has shown that there can be clear and consistent dialectal features found in a Middle Breton text of the classical period (1450-1600), and all of the Middle Breton texts could therefore be reexamined in that light.

FORTY-SECOND CELTIC COLLOQUIUM

In this paper I propose to examine the dialectal features found in the two fragments of Bignan, to determine if they do show clear and consistent dialect features from Gwened. In order to do that I will base my dialect examination on the two Breton dialect atlases that have been published (ALBB and NALBB) as well as various local dialectal studies that have been conducted for Breton.

Secondary Predication in Irish

Anabelle Caso & Oisín Ó Muirthile

Secondary predicates convey information about major arguments in a clause and are distinct from adverbial, adjectival, prepositional, and non-finite structures which modify events or individuals. Resultative secondary predicates denote states attained by their subject as a result of the action indicated by a lexical verb (Kaufmann and Wunderlich 1998; Kratzer 2005; Irimia 2012). Depictive secondary predicates describe the state of their subject at the time when the action indicated by the lexical verb occurs (Schultze-Berndt and Himmelmann 2004; Pylkk"anen 2008; Bruening 2018). This paper examines the behavior of secondary predicates in Irish, which can form periphrastic resultative (1), resultative (2), depictive absolute (3), and depictive (4) constructions, as exemplified below:

> (1) *tharraing na capaill na cearchaillí (nó) go rabhadar mín*
> draw.pst det horse.pl det log.pl (or) until be.3pl.pst.dep smooth
> "the horses dragged the logs (until) smooth" (periphrastic resultative)
>
> (2) *leag sí mín marbh é*
> knock.down.pst 3sg.f smooth dead 3sg.m
> "she killed him stone dead" (resultative)
>
> (3) *d'fhág Seán an chóisir agus fearg air*
> leave.3sg.pst John det party and anger upon.him
> "John left the party angry" (depictive absolute)

ABSTRACTS

(4) *níor tháinig tú folamh*
neg.pst come.pst 2sg empty
"you did not come empty-handed" (depictive)

Unlike English or German, which regularly express secondary predication with bare adjectival and prepositional phrases, equivalent structures have a restricted distribution in Modern Irish. We explore the synchronic and diachronic nature of this restriction and the productivity of corresponding periphrastic constructions. Further, we identify the application of the Irish initial mutation system as a significant diagnostic of depictive and resultative secondary predication. This paper will therefore fill an outstanding gap in the literature on Irish syntax and syntax-prosody mapping, placing the language within the more broadly understudied typology of secondary predication.

The first commercial discs of Breton language in 1910

Tudi Crequer

In the beginning of the last century, the commercial opportunities of the new technology of sound recording started to be understood (Chamoux : 2015). In 1910, Pathé, one of the biggest companies in the world, decided to record some traditional music from different French regions. Two Breton singers were selected by the Breton musician Maurice Duhamel to feature in the new Pathé's catalog : François Jaffrennou, known as Taldir, and Loeiz Herrieu. The two popular bards and singers went to Paris in 1910 and recorded 20 songs with full orchestra. For the first time in history, the Breton language was recorded for a commercial sale to the masses. This presentation will examine why these two singers were selected and how Pathé chose them. Moreover, reading archives, old newspapers, and particularly the letters between Maurice Duhamel, Loeiz Herrieu and Pathé, we're going to explain the conditions of recording, the selections of the songs and their origins, and the way these commercial discs were sold. During this presentation we will compare the Breton catalogue to the other regional artists selected by the sound recording company to expose Pathé's will in recording these local artists. We will also make a parallel with the other Celtic languages in regards to the production of commercial discs in the early twentieth century.

nitatsoír huili oc tintuúth abélru innalaill ɫ ocsaigid forsunu ɫ octabairtruún essib: **Questionable New Translations in the Universal Dependencies Treebank of the St. Gall Glosses, and Why they Don't Matter**

Adrian Doyle

The Diplomatic St. Gall Glosses Treebank is a new digital edition of the Old Irish glosses, annotated with both lexical and syntactic information. Its creation has required reassessment of many of the glosses from that corpus. This paper will discuss manners relating to Universal Dependencies (UD) corpora, as well as digital editions more generally. It will address the value of digital editions, as well as concerns which may prevent scholars from interacting with them. The CoNLL-U file format and upload cycle utilised by UD will be held up as an example of effective version control. While translations to English are not a requirement for Universal Dependencies corpora, such translations can be included as metadata in CoNLL-U files if required. In the case of the new St. Gall treebank, translations have been included to increase the utility of the resource for Natural Language Processing purposes. Tasks like Machine Translation, for example, can necessitate the training of language models on parallel corpora, collections of the same text written in two or more languages. As such, the St. Gall treebank can act as a parallel corpus with translations from Old Irish to English being aligned at the sentence level. This required that translations be provided for some glosses for which earlier editions provided none. Updates were also made for certain glosses where pre-exis.ng translations were deemed to be either too-direct to be idiomatic, or otherwise obtuse. Among these are reanalyses of Ogam glosses, and the somewhat enigmatic poem beginning, *gaib do chuil isin charcair*. While some of these translations may be objectionable, it will be argued that they are nevertheless, fit for purpose.

ABSTRACTS

Celtic in Greek characters and implications for phonology

Joseph F. Eska

In recent years, I have argued that the Celtic languages did not contrast their plosive series via voicing, i.e., /p t k/ vs. /b d g/, as has been traditionally assumed, but via aspiration, i.e., /ph th kh / vs. /p t k/. Thus, orthographic ⟨p t k b d g⟩ represent phonemic /ph th kh p t k/. This is certain for the modern Celtic languages (save for Breton, which acquired a voicing distinction via contact with Late Latin and/or French), which can be measured with acoustic instrumentation. It is also demonstrated for the medieval and early modern periods in Irish and Welsh by the use of orthographic ⟨sb sd sg⟩ to represent phonetic [sp st sk]. These orthographies are continued to the present day in Scottish Gaelic and Welsh. That an aspiration contrast existed in the Continental Celtic languages, which are recorded in a variety of scripts, is more difficult to ascertain. This paper examines the matter with regard to the inscriptions of Transalpine Gaul that are engraved in Greek characters with a focus on issues related to script transfer, especially the use of the characters ⟨θ χ⟩ .

Dress, Clothing and Accessory in Late Medieval Ireland *c.* 1100–*c.* 1550

Mairéad Finnegan

Research on dress, clothing and accessory of the Middle Ages has proven the increasingly important role it played in the medieval world. For those living in the medieval period, the garments a person wore could be read as an indicator of their status, gender, religion and regional identity. From the early fourteenth century onwards, this became clearly evident as 'fashionable' dress emerged and with regional variations becoming even more apparent. Despite this trend, the exchange and sharing of clothing and accessory remained as a common occurrence in medieval society.

Within Ireland, clothing was also exchanged. There is evidence that clothing was not only shared between the different communities in Ireland, but between Ireland and its neighbouring regions in the medieval world. Through information gleaned from archaeology, linguistics and literary sources, we can begin to piece together how dress in Ireland compared and contrasted to its close neighbours and, moreover, how one region's style of clothing could influence another.

    The aim of this paper is to delve into select evidence for the exchange of dress, clothing and accessory between Ireland and its neighbours, and provide some comparison. Ultimately, the paper will explore how dress in Ireland cannot be fully analysed without the context of the broader material culture in which it is set. By placing Ireland within the wider medieval world, the study of dress, clothing and accessory becomes richer as the patterns of influence and sharing between these regions is made clear and evident.

Crafting a drinking-cup: the verbal artistry of *Cuach ríogh Connacht cuanna séad*

Margo Griffin-Wilson

    This paper will examine the poetic diction and metrical ornamentation in an anonymous bardic poem composed in praise of a drinking cup (*cuach*), the prized possession of Aodh Ó Conchobhair, a king of Connacht. The figure of the king recedes into the background, as the poet directs attention to the crafted object which adorns the feast—its interlaced gold ornamentation and life-like zoomorphic engravings. Through verbal repetition, metrical ornament and an imaginative search for its Otherworld orgins, the poet-craftsman shapes the goblet in language. The poem is undated, but two citations in the Irish Grammatical Tracts and the highly ornate form of the metre *rannaigheacht mhór* suggest that it was composed sometime between 1200-1400 and was highly regarded within the bardic schools. The analysis will draw on my edition of the poem from Dublin, RIA MS 23 O 78 (1387). As time allows, I will comment briefly on other poems which focus on prized objects and their varied presention in bardic verse.

ABSTRACTS

The Sword in the Mere: The Case for Brittonic Influence in *Beowulf*

Tristan Gutbezahl

Previous studies exploring the possibility of Celtic influence in Beowulf have categorically neglected Brittonic parallels, even though the Anglo-Saxons historically had more direct contact with the Britons during the early settlement period than any other Celtic people. The present study brings to light a range of ancient Brittonic traditions whose resonances arguably may be detected within the lines of the poem. Many of these were very widespread, predating even the period of Roman occupation in Britain, but all of them persisted throughout the Anglo-Saxon period. The analysis suggests that these themes may have provided an effective foil for English ideologues–an antagonist 'Other,' in a sense–during the earliest stages of Anglo-Saxon nation-building. These in turn stood to affect the emergence of early English cultural consciousness generally. With respect to Beowulf specifically, they may inform new interpretations of the imagery of the haunted mere, the cavernous lair of the Grendel-kin which Beowulf finds beneath the surface of the mere, and the hero's subsequent discovery of the "giant's sword." In sum, reading Beowulf through this Brittonic lens may serve to unveil dynamic strains of Celtic influence within its verse that have not been considered previously. It is remarkable to note that essentially all previous scholarship on the subject has exclusively addressed Irish literary parallels and other Gaelic traditions. Indeed, this oversight appears particularly egregious when we consider the stark animus meted out to the Britons in other foundational English texts, notably The Anglo-Saxon Chronicle and *Vita S. Guthlaci*.

Brittonic and Gaelic Hagiography in the Latin "Lives" of St. Lorcán Ua Tuathail

Jesse Harrington

St. Lorcán Ua Tuathail (Laurence O'Toole, c. 1128–80), abbot of Glendalough, archbishop of Dublin, and papal legate in Ireland, stands alongside St. Malachy as one of only two twelfth-century Irish churchmen to have been made the subject of a dedicated biography by his contemporaries. No fewer than five or six hagiographical *vitae S. Laurentii* survive in some fourteen manuscripts. Only two of these *vitae*, both from the Norman/Picard frontier, have hitherto been edited, by the Bollandists in 1893 and Charles Plummer in 1913, albeit with incomplete reference to the full manuscript source base.

Often dismissed as continental productions, the hagiographical dossier has gone largely overlooked by scholars of Celtic Studies and of medieval Ireland and has never received the systematic attention warranted by a figure of Lorcán's stature. Moreover, the possibility of Celtic linguistic and literary influences has been unjustifiably downplayed. Nonetheless, all of these *vitae* made use of biographical materials gathered in Ireland, while it will be argued that at least two, both unpublished, display hitherto unnoticed linguistic and literary evidence of having been composed by native Brittonic and Gaelic speakers. This paper, which is based on an ongoing examination of the hitherto unedited manuscript originals, will examine collectively the *vitae S. Laurentii* and argue for important, but hitherto unnoticed, literary influences from Ireland, Cornwall, and Brittany.

Language, Education and Medical Learning in the Premodern Gaelic World: An Introduction to the LEIGHEAS Project

Deborah Hayden

The first part of this paper will introduce the major new Celtic Studies research project LEIGHEAS ('Language, Education and Medical Learning in the Premodern Gaelic World'), which is based in the Department of Early Irish at Maynooth University from 2022–2026. The central aim of LEIGHEAS is to advance our knowledge of the nature and scope of medical learning in the premodern Gaelic world by charting the vernacular translation and transmission of medical texts across Ireland and Scotland, ca 1350–1700. The project will integrate digital tools for the network analysis of vernacular medical sources from this region with detailed philological and historical research on a subset of manuscripts associated with scribes from Connacht, Ireland. It is argued that the sources at the heart

ABSTRACTS

of this case study shed new light on the relationship between Irish-language medical learning and other aspects of contemporary literary culture, including narrative, legal, religious and historical writing. The project aims to illuminate the social, pedagogical and manuscript context for the production and circulation of medical texts throughout the Gaelic world, while also positioning this corpus more firmly within a wider intellectual framework by exploring the complex multilingual and cross-cultural interactions that shaped the development of scientific writing across northern Europe more broadly. To illustrate some aspects of this ongoing work, the second part of the paper will consider some examples from a collection of remedies for women's ailments that is being edited for the project.

Beannacht duit, beannacht d'fhearaibh th'oileamhna: Insights from the elegy for Dáibhíth Óg de Barra (†c.1605)

Philip Mac a' Ghoill

Dáibhíth Óg de Barra–the son of Dáibhíth de Barra (David Barry), fifth Viscount Buttevant–died in 1604/5. Soon after his death, the professional court poet Domhnall (mac Taidhg) Ó Dálaigh composed an elegy in praise of him providing us with various insights into his life. Central to the poem is the patron's unwavering faith which contributed to his success in life; his fruitful submission to the English king and details of Dáibhíth's otherwise unrecorded visit to London; and his education, where the poet provides us with a unique source of insights into how members of the Anglo-Irish nobility of Munster were educated in the early modern period. The poet also included envois to St. Paul and to David's wife, Eilís Puidhéar (Elizabeth Power), at the end of the poem which was characteristic of Gaelic praise poetry at the time. This paper will explore the insights we gain from this poem, which to this day remains without a full critical edition or English translation. The poem will be discussed for its value as a source of historical information and as a multifaceted sample of Gaelic syllable poetry during those turbulent years at the turn of the seventeetnth century.

FORTY-SECOND CELTIC COLLOQUIUM

Dialects, Demographics and Development: The Irish Language Summer College in Ulster, 1905-1930

Máire McCafferty

The Irish Language Summer College has been a rite of passage for thousands of people on the island of Ireland for nearly 120 years. Despite this, the cultural, linguistic and political significance of this institution has been largely overlooked by academic scholarship thus far. So too has the role of the Ulster Irish College in the Irish language movement during the revolutionary and post-partition period been underexamined. Within two years of establishment of the first Irish Language Summer College in Co. Cork in 1904, half of the total number of Irish Colleges were located in Ulster. During this period these institutions were largely occupied with adult teacher-training, and Ulster Irish Colleges were instrumental to this work prior to the partitioning of Ireland in 1921.

Following 1922 and the establishment of the Irish Free State, however, the Irish language experienced direct persecution in the new Northern Irish state, and Ulster Irish speakers began to express increasing concern about the future of their own dialects. It was in the early 1920s, then, that schemes to send children from the Six Counties to the Gaeltachtaí, or Irish-speaking areas, were accelerated, and pioneering Irish Colleges in Donegal set the pattern for youth-centric courses. This pattern would be followed by the rest of the Irish Colleges in the South from the 1930s.

This paper will examine the significance of the Ulster Irish College to the language movement in Ireland prior to partition in 1921, and in the initial years following the creation of Northern Ireland. It will provide an insight into a period crucial to the understanding of the relevance of the Irish Summer College as a cross-border institution that continues to provide an alternative education to Irish youth today in 2023.

ABSTRACTS

A Tumultuous Noise: Music in the Mabinogi

Shannon Rose Parker

This paper aims to identify and analyze references to music (of which there are many) in the Four Branches of the *Mabinogi*. Despite this there is very little written on the subject aside from a brief report in Helen Fulton's "Words for Music" in *A History of Welsh Music* (2022). Music (or lack thereof) ties the branches together and I propose to analyze the Four Branches to find its narrative functions. Thus far, I have identified the following categories of references: 1. Music for signaling events; 2. Music as contentment; 3. Birdsong; 4. The supernatural effects of music; 5. *Englynion*; 6. Information about musicians; 7. Liturgical music; and 8. the value of stringed instruments.

Curiously, there is no music or sound imagery in the third branch apart from 'a tumultuous noise' (twrwf). One aim of this paper is to investigate the significance of this in relation to the storyline and in relation to the other branches.

Beyond Poetry: Viewing Clanship through Highland Letters and Family Papers

Roxanne Reddington-Wilde

Scottish Highland clans existed in the Early Modern Era, right? We admire them in Outlander and on the covers of Romance novels. But . . . clan tartans during this period are a myth, and Gaelic poetry presents an idealized, equally–albeit indigenous–'romanticizing' perspective. Where to find on the ground evidence that clanship remained a functional part of Highland society in the seventeenth and eighteenthth centuries? The answer: letters between and from the elite, especially during times of war and social stress when the concept of 'clan' enabled the major landowners (and thus 'elite') in Highland society to rally their 'men' and defend their lands, king and country.

Grant, Campbell and other family letters and papers of the period confirm the hierarchical concept of chief and clan members, such as "the true way of doing service in the Highlands . . . a [military] corps being formed out of one clan under the command of their chieftains or a near relation of his family (in Fraser, *Chiefs of Grant:* 218)." Beyond warfare, though, was 'clan' as the poets (and we today) understand it, a functional, useful *everyday* feature of society? Unromantically, I doubt it.

Betwixt Earth and Heavens: The Theological Inspiration for Robert Kirk's The Secret Commonwealth of Elves, Fauns, and Fairies in the Works of Origen of Alexandria

Natalia Schwien

In *The Secret Commonwealth of Elves, Fauns, and Fairies,* Episcopalian minister Robert Kirk details the nature of second sight and belief in fairies amongst his Highland parishioners in the late 1600's. Kirk's essay has been labeled as a curious anomaly, born from his desire to validate his community. However, Celtic Studies scholars have thus far neglected to note that in the seventeenth century amongst the educated elite, there was a resurgence of interest in the work of Origen of Alexandria (185-253CE), a Church Father who articulated an expanded theology of souls moving within a hierarchy towards *apokatastasis*. Kirk's arguments closely mirror Origen's cosmological outline, and this paper compares those similarities.

How to Swear in Manx: Curses from the Ecclesiastic Court Records in the Eighteenth Century

Tim Swales

It used to be said that there were no curse words in Manx Gaelic. Victorian travel writers wrote that the pious inhabitants of the Isle simply had no need for them. Back then, older generations didn't teach their children the language, let alone any of its rude words. Likewise, the younger generations found it rude to speak Manx itself, and had no appetite to hear any more of it. Now, during the Revival, profanities rarely come up when learning Manx over tea and biscuits. This, however, is not the full picture,

ABSTRACTS

and for all the tea and biscuits consumed in morning classes there are equally as many ales and lagers consumed in late night pub sessions.

Therefore, it *is* possible to swear in Manx, and examples can be found in the spoken language, literature, legal documents and court records. One source of profanities is the ecclesiastic court of the eighteenth century. The records of these courts contain legal cases regarding cursing and swearing. They are a mixture of Latin and English, though an occasional Manx word is recorded. This presentation gives examples of these Manx words from the ecclesiastic court records and addresses the topic of how to swear in Manx.

"Progress ... in the Old World and the New":
The Preservation Society's transnational revival efforts post-1900

Aoife Whelan

In the annual report of the Society for the Preservation of the Irish Language for the period 1901-02, a letter from Rev. J.L. Ahern from Auckland, New Zealand states: "It afforded me very great pleasure to see the progress the study of our dear old language is making both in the Old World and the New." Additional correspondence received from language enthusiasts in Europe, the US and Australia demonstrates that the Society's campaigns and publications had reached a transnational readership by the turn of the twentieth century. International academic collaborations are also noted, including a visit to the Society's Council Meeting by Dr. F.N. Robinson, Professor of Celtic at Harvard University.

Yet many Irish language scholars and speakers are unaware of this Society's achievements as the success of the Gaelic League eclipsed that of the language organisations which preceded it. The Society was originally founded in 1876 and the Gaelic Union sprang from a breakaway group within a few years. It was under the auspices of these organisations that *Irisleabhar na Gaedhilge* [The Gaelic Journal] was founded in 1882 and that Irish was first established on the official school curriculum.

Despite the prominence of the Gaelic League from 1893 onwards, the Preservation Society persevered in its efforts on behalf of the language, including extending the teaching of Irish in schools. The Society's financial reports present evidence of its publication sales and the literary prizes awarded to Fr. O'Dinneen and Douglas Hyde, among others. The Society's report also details a comprehensive list of newspapers and journals that published Irish language material in Ireland and overseas at the time, thereby disseminating revivalist ideals on a transnational basis.

This paper will analyse the Society's role in reclaiming a cultural space for Irish language, literature and scholarship. The Society's reports for this period serve as a bridge between the earliest revival organisations and the Gaelic League, all of whom were striving for a common cause. This paper will remind audiences that the Irish language revival did not begin with the foundation of the Gaelic League in 1893. In the words of David Comyn, editor of *The Gaelic Journal*: "The Gaelic League people have very short memories. All before 1893 is darkness."

A Storm, a Harvest, and a Mischief of Mice: Locating the Context for a Poem by 'Ricmarchus'

Sarah Zeiser

This paper will explore the literary and historical context for a short Latin quatrain attributed to Rhygyfarch ap Sulien in the early-twelfth-century manuscript British Library MS Cotton Faustina C.I., part II. The sole recorded instance of the poem "De Messe Infelici" (so titled by Michael Lapidge) attests to damaging storms and an abandoned harvest. Its contents have not been rigorously examined, often neglected in the shadow cast by the more complex and compelling Latin and Old Welsh poetry attributed to Rhygyfarch and his brother Ieuan, both monks and famed scholars at Llanbadarn Fawr at a time when that foundation faced tumultuous changes. I will not only examine "De Messe Infelici" within its manuscript context, but also connect its content to key references in the chronicles and contemporary literary records with two aims: to more clearly pinpoint the period in which the BL Cotton Faustina manuscript was written, and to bring "De Messe Infelici" further into the light of medieval Welsh poetic traditions, confirming the canny creative and political maneuvering of the community at Llanbadarn Fawr under Norman control.